Fodor's InFocus

SAVANNAH

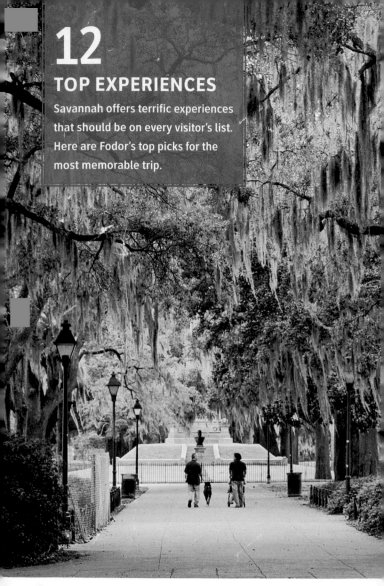

12
TOP EXPERIENCES

Savannah offers terrific experiences that should be on every visitor's list. Here are Fodor's top picks for the most memorable trip.

1 Forsyth Park

Spending time in Forsyth Park is a must for any visitor. People-watching from a bench, seeing a concert at the bandshell, or simply strolling beneath a canopy of Spanish moss–draped branches are wonderful ways to explore. *(Ch. 2)*

2 Tybee Island

Whether you want to relax on the beach, visit the lighthouse, or paddle around in kayaks, there are plenty of ways to enjoy this fun-loving island town. *(Ch. 2)*

3 Antique Shops

In a city this old, there's no shortage of amazing antiques stores. Some of them are more like museums of everyday life. Explore the shops around the Historic District. *(Ch. 7)*

4 Savannah Music Festival

Savannah is in full bloom in late March and early April, providing a magical backdrop for two weeks of performances by some of the world's most talented musicians and vocalists from every genre. *(Ch. 5)*

5 Jepson Center for the Arts

The building's modern architecture might not mesh with the Historic District's stately town homes, but the museum's changing exhibits of contemporary art delight residents and visitors alike. *(Ch. 2)*

6 White Shrimp

Georgia white shrimp are delicious, especially when you taste one fresh from the ocean. Whether served over grits, grilled on a salad, or in any of the myriad other preparations, these crustaceans are a decadent delight. *(Ch. 3)*

7 The Riverfront

Buildings that were once cotton warehouses, shipping offices, and markets have been converted to some of Savannah's liveliest restaurants, bars, and shops. Take a ferry ride across the river to enjoy one of the city's iconic views. *(Ch. 2)*

8 Horse-Drawn Carriage Rides

There is something magical about riding past pristinely restored historic town homes in a horse-drawn carriage. If you're traveling with that special someone, look into deals that include flowers and Champagne. *(Ch. 1)*

9 Bonaventure Cemetery

Situated along the Bull River and shaded by moss-draped live oaks, this cemetery is one of the city's truly memorable sights, full of ornate headstones. It's also the final resting place of local notables like Johnny Mercer. *(Ch. 2)*

10 Mercer Williams House

The former home of Jim Williams—the central figure in John Berendt's *Midnight in the Garden of Good and Evil*—is now a museum. Reading the book makes a visit even better. *(Ch. 2)*

11 Ghost Tours

In "one of the most haunted cities in America," a brush with the paranormal can happen in "haunted buildings" like the Eliza Thompson House. *(Travel Smart)*

12 Fort Pulaski

This 19th-century fortification was considered impenetrable until the Civil War, when weapons technology caught up with it. Walk the ramparts for an incredible view and then follow trails out to the Cockspur Lighthouse. *(Ch. 2)*

CONTENTS

MAPS

ABOUT THIS GUIDE

Fodor's Ratings

Everything in this guide is worth doing—we don't cover what isn't—but exceptional sights, hotels, and restaurants are recognized with additional accolades. **Fodor's Choice★** indicates our top recommendations. Care to nominate a new place? Visit Fodors.com/contact-us.

Trip Costs

We list prices wherever possible to help you budget well. Hotel and restaurant price categories from $ to $$$$ are noted alongside each recommendation. For hotels, we include the lowest cost of a standard double room in high season. For restaurants, we cite the average price of a main course at dinner or, if dinner isn't served, at lunch. For attractions, we always list adult admission fees; discounts are usually available for children, students, and senior citizens.

Hotels

Our local writers vet every hotel to recommend the best overnights in each price category, from budget to expensive. Unless otherwise specified, you can expect private bath, phone, and TV in your room. For expanded hotel reviews, facilities, and deals visit Fodors.com.

Restaurants

Unless we state otherwise, restaurants are open for lunch and dinner daily. We mention dress code only when there's a specific requirement and reservations only when they're essential or not accepted. To make restaurant reservations, visit Fodors.com.

Credit Cards

The hotels and restaurants in this guide typically accept credit cards. If not, we'll say so.

Top Picks
★ **Fodor's Choice**

Listings
⊠ Address
⊠ Branch address
⌂ Mailing address
☎ Telephone
🖶 Fax
⊕ Website
✎ E-mail

🎟 Admission fee
🕓 Open/closed times
Ⓜ Subway
✛ Directions or Map coordinates

Hotels & Restaurants
🏨 Hotel
🛏 Number of rooms
🍽 Meal plans

✗ Restaurant
☖ Reservations
🏛 Dress code
🚫 No credit cards
$ Price

Other
⇨ See also
☞ Take note
⛷ Golf facilities

EXPERIENCE
SAVANNAH

WHAT'S WHERE

1 The Historic District. This area is home to the city's historic squares as well as many of its finest hotels, restaurants, and shopping. The borders of the district are River Street to the north, Gaston Street to the south, and East Broad Street and Martin Luther King Jr. Boulevard to the east and west.

2 The Victorian District and Eastside. One of Savannah's oldest neighborhoods, the Victorian District is where you'll find gorgeous homes that date to the 1800s.

3 The Starland District, Thomas Square, and Midtown. The up-and-coming neighborhoods of Starland District and Thomas Square have funky shops and great restaurants. Midtown is home to Grayson Stadium and the Savannah Bananas.

4 The Moon River District. 20 minutes south of the Historic District, this area includes the Sandfly, Isle of Hope, and Skidaway Island neighborhoods.

5 The Islands and Thunderbolt. About 15 minutes east of the Historic District, this area includes Wilmington and Whitemarsh Islands as well as the town of Thunderbolt.

6 Southside, Gateway, and Greater Savannah. Southside is near the Savannah/Hilton Head International Airport and close to downtown. Gateway is home to Coastal Georgia Botanical Gardens.

7 Tybee Island. A barrier island 18 miles east of Savannah, Tybee is a quirky beach town with kitschy shops, interesting restaurants, and outdoor activities.

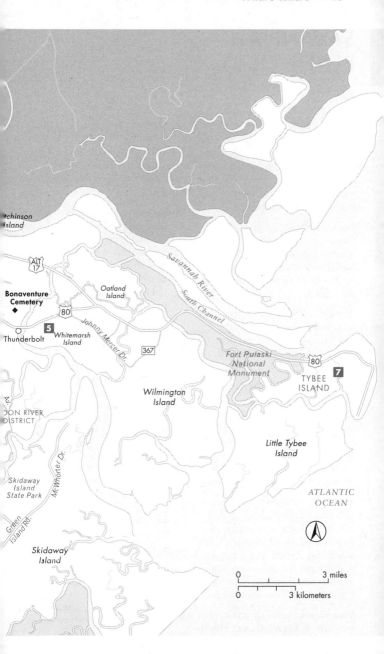

*chinson
Island*

ALT 17

**Bonaventure
Cemetery** ◆

80

*Oatland
Island*

Savannah River

South Channel

5

*Whitemarsh
Island*

Thunderbolt

Johnny Mercer Dr.

367

*Fort Pulaski
National
Monument*

80

7

TYBEE
ISLAND

*Wilmington
Island*

ON RIVER
DISTRICT

McWhorte, Dr.

*Little Tybee
Island*

ATLANTIC
OCEAN

*Skidaway
Island
State Park*

*Green
Island Rd.*

*Skidaway
Island*

0   3 miles

0   3 kilometers

SAVANNAH PLANNER

Visitor Resources

Savannah and Tybee Island each have official resources (⊕ *www.visitsavannah.com*, ⊕ *www.visittybee.com*) for travelers that include information on tours, dining, attractions, and more.

For information on several prominent local museums, look at the websites of the Coastal Heritage Society (⊕ *www.chsgeorgia.org*) or Telfair Museums (⊕ *www.telfair.org*).

The city's Riverfront Association (⊕ *www.riverstreetsavannah.com*) has information on events and member businesses along River Street.

Getting Here and Around

You can fly into Savannah and catch a cab into downtown, but you'll probably need a car if you want to explore attractions like Bonaventure Cemetery, Tybee Island, and Fort Pulaski, which are several miles east of downtown.

Getting to Savannah: There are a handful of direct flights into Savannah, but unless you're visiting from New York City, Chicago, or a few other major metropolitan areas, you'll have a connecting flight, most often through Atlanta or Charlotte.

More Flights: Although the airport serves both Savannah and Hilton Head, there is another, considerably smaller airport on Hilton Head Island. If you're looking for additional flight options, it is only about 45 to 60 minutes from Savannah.

On the Ground: Savannah is roughly 10 miles east of Interstate 95, so if you're heading up or down the Eastern seaboard through Georgia, it is an easy stopover. Follow Interstate 16 east until it dead-ends in the Historic District. Interstate 16 traverses west through Georgia to intersect with Interstate 75, the fastest route to or from Atlanta by car.

Other Options: You can reach Savannah by train; there's an Amtrak station several miles west of downtown. Bus travel is also an option. The Greyhound station is located on West Oglethorpe Avenue.

Renting a Car: There are several major car rental companies with offices at the airport, including Avis, Budget, Dollar, Enterprise, Hertz, National/Alamo, and Thrifty.

Planning Your Time

Savannah is not large, but it is atmospheric, so make sure you allow sufficient time to soak in the ambience and see the sights. You'll need at least two or three days to fully appreciate the Historic District and its many sights, not to mention the food, which is an integral part of the Savannah experience. You'll need another day or two to see the sights in the surrounding area, including a jaunt out to Tybee Island for a fishing trip, kayaking tour, or relaxing on the beach. Some travelers head north to Hilton Head or Charleston to round out their Lowcountry experience.

Saving Money

Savannah's low season is around November through the end of January, and there are significantly better deals to be found, generally speaking, to compensate for the chilly weather.

For savings on hotels, Stay in Savannah (⊕ *www.stayinsavannah. com*) offers discounts at member hotels. The best deals can be found during the off-season. Another way to save on hotels is to book a place south of the Historic District. There are a number of hotels along Abercorn Street, south of DeRenne Avenue, that provide easy access to downtown for less money per night.

Reservations

If you have your heart set on a specific restaurant (particularly one of the city's nicer places), then reservations are essential during the high season (spring and fall). However, it's not unheard of to walk in and get a table, particularly midweek.

Although the city is bustling, there are relatively few instances where reservations are necessary. It's advisable to get tour tickets in advance if you're looking for something like the "haunted hearse" tours or others with relatively limited seating. Walking tours should also be set up in advance, particularly with the smaller tour companies.

WHEN TO GO

Spring and fall are Savannah's peak seasons, when the climate is at its most pleasant and activities are abundant. In March the azaleas bloom and St. Patrick's Day turns the city green. This is hands-down the prettiest, priciest, and most popular time to visit. If you plan on staying in the Historic District in March, it's wise to book at least six months ahead—longer if you plan on snagging a spot along the St. Pat's parade route. April and May are also considered peak, but as humidity and temperatures begin to spike in summer—particularly July and August—Savannah dips into a small lull, a great time for deal-seekers to hunt for hotel offers. Similarly, from December through February, hotel occupancies fall again and you can find the best deals of the year.

Climate

Savannah's climate is mild and comfortable much of the year, and sunny days are abundant. In spring and fall, temperatures typically range from the low 70s to the mid-80s. Locals begin flocking to beaches as early as March and linger long into October. Winter temperatures average in the low 60s and rarely dip below freezing. Summer sees Savannah at its most extreme, particularly in July and August, when highs peak around 100 and humidity soars.

This is also hurricane season, and although major storms rarely brush Georgia's coast, you can count on a brief downpour nearly every afternoon, leaving behind steamy conditions.

Festivals

Spring is packed with popular events, like the Savannah Music Festival, Savannah Stopover Music Festival, Savannah College of Art and Design Sidewalk Arts Festival, and the annual Tour of Homes and Gardens, which invites visitors into some of the city's best-preserved private residences. But the star of Savannah's festival calendar is St. Patrick's Day, which boasts the second-largest parade of its kind in the world and leaves the city a swirl of leprechaun hats and green beads. On years when March 17 falls on a weekend, attendance can reach a whopping one million. The slightly calmer fall season features the Craft Beer Festival, the Tybee Island Pirate Festival, and the glitzy Savannah Film Festival. And on the first Friday of nearly every month visitors can enjoy live music, art, vendors, and fireworks on River Street.

PERFECT DAYS IN SAVANNAH

Here are a few ideas on how to spend a day in Savannah.

Getting to Know the Historic District

Walk over to the Colonial Park Cemetery at the corner of Oglethorpe and Abercorn. Its dramatic iron gateway is a popular spot to pose for photos, and inside you'll find graves dating back to the Revolutionary War. Walk west along Oglethorpe until you reach Bull Street and then turn north toward Wright Square. There you'll find two impressive 19th-century courthouses overlooking the lovely shaded square. For a sweet treat, drop into the Wright Square Café, where you'll find a selection of artisan chocolates. Continue west on York or State streets until you reach Telfair Square. The Jepson Center for the Arts and Telfair Academy are here, and each hosts a diverse array of exhibitions. From there, follow Barnard north until you reach the statue of Johnny Mercer in Ellis Square, which is Savannah's most recently restored square. Stroll west through the colorful City Market. From there you can either cross Martin Luther King Jr. Boulevard to visit the beautiful walled gardens at the Ships of the Sea Museum, or turn to the north until you reach River Street, to hit the restaurants and bars.

Beyond the Historic District

To explore farther outside the downtown Historic District, you'll need a car. Start by heading south toward Victory Drive. Stop at Forsyth Park, if you haven't already; there's usually parking along the southern edge. Proceed to Victory Drive and head east. Visit the historic Bonaventure Cemetery, which sits along the banks of the Bull River and is the final resting place of local notables like Johnny Mercer and Conrad Aiken. Afterward, continue east on Victory, which becomes Highway 80, and head to Fort Pulaski, a national park site with a small museum within the walls and trails that wind out into forest and marsh. On your way back into town, stop for some barbecue at Wiley's Championship BBQ on Whitemarsh Island.

Sun and Sand

Tybee Island is only about 18 miles east of downtown Savannah, but it feels like a different world. This quaint and quirky beach town is definitely worth a visit, especially if you're looking to get some sun on your trip. Arrange to take a guided kayak tour, or rent boats and explore on your own in the morning. Grab lunch on the island, and then slather on some sunscreen and head out to the beach to swim, relax, or build a sandcastle in the afternoon.

IF YOU LIKE

Eating Locally

Foodies have plenty of reasons to love dining in Savannah. An influx of young, talented chefs and entrepreneurs have helped put the focus back on locally grown food here.

Green Truck Pub. Don't be fooled by the burger-and-fries-centric menu, because this place is a must-try. The Green Truck uses only grass-fed beef for its burgers, and everything else is made in-house, including the veggie burgers, salad dressings, and even the ketchup.

The Grey. James Beard–winner Chef Mashama Bailey creates Port City Southern dishes that have won national awards. The service is impeccable, the wine list renowned, and the city's best meal lies within its remodeled Greyhound station walls.

The Olde Pink House. The chef at the Pink House, one of Savannah's most iconic restaurants, isn't afraid to update local traditions, such as its "Southern Sushi," which wraps smoked shrimp and grits in coconut-crusted nori.

The Savannah Bee Company. Its Broughton Street flagship store carries more honey-based products than you'd think possible. Its honey varietals are some of the most delicious you'll find. There are also treats like honey lattes at the barista counter.

Strolling the Squares

With more than 20 to choose from, you never walk far in the Historic District before coming across a square, each with its own personality. Here are a few notable squares to look for as you stroll around downtown.

Chippewa Square. Travelers know this swath of green as the location for the bus-stop scenes in *Forrest Gump*. You won't find the bench here anymore, but you will see the historic Savannah Theatre, several lovely B&Bs, and a great coffee shop.

Ellis Square. Situated at the west end of City Market, the square had been a parking garage for decades until a massive public project restored the public space, which now includes an interactive fountain, a visitor information kiosk, and public restrooms.

Lafayette Square. Here you'll find historic charm and plenty of trees. Flanked by two notable house museums—the Andrew Low House and the Flannery O'Connor Childhood Home—as well as St. John the Baptist Cathedral, Lafayette is like a trip back in time.

Monterey Square. For a look at some of the city's finest historic homes, including the famous Mercer House, which was the center of the action in *Midnight in the Garden of Good and Evil,* head to Monterey Square.

Telfair Square. Bounded by the Telfair Museum, the Jepson Center, and the Trinity United Methodist Church, this park is a popular meet-up spot.

Shopping

If you believe that shopping is the great American pastime, you'll find the scene in Savannah's Historic District incredibly patriotic. The Historic District hosts an eclectic selection of locally owned boutiques and national brands.

Antiques. There are plenty of amazing spots to find everything from 18th-century desks to mid-century modern baubles, but Jere's, Alex Raskin Antiques, or Picker Joe's are good places to start your hunt.

Broughton Street. Home to a variety of shops, you can find national retailers like J. Crew, Urban Outfitters, and Banana Republic, along with local favorites like the Savannah Bee Company, Paris Market, and 24e.

City Market. A four-block stretch of galleries, boutiques, sidewalk cafés, and artists' studios, this market is a stroller's delight.

The Design District. This stretch of Whitaker Street from Gaston north to Charlton has emerged in recent years as one of the city's most stylish hidden gems, with local shops offering fashion, home goods, and more.

River Street. Although this stretch of Savannah has a reputation as a tourist trap, River Street Sweets sells incredible pralines and other treats. And if you need souvenirs like shot glasses or T-shirts, this is the spot.

KIDS AND FAMILIES

Savannah's Historic District offers a number of wonderful family activities, and not all of them are historic home tours. The surrounding areas, particularly the islands to the east of downtown, provide plenty of other options for family fun.

In the Historic District
One good bet for the kids is the Tricentennial Park, which includes the **Savannah Children's Museum,** the **Savannah History Museum,** and the **Georgia State Railroad Museum,** where you can catch a ride on an antique steam engine during warmer months. Another spot where families flock is the ArtZeum section of the **Jepson Center for the Arts,** which includes interactive exhibits designed to entertain the younger crowd. When it starts to get hot outside, hit the fountain at **Ellis Square,** a popular destination for kids of all ages who want to run through the jets of water shooting up from the ground. **Forsyth Park** is another great spot to spend some quality time. There's a large playground, as well as open fields perfect for tossing a Frisbee or football. The restored historic fort across from the Mansion on Forsyth offers public restrooms, a café, and a visitor information kiosk. For older kids who want their own scene, the **Sentient Bean** coffee shop on the south end of Forsyth Park is one of the city's few all-ages venues and features a variety of live music, films, and other programs during the evening.

Elsewhere in Savannah
Among the most popular destinations for families in the area is **Tybee Island.** Whether it's a day relaxing on the beach, or something more adventurous, like renting bicycles, kayaks, or other equipment. The **Crab Shack** capitalizes on family traffic with a large display of baby alligators that allows for up-close viewing of the indigenous reptiles. The **Oatland Island Wildlife Center** is a few miles east of downtown Savannah, and features a zoo, among other exhibits related to local history, flora, and fauna.

EXPLORING
SAVANNAH

Updated
by Anna
Chandler

SAVANNAH, GEORGIA'S OLDEST CITY, BEGAN its modern history on February 12, 1733, when General James Oglethorpe and 120 colonists arrived at Yamacraw Bluff on the Savannah River to form what would be the last British colony in the New World. For a century and a half, the city flourished as a bustling port, serving as a hub of import and export that connected Georgia to the rest of the world.

The past plays an important role in Savannah. Standing in a tranquil square surrounded by historic homes, it's easy to feel as if you have stumbled through a portal into the past. Don't be fooled, though, as the city offers much more than antebellum nostalgia for moonlight and magnolias. Savannah is home to several colleges and universities, including the prestigious Savannah College of Art and Design. In the last decade the city has seen a surge of creative energy that has helped infuse a youthful vibe into the traditions of the Hostess City.

When Oglethorpe founded Savannah, one of the original rules forbade strong drink. Temperance didn't last long, and these days Savannah is one of only a few places in the country without an open container law, meaning that you can walk around downtown with a beer or cocktail so long as it's in a plastic cup—known locally as a "to-go cup." Residents joke that in Atlanta they ask what you do for a living, in Macon they ask where you go to church, and in Savannah they ask what you drink.

Maybe it's the heat, but things move a little more slowly in Savannah. If you're visiting from out of town, take a deep breath, relax, and enjoy the languid pace of "Slow-vannah."

EXPLORING SAVANNAH

With an eclectic array of shops, restaurants, museums, and monuments spread across the Historic District, the best way to explore downtown Savannah is on foot. Whether you plan a route ahead of time or just wander aimlessly, a leisurely stroll will always result in unique discoveries. If your feet start to ache, flag down a pedicab driver—these people-powered vehicles are a great way to get around, and the drivers usually tell a good story or two. Or hop on one of the many meandering trolleys, a great way to see the city. The Victorian District and much of Midtown are just a few minutes' drive away from downtown, while the Islands, Moon River District, Southside, and Gateway will take 10–15 minutes to reach by car.

When you explore beyond Savannah's historic heart, you'll be reminded that it's a place where past and present mingle. Several colleges and universities bring a certain youthful energy to the area, which balances the old history that's preserved in the Bonaventure Cemetery and Fort Pulaski. To explore farther outside the downtown Historic District, you'll need a car. Start by heading south toward Victory Drive, then head east. Visit the Bonaventure Cemetery, which sits along the banks of the Bull River and is the final resting place of local notables like Johnny Mercer and Conrad Aiken. Afterward, continue east on Victory, which becomes Highway 80, and head to Fort Pulaski, a national park site with a fort, a small museum, and trails that wind out into the forest and marsh

THE HISTORIC DISTRICT

General James Oglethorpe, founder of Georgia, plotted Savannah on a grid in a city plan that has won countless awards in the centuries since. The Historic District is neatly hemmed in by the Savannah River, Gaston Street, East Broad Street, and Martin Luther King Jr. Boulevard. Streets are arrow-straight, and public squares are tucked into the grid at precise intervals. Bull Street, anchored on the north by City Hall and the south by Forsyth Park, charges down the center of the grid and maneuvers around the five public squares that stand in its way. The squares all have some historical significance; many have elaborate fountains, monuments to war heroes, and shaded resting areas with park benches. Beautiful homes and mansions speak lovingly of another era.

American Prohibition Museum. In the heart of City Market, America's only museum dedicated to the Prohibition era shares history from 1907 to 1933. In the 6,000 square feet space, guests wander 13 galleries, a theater, and a real speakeasy. From stories of Southern rum runners to the history of moonshine, the museum offers a fun and informative look at the past—there are even four antique cars on the premise. Make sure to enjoy a specially crafted cocktail at the museum speakeasy bar, Congress Street Up, which stays open long after the museum closes. ⌗ *209 W. Julian St., Downtown ✛ In City Market* ☎ *912/220–1249* ⊕ *www.americanprohibitionmuseum.com* ⌗ *$15.*

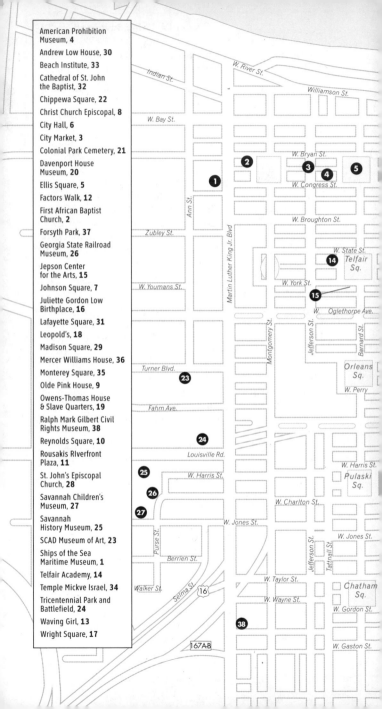

Savannah Historic District and Victorian District

Andrew Low House. Built on the site of the city jail, this residence was constructed in 1848 for Andrew Low, a native of Scotland and one of Savannah's merchant princes. Designed by architect John S. Norris, the residence later belonged to Low's son, William, who inherited his father's wealth and married his longtime sweetheart, Juliette Gordon. The couple moved to England and several years after her husband's death, Juliette returned to this house and founded the Girl Scouts here on March 12, 1912. The house has 19th-century antiques, stunning silver, and some of the finest ornamental ironwork in Savannah, but it is the story and history of the family—even a bedroom named after the family friend and visitor General Robert E. Lee—that is fascinating and well told by the tour guides. ✉ *329 Abercorn St., Historic District* ☎ *912/233–6854* ⊕ *www.andrewlow-house.com* 🎟 *$10; $21 includes admission to Davenport House and Ships of the Sea Museum* ⊙ *Closed early Jan.*

Beach Institute. Works by African American artists from the Savannah area and around the country are on display in this building, which once housed the first school for African American children in Savannah. On permanent exhibit are more than 230 wood carvings by renowned folk artist Ulysses Davis. ✉ *502 E. Harris St., Historic District* ☎ *912/234–8000* ⊕ *www.beachinstitute.org* 🎟 *$7* ⊙ *Closed Sun. and Mon.*

Cathedral of St. John the Baptist. Soaring over the city, this French Gothic–style cathedral, with pointed arches and free-flowing traceries, is the seat of the Catholic diocese of Savannah. It was founded in 1799 by the first French colonists to arrive in Savannah. Fire destroyed the early structures; the present cathedral dates from 1876. Its architecture, gold-leaf adornments, and the entire edifice give testimony to the importance of the Catholic parishioners of the day. The interior spaces are grand and dramatic, including incredible stained glass and an intricately designed altar. ✉ *222 E. Harris St., at Lafayette Sq., Historic District* ☎ *912/233–4709* ⊕ *www.savannahcathedral.org* ⊙ *No tours Sun.*

Chippewa Square. Anchoring this square is Daniel Chester French's imposing bronze statue of General James Edward Oglethorpe, founder of both the city of Savannah and the state of Georgia. The bus-stop scenes of *Forrest Gump* were filmed on the northern end of the square. Savannah Theatre, on the corner of Bull and McDonough Streets, claims to be the oldest continuously operated theater site in North America and offers a variety of family-friendly shows. ⊠ *Bull St., between Hull and Perry Sts., Historic District.*

Christ Church Episcopal. This was the first church—then Anglican—established in the Georgia colony in 1733. It is often called the "Mother Church of Georgia." Located on Johnson Square, the centuries-old building with its columns and wrought-iron railings is an imposing sight. ⊠ *28 Bull St., Historic District* ☎ *912/236–2500* ⊕ *www. christchurchsavannah.org.*

City Hall. Built in 1906 on the site of the Old City Exchange, this imposing structure is now home to the city council. Its landmark tower clock and bells played a significant role in the day-to-day business of Savannah in the days before everyone owned a pocket watch. City Hall is open to the public on weekdays, and visitors can admire the dramatic four-story rotunda crowned with a stained-glass inner dome, mosaic tiles, marble wainscoting, mahogany and live-oak pediments and banisters, and stately fountain. ■ TIP→ Free tours are offered the first Tuesday of each month at noon, but reservations are a must. ⊠ *2 E. Bay St., Historic District* ☎ *912/651–6415* ⊕ *www.savannah.gov.*

City Market. Although the 1870s City Market was razed years ago, its atmosphere and character are still evident. Adjacent to Ellis Square, the area is a lively destination because of its galleries, boutiques, street performers, and open-air cafés. Local favorites include Byrd Cookie Co., a popular Savannah-based bakery with great edible souvenirs, and Pie Society, offering specialty British meat pies. City Market is also a good spot to purchase trolley tickets, take a ride in a horse-drawn carriage, or dive into history at the American Prohibition Museum. ⊠ *W. St. Julian St., between Barnard and Montgomery Sts., Historic District* ☎ *912/232–4903* ⊕ *www.savannahcitymarket.com.*

Colonial Park Cemetery. Stroll the shaded pathways and read some of the old tombstone inscriptions in this park, the final resting place for Savannahians who died between 1750 and 1853. Many of those interred here succumbed during the yellow fever epidemic in 1820. Notice the dramatic entrance gate on the corner of Abercorn and Oglethorpe Streets. Local legend tells that when Sherman's troops set up camp here, they moved some headstones around and altered inscriptions for their own amusement, which partially explains the headstones mounted against the far wall. This spooky spot is a regular stop for ghost tours. ⊠ *Oglethorpe and Abercorn Sts., Historic District.*

Davenport House Museum. Semicircular stairs with wrought-iron railings lead to the recessed doorway of the redbrick Federal home constructed by master builder Isaiah Davenport for his family between 1815 and 1820. Three dormered windows poke through the sloping roof of the stately house, and the interior has polished hardwood floors and fine woodwork and plasterwork. The proposed demolition of this historic Savannah structure galvanized the city's residents into action to save their treasured buildings. The home endured a history of dilapidation that lingered since the 1920s, when it was divided into tenements. When someone proposed razing it to build a parking lot in 1955, a small group of neighbors raised $22,000 to buy and restore this property. This was the inception of the Historic Savannah Foundation and the first of many successful efforts to preserve the architectural treasure that is the city today. ⊠ *324 E. State St., Historic District* ☎ *912/236–8097* ⊕ *www.davenporthousemuseum.org* 🖅 *$9; $21 includes admission to Andrew Low House and Ships of the Sea Museum* ☉ *Closed mid-Jan.*

★ **Fodor's**Choice **Ellis Square.** Converted from a public square to a
FAMILY parking garage in the 1970s, Ellis Square has been restored in recent years and is once again one of Savannah's most popular spots. Near the western end stands a statue of legendary songwriter Johnny Mercer, a Savannah native. Nearby is a visitor center with a touch-screen city guide, maps and brochures, and public restrooms. To the east is a life-size chess board; the pieces can be requested at the visitor center. A treat for youngsters (and the young at heart) is the square's interactive fountain, which is entertaining and refreshing in the warmer months. ⊠ *Barnard St., between W. Congress and W. Bryan Sts., Historic District.*

Factors Walk. A network of iron crosswalks and steep stone stairways connects Bay Street to Factors Walk below. The congested area of multistory buildings was originally the center of commerce for cotton brokers (also called factors), who walked between and above the lower cotton warehouses. Ramps lead down to River Street. ■ TIP→ **This area is paved in cobblestones, so wear comfortable shoes.** ⊠ *Bay St. to Factors Walk, Historic District.*

First African Baptist Church. Slaves constructed this church at night by lamplight after having worked the plantations during the day. It is one of the first organized black Baptist churches on the continent. The basement floor still shows signs of its time as a stop on the Underground Railroad. Designs drilled in the floor are thought to actually have been air holes for slaves hiding underneath, waiting to be transported to the Savannah River for their trip to freedom. It was also an important meeting place during the civil rights era. ⊠ *23 Montgomery St., Historic District* ☎ *912/233–6597* ⊕ *www.firstafricanbc.com* ⊠ *$10* ⊗ *Closed Mon.*

FAMILY **Georgia State Railroad Museum.** This museum preserves the legacy of the Central of Georgia Railway, an integral part of Savannah's industrial heritage. A step into a different era, the museum is home to numerous railcars and boxcars, working diesel and steam locomotives, and a rare functioning railroad turntable. Around the corner is an iconic 125-foot-tall smokestack and the original quarters for workers and managers. Children of all ages will appreciate the expansive model-train exhibit, a fully operable rendition of a train traveling through the region. Ride on a historic diesel or steam locomotive. ⊠ *Tricentennial Park, 303 Martin Luther King Jr. Blvd., Historic District* ☎ *912/651–6823* ⊕ *www.chsgeorgia.org/GSRM* ⊠ *$10.*

★ **Fodor's**Choice **Jepson Center for the Arts.** This contemporary
FAMILY building is one of a kind among the characteristic 18th- and 19th-century architecture of historic Savannah. The modern art extension of the Telfair Academy museum, the Jepson was designed by renowned architect Moshe Safdie. Within the marble-and-glass edifice are rotating exhibits, on loan and from the permanent collection, ranging from European masters to contemporary locals. There's also an outdoor sculpture terrace and an interactive, kid-friendly area on the third level called the ArtZeum. ⊠ *207 W. York St., Historic District* ☎ *912/790–8800* ⊕ *www.telfair.org/visit/jepson-center* ⊠ *$20, includes admission to the Owens-Thomas House & Slave Quarters and the Telfair Academy.*

Johnson Square. The oldest of James Oglethorpe's original squares was laid out in 1733 and named for South Carolina Governor Robert Johnson. A monument marks the grave of Nathanael Greene, a hero of the Revolutionary War. The square has always been a popular gathering place: Savannahians came here to welcome President Monroe in 1819, to greet the Marquis de Lafayette in 1825, and to cheer for Georgia's secession in 1861. ■TIP→ **Locals call this**

FAMOUS FACES IN SAVANNAH

Here's a sampling of the figures who have etched themselves into Savannah's collective memory.

Antwan "Big Boi" Patton (born 1975), best known as half of the legendary hip-hop duo OutKast, was born on the west side of the city.

Fiction writer **Flannery O'Connor** (1925–64) spent the first 13 years of her life in Savannah. Known for her Southern-Gothic style, her greatest achievement is found in her short stories, published in the collections *A Good Man Is Hard to Find* and *Everything That Rises Must Converge*.

James L. Pierpont (1822–93) probably wrote a classic Christmas carol in Savannah, despite the total lack of snow. A native of Medford, Massachusetts, Pierpont became music director of Savannah's Unitarian church in the 1850s.

In 1857 he obtained a copyright for "The One Horse Open Sleigh" (more popularly known as "Jingle Bells"). All was jolly until the 1980s: Tempers flared when Medford claimed that Pierpont had written the song there instead. The dispute over where he wrote the timeless tune remains unresolved.

Johnny Mercer (1909–76), who penned such classic songs as "Moon River" and "Accentuate the Positive," was a fourth-generation Savannah native and helped found Capitol Records. He is buried in Bonaventure Cemetery next to his wife, Ginger.

John Wesley (1703–91), the founder of Methodism, arrived in 1735 and is commemorated by a statue in Reynolds Square. After returning to England, he became one of the towering figures in the history of Protestantism.

Bank Square because of the plethora of nearby banks—perfect if you need an ATM. ⊠ *Bull St., between Bryan and Congress Sts., Historic District.*

FAMILY **Juliette Gordon Low Birthplace.** This early-19th-century town house, attributed to William Jay, was designated in 1965 as Savannah's first National Historic Landmark. "Daisy" Low, founder of the Girl Scouts, was born here in 1860, and the house is now owned and operated by the Girl Scouts of America. Mrs. Low's paintings and other artwork are on display in the house, restored to the style of 1886, the year of Mrs. Low's marriage. Droves of Girl Scout troops make the regular pilgrimage to Savannah to see their founder's birthplace and earn merit badges. ■ TIP→ **Tickets sell fast, so** book in advance if you want to tour the house on a specific day. ✉ *10 E. Oglethorpe St., Historic District* ☎ *912/233–4501* ⊕ *www.juliettegordonlowbirthplace.org* 🎫 *$15* ⊙ *Closed Sun. and early Jan.*

Lafayette Square. Named for the Marquis de Lafayette, who aided the Americans during the Revolutionary War, the square contains a graceful three-tier fountain donated by the Georgia chapter of the Colonial Dames of America. The Cathedral of St. John the Baptist is located on this square, as are the Andrew Low House and the impressive Hamilton-Turner Inn. The childhood home of celebrated Southern author Flannery O'Connor also sits on this square. ✉ *Abercorn St., between E. Harris and E. Charlton Sts., Historic District.*

Leopold's. One of the best ice-cream parlors in the area is Leopold's, a Savannah institution since 1919. It's currently owned by Stratton Leopold, grandson of the original owner and the producer of films like *Mission Impossible 3*. Movie posters and paraphernalia make for an entertaining sideline to the selection of ice cream made with the old family recipe. Try the delicious lemon custard or honey almond and cream flavors, or unique seasonal inventions like lavender, orange blossom, or rose petal. ✉ *212 E. Broughton St., Historic District* ☎ *912/234–4442* ⊕ *www.leopoldsicecream.com.*

Madison Square. Laid out in 1839 and named for President James Madison, this square is home to a statue depicting Sergeant William Jasper hoisting a flag, a tribute to his bravery during the Siege of Savannah. Though mortally wounded, Jasper rescued the colors of his regiment in the assault on the British lines. A granite marker denotes the southern line of the British defense during the 1779 battle. The Green-Meldrim House is here. ✉ *Bull St., between W. Harris and W. Charlton Sts., Historic District.*

Mercer Williams House. A staple on the tourist circuit, this house museum has been the stuff of legend since the release of the longtime bestselling novel *Midnight in the Garden of Good and Evil*, which was based on the murder trial of local antiques dealer Jim Williams. Williams, who purportedly killed his lover in the front den while sitting at the desk where he later died, purchased the house in 1969. Scandal aside, Williams was an aficionado of historic preservation, and the Mercer House was one of some 50 properties that he purchased and restored. Designed by New York architect John S. Norris for General Hugh Mercer, great-grandfather

FAMILY-FRIENDLY SAVANNAH

Savannah has its share of kid-appropriate activities. Juliette Gordon Low's Birthplace is the original home of the founder of the Girl Scouts, and girls of scouting age flock here annually, especially during the summer. The house is full of period furnishings and memorabilia from the early days of the Girl Scouts. On the second floor is Juliette's childhood room with vintage toys and dolls and two dollhouses, one a Georgia Plains–style farmhouse.

City Market is always popular with younger children. Even if your child isn't keen on a horse-drawn carriage tour, they may enjoy petting the horses and taking pictures with them. A short stroll farther lands you at the Ellis Square fountain, a popular spot to run through the jets of water when the weather is warm.

Kids flock to Savannah's Tricentennial Museums, which include the Savannah Children's Museum, Georgia State Railroad Museum, and Savannah History Museum, all within walking distance of one another. Entertaining and educational activities include story-time sessions, the backyard science program, rides on a historic steam engine, and programs about archaeology.

Forsyth Park is a great place to let kids run free, with wide-open fields, perfect for Frisbee or a game of catch, and two playgrounds—one for younger children and one for older.

The Jepson Center for the Arts is a terrific venue for children and helps instill an appreciation for art. ArtZeum, located on the upper levels, is an interactive, two-story space especially designed to entertain and educate.

Belles Ferry, the free water taxi that goes back and forth to the Westin, can also be a kid-pleasing opportunity to ride across the river. The trip offers great views of the old buildings lining the riverfront.

East of the Historic District is Oatland Island, a wildlife preserve that is popular with youngsters. Fenced habitats for wolves, bobcats, bison, and numerous birds are dotted along walking trails that run through the forest and marsh.

With long stretches of beach, quirky shops, and casual restaurants, Tybee Island is another popular destination for families.

of Johnny Mercer, the home was constructed in 1860 and completed after the end of the Civil War in 1868. Inside are fine examples of 18th- and 19th-century furniture and art from Jim Williams's private collection. ■ TIP→ **Don't miss a look around the charming gift shop.** ✉ *429 Bull St., Historic District* ☎ *912/236–6352* ⊕ *mercerhouse.com* 🖅 *$13.*

Monterey Square. Commemorating the victory of General Zachary Taylor's forces in Monterrey, Mexico, in 1846, this is the southernmost of Bull Street's squares. A monument honors General Casimir Pulaski, the Polish nobleman who lost his life in the Siege of Savannah during the Revolutionary War. On the square sits Temple Mickve Israel (one of the country's oldest Jewish congregations) and some of the city's most beautiful mansions, including the infamous Mercer House. ✉ *Bull St., between Taylor and Gordon Sts., Historic District.*

Olde Pink House. Built in 1771, this is one of the oldest buildings in town. Now a restaurant, the portico pink-stucco Georgian mansion has also been a private home, a bank, and headquarters for a Yankee general during the Civil War. In its lower level is the city's most beloved piano bar, Planters Tavern, and on the southern side there's a bar and sidewalk café. ✉ *23 Abercorn St., Historic District* ☎ *912/232–4286* ⊕ *www.plantersinnsavannah.com/the-olde-pink-house.*

★ Fodor'sChoice **Owens-Thomas House & Slave Quarters.** Designed by William Jay, the Owens-Thomas House is widely considered to be one of the finest examples of English Regency architecture in America. Built in 1816–19, the house was constructed with local materials. Of particular note are the curving walls of the house, Greek-inspired ornamental molding, half-moon arches, stained-glass panels, original Duncan Phyfe furniture, the hardwood "bridge" on the second floor, and the indoor toilets, which it had before the White House or Versailles. In 2018, the site renamed itself the Owens-Thomas House & Slave Quarters and revealed a new interpretive exhibition that includes the home's restored slave quarters. Owned and administered by the Telfair Museum of Art, this home gives an inside perspective on Savannah's history. ✉ *124 Abercorn St., Historic District* ☎ *912/790–8889* ⊕ *www.telfair.org/visit/owens-thomas* 🖅 *$20, includes admission to Jepson Center for the Arts and the Telfair Museum of Art.*

Ralph Mark Gilbert Civil Rights Museum. This history museum, named after the late Dr. Ralph Mark Gilbert, the father of Savannah's modern day Civil Rights Movement and leader of the NAACP, has a series of engaging exhibits on segregation, from emancipation through the civil rights movement. The role of black and white Savannahians in ending segregation in their city is well detailed and includes archival photographs and videos. There's also a replica of a lunch counter where black patrons were denied service. ✉ *460 Martin Luther King Jr. Blvd., Historic District* ☎ *912/777–6099* ✍ *$8* ⊘ *Closed Sun. and Mon.*

Reynolds Square. Anglican cleric and theologian John Wesley is remembered here. He arrived in Savannah in 1736 at the behest of General James Oglethorpe. During his short stay, the future founder of the Methodist Church preached and wrote the first English hymnal in the city. His monument in Reynolds Square is shaded by greenery and surrounded by park benches. The landmark Planters Inn, formerly the John Wesley Hotel, is also located on the square. Ironically, though it was named after a man of the cloth, it was considered the best brothel in town at the turn of the century. ✉ *Abercorn St., between E. Congress and E. Bryan Sts., Historic District.*

Rousakis Riverfront Plaza. From River Street's main pavilion you can watch a parade of freighters and pug-nosed tugs glide by along the river. River Street is the main venue for several of the city's grandest celebrations, including the First Friday Fireworks. The plaza is named for former Savannah mayor John Rousakis and fills with locals for Savannah's signature St. Patrick's Day festivities and Fourth of July celebration. Rousakis, like greater River Street, is flanked by an abundance of shops and restaurants and draws colorful street entertainers. ✉ *River St., near Abercorn St., Historic District.*

St. John's Episcopal Church. Built in 1852, this church is famous for its whimsical chimes and stained-glass windows. The extraordinary parish house is the revered Green-Meldrim House. One interesting bit of trivia: on Christmas 1864, after General Sherman moved into the Green-Meldrim House, his army chaplain conducted the church's Christmas service. ✉ *1 W. Macon St., at Madison Sq., Historic District* ☎ *912/232–1251* ⊕ *www.stjohnssav. org.*

★ **Fodor'sChoice Savannah Children's Museum.** Adhering to the
FAMILY principle of learning through doing, the Savannah Children's Museum has open green spaces with several stations geared for sensory play, including a water–sand play excavation station, sound station of percussion instruments, and

FULL STEAM AHEAD

The first steam-powered ship to cross the Atlantic was the SS *Savannah*, which sailed from Savannah north to Newark and then finally to Scotland, England, and Russia during its maiden voyage in 1819. The ship was funded by local shipping magnate William Scarborough, whose home still stands on Martin Luther King Jr. Boulevard (formerly West Broad Street). While the SS *Savannah*'s first trip was a success as a major landmark in the evolution of maritime travel and commerce, the endeavor didn't work out so well for Scarborough as a businessman. He ended up bankrupt and eventually was forced to sell his newly constructed home, which is now the Ships of the Sea Maritime Museum—an appropriate homage to its original tenant. Before the building underwent substantial restorations prior to becoming the museum, it spent nearly a century as a public school. Opened in the 1870s, the West Broad Street School was the first officially sanctioned school for African American children in the city.

an organic garden. The storybook nook is a partnership with the Savannah public library and encourages visiting youngsters to balance physical and mental recreation. One station includes costumes for stage performances. ✉ *Tricentennial Park, 655 Louisville Rd., Historic District* ☎ *912/651–4292* ⊕ *www.chsgeorgia.org/scm* 🎟 *$8* ⊗ *Closed Sun. in June–Aug., and Mon. and Tues. in Sept.–May.*

FAMILY **Savannah History Museum.** This history museum houses exhibits on Savannah's cultural and military history. Inside you'll find much about the lives of early Native American settlers, including the development of tabby (crushed oyster shells with lime, sand, and water) for use in early construction. Subsequent historical periods are portrayed, including the Revolutionary and Civil War eras and the Industrial Revolution. More modern highlights include the city's countless Hollywood film appearances over the years, the most memorable of which might be *Forrest Gump*. The very bench that Tom Hanks sat on can be seen here. ✉ *Tricentennial Park, 303 Martin Luther King Jr. Blvd., Historic District* ☎ *912/651–6825* ⊕ *www.chsgeorgia.org* 🎟 *$7.*

★ Fodor'sChoice **SCAD Museum of Art.** This architectural marvel rose from the ruins of the oldest surviving railroad building in the United States. Appropriately, the architect chosen for the lofty design and remodel project was Christian Sottile, the valedictorian of Savannah College of Art and Design's 1997 graduating class and the current dean of the School of Building Arts. Sottile rose to the hearty challenge of merging the past with the present, preserving key architectural details of the original structure while introducing contemporary design elements. SCAD Museum of Art houses two main galleries with rotating exhibits by some of the most acclaimed figures in contemporary art: the Evans Gallery features works of African American arts and culture, while the André Leon Talley Gallery is devoted to fashion and high style. ✉ *601 Turner Blvd., Historic District* ☎ *912/525–7191* ⊕ *www.scadmoa.org* 🎟 *$10* ☾ *Closed Mon.*

★ Fodor'sChoice **Ships of the Sea Maritime Museum.** This exuberant
FAMILY   Greek Revival mansion was the home of William Scarborough, a wealthy early-19th-century merchant and one of the principal owners of the *Savannah*, the first steamship to cross the Atlantic. The structure, with its portico capped by half-moon windows, is another of architect William Jay's notable contributions to the Historic District. These days, it houses the Ships of the Sea Museum, with displays of model ships and exhibits detailing maritime history. The ambitious North Garden nearly doubled the original walled courtyard's size and provides ample space for naturalist-led walks and outdoor concerts. ✉ *41 Martin Luther King Jr. Blvd., Historic District* ☎ *912/232–1511* ⊕ *www.shipsofthesea.org* 🎟 *$9* ☾ *Closed Mon.*

★ Fodor'sChoice **Telfair Academy.** The oldest public art museum in the Southeast was designed by William Jay in 1819 for Alexander Telfair. Within its marble rooms are a variety of paintings from American and European masters, plaster casts of the Elgin Marbles and other classical sculptures, and some of the Telfair family furnishings, including a Duncan Phyfe sideboard and Savannah-made silver. ✉ *121 Barnard St., Historic District* ☎ *912/790–8800* ⊕ *www.telfair.org* 🎟 *$20, includes admission to the Jepson Center for the Arts and the Owens-Thomas House & Slave Quarters.*

Temple Mickve Israel. This unique Gothic-revival synagogue on Monterey Square houses the third-oldest Jewish congregation in the United States; its founding members settled in town only five months after the establishment of Savannah in 1733. The synagogue's permanent collection includes documents and letters (some from such notables as George Washington, James Madison, and Thomas Jefferson) pertaining to early Jewish life in Savannah and Georgia. ✉ *20 E. Gordon St., Historic District* ☎ *912/233–1547* ⊕ *www. mickveisrael.org* ☜ *$8 tour.*

FAMILY **Tricentennial Park and Battlefield.** This 25-acre complex is home to the Savannah History Museum, the Georgia State Railroad Museum, and the Savannah Children's Museum, as well as Battlefield Memorial Park. This site offers an unbeatable introduction to the city and a full day of fun for the whole family. The battlefield was the site of the second bloodiest battle of the Revolutionary War where, on October 9, 1779, 800 of the 8,000 troops who fought lost their lives. ✉ *303 Martin Luther King Jr. Blvd., Historic District* ☎ *912/651–6840* ⊕ *www.savannah.com/tricentennial-park.*

Waving Girl. This statue at River Street and East Broad Ramp is a beloved symbol of Savannah's Southern hospitality. It commemorates Florence Martus, a sister to the lighthouse keeper, who waved to ships in Savannah's port for more than 44 years. She would wave a white towel and, when young, always had her dog by her side. Late in her life, locals threw her a huge birthday party at Fort Pulaski with more than 5,000 guests. Despite having welcomed so many sailors to port, she died without ever having been wed. ✉ *River St. near E. Broad Ramp, Historic District.*

Wright Square. Named for James Wright, Georgia's last colonial governor, this square has an elaborate monument in its center that honors William Washington Gordon, founder of the Central of Georgia Railroad. A slab of granite from Stone Mountain adorns the grave of Tomochichi, the Yamacraw chief who befriended General Oglethorpe and the colonists. ✉ *Bull St., between W. State and W. York Sts., Historic District.*

VICTORIAN DISTRICT AND EASTSIDE

Bordered by Gwinnett, Abercorn, and 31st Street, the Victorian District is Savannah's first neighborhood with the picturesque Forsyth Park at its heart. You'll find many historic bed-and-breakfasts here, including Catherine Ward House Inn and Azalea Inn & Villas. The Mansion on Forsyth Park is nestled alongside Forsyth Park.

★ Fodor'sChoice **Forsyth Park.** The heart of the city's outdoor life, FAMILY Forsyth Park hosts a number of popular cultural events, including film screenings, sports matches, and the annual Savannah Jazz Festival. Built in 1840 and expanded in

MOSS MYSTIQUE

Spanish moss—the silky gray garlands that drape over the branches of live oaks—has come to symbolize the languorous sensibilities of the Deep South. A relative of the pineapple, the moisture-loving plant requires an average year-round humidity of 70%, and thus thrives in subtropical climates—including Georgia's coastal regions.

Contrary to popular belief, Spanish moss is not a par-asite; it's an epiphyte, or "air plant," taking water and nutrients from the air and photosynthesizing in the same manner as soil-bound plants. It reproduces using tiny flowers. When water is scarce, it turns gray, and when the rains come it takes on a greenish hue. Although it is tempting to grab handfuls of Spanish moss as a souvenir, be careful. It often harbors the biting menaces commonly known as chiggers.

1851, the park was part of General Oglethorpe's original city plan and made possible by the donation of land from Georgia Governor John Forsyth. A glorious white fountain dating to 1858, Confederate and Spanish-American War memorials, a rose garden, multiple playgrounds, tennis and basketball courts, and an old fort are spread across this grand park. Be sure to stop by Saturday for the bustling farmers' market. The park's 1-mile perimeter is among the prettiest walks in the city and takes you past many beautifully restored historic homes. ⊠ *Gaston St., between Drayton and Whitaker Sts., Historic District.*

THE STARLAND DISTRICT, THOMAS SQUARE, AND MIDTOWN

Midtown Savannah includes neighborhoods south of Forsyth Park to Derenne Avenue, including the Starland District, Thomas Square Streetcar Historic District, Baldwin Park and Ardsley Park. The area is home to numerous B&Bs, fabulous dining (try an award-winning burgers at Green Truck Neighborhood Pub or beautiful seasonal fare at Atlantic) and a vibrant arts and culture scene.

MOON RIVER DISTRICT

Experience marshside tranquillity in the Moon River District, named after the tune that made Savannah native Johnny Mercer famous. The area includes the Sandfly, Isle of Hope, and Skidaway Island neighborhoods and is a necessary stop for outdoor adventurers and history buffs. Learn about Gullah Geechee culture at Pin Point Heritage Museum, see the area by water with Moon River Kayak Tours, and sip a handcrafted cocktail on the dock at The Wyld Dock Bar. See beautiful coastal homes on Isle of Hope, a historic community flanked by Herb River and Skidaway River. Wormsloe Historic Site, on Skidaway Road, is a beautiful visit. Carry on to Skidaway Island and enjoy a nature walk at Skidaway Island State Park.

Isle of Hope. In 1736, General James Oglethorpe, who founded the colony of Georgia, parceled out 1,500 acres along the Intracoastal Waterway on the condition that the owners would help defend the city. The northernmost tract, today known as the Isle of Hope, was bequeathed to Henry Parker, who became the first acting governor in 1752. In the 1840s, the island had become a popular community for summer homes and, by 1875, the terminus for the Savannah, Skidaway, and Seaboard railroads, three major transit routes that transported travelers from far up the east coast and across the South. Today, the horseshoe-shape island provides sweeping views and cool breezes from almost any point along the bluff, as well as an array of beautiful, historic homes. ✉ *Thunderbolt.*

Pin Point Heritage Museum. The culturally rich community surrounding this museum has lived in relative isolation for nearly 100 years. Residents of Pin Point are Gullah/Geechee descendants of first-generation freed slaves from Ossabaw Island. Founded in 1890 on the banks of Moon River, this fishing community has a deep connection to the water. Many residents once worked at the A.S. Varn & Son oyster and crab factory, which has been transformed into this museum to honor the life, work, and history of the community. ✉ *9924 Pin Point Ave.* ☎ *912/355–0064* ⊕ *www.chsgeorgia.org/phm* ☺ *Closed Sun.–Wed.*

FAMILY **UGA Marine Education Center and Aquarium.** On the grounds of the former Modena Plantation, the University of Georgia runs this aquarium with exhibits about the state's coastal wildlife and ecosystems. Kids love seeing the tidal creeks of the salt marshes, the ocean beaches, and the open waters

Greater Savannah

ATLANTIC OCEAN

Tybee Island Lighthouse and Museum

Tybee Island Marine Science Center

TYBEE ISLAND

80

Fort Pulaski National Monument

Little Tybee Island

Fort Pulaski National Monument

Savannah River

South Channel

THE ISLANDS

367

Oatland Island Wildlife Center

Oatland Island

Johnny Mercer Dr.

Wilmington Island

Whitemarsh Island

80

UGA Marine Education Center and Aquarium

TO HILTON HEAD

The Eugene Talmadge Memorial Bridge

ALT 17

Old Fort Jackson

ALT 17

Hutchinson Island

Back River

Savannah River

Liberty St.

Gwinnett St.

HISTORIC DISTRICT

Bonaventure Cemetery

THUNDERBOLT

Skidaway Rd.

McWhorter Dr.

Skidaway Island State Park

Skidaway Island

Green Island Rd.

Skidaway Rd.

Isle of Hope

Laroche Av.

Diamond Cswy.

Wormsloe State Historic Site

ALT 17

SAVANNAH

Victory Dr.

Skidaway Rd.

Derenne Av.

Waters Av.

Harry S. Truman Pkwy.

Ferguson Av.

Whitfield Av.

MOON RIVER DISTRICT

Pin Point Heritage Museum

516

Mills B. Lane Blvd (52nd St.)

516

80

204

Abercorn

White Bluff

GATEWAY

Montgomery Cross Rd.

SOUTH-SIDE

Vernon River

Coffee Bluff

Little Ogeechee River

21

GARDEN CITY

Louisville Rd.

516

17

Chatham Pkwy.

Amtrak Station

80

16

17

307

White Bluff Rd.

Middle Ground Rd.

204

Savannah Int'l Airport

Mighty Eighth Air Force Heritage Museum

EXIT 102

EXIT 99B

POOLER

Quacco Rd.

Pooler Pkwy.

95

SAVANNAH

Atlantic Coast Hwy.

Veterans Pkwy.

Quacco Rd.

EXIT 94

Abercorn Pkwy.

Coastal Georgia Botanical Gardens

204

80

16

17

95

Ogeechee River

17

Ford Av.

3 miles

3 kilometers

of the continental shelf up close. The sea turtles are especially popular. Don't miss the nearby nature trails. ✉ *30 Ocean Science Circle, Skidaway Island* ✛ *8 miles south of Savannah* ☎ *912/598–3325* ⊕ *gacoast.uga.edu/uga-aquarium* ✉ *$6* ☉ *Closed Sun.*

Wormsloe State Historic Site. In 1736, General James Oglethorpe gave 500 acres to Noble Jones, who was required to build a small fort to protect Savannah from an attack up the Skidaway River. Wormsloe is the only property in Georgia remaining in the hands of descendants of the original owners. Over the years, the land was used to produce cotton, as well as fruits, vegetables, and silk. In later years it served as a dairy farm and rice mill. Many of the 400 oaks planted along the mile-and-a-half entry in 1891 still stand proud today—you might recognize them from the movie *Forrest Gump*. Today, you can tour the tabby fort ruins, wander around the historic cemetery, and take in colonial plantation reenactments. ✉ *7601 Skidaway Rd.* ☎ *912/353–3023* ⊕ *www.gastateparks.org/wormsloe* ✉ *$10.*

SOUTHSIDE, GATEWAY, AND GREATER SAVANNAH

For bigger chains and shopping malls, head to the Southside; it's also where you'll find the majority of Savannah's movie theatres and cheaper rates on chain hotels. Gateway is conveniently located close to the Savannah/Hilton Head Airport off of I–95 about 20 minutes from downtown. While it doesn't offer the Historic District's charm, the hotel and motel rates can't be beat.

Coastal Georgia Botanical Gardens. In 1890, Mrs. Herman B. Miller planted three clumps of Japanese timber bamboo near her farmhouse 15 miles south of Savannah. As the bamboo took to the warm Southern climate, it spread to what now stands today at the Bamboo Farms at the Coastal Georgia Botanical Gardens. The gardens, deeded to the University of Georgia in 1983, now also boast a 4-acre bamboo maze, a children's garden, formal and shade gardens, and a water garden. Seasonally, visitors can enjoy the pick-your-own berries garden. ✉ *2 Canebrake Rd.* ☎ *912/921–5460* ⊕ *www.coastalgeorgiabg.org* ✉ *$5.*

Mighty Eighth Air Force Heritage Museum. A famous World War II squadron called the Mighty Eighth was formed in Savannah in 1942. Within one month, they answered the call to arms and shipped out to the United Kingdom. Flying in Royal Air Force planes, the Mighty Eighth became the largest air force of the period. Exhibits at this museum begin with the prelude to World War II and the rise of Adolf Hitler, and continue through Desert Storm. You can see vintage aircraft, fly a simulated bombing mission with a B-17 crew, test your skills as a waist gunner, and view interviews with courageous World War II vets. The museum also has three theaters, an art gallery, and a 7,000-volume library. ⊠ *175 Bourne Ave.* ☎ *912/748–8888* ⊕ *www.mightyeighth. org* ⊠ *$12.*

THE ISLANDS AND THUNDERBOLT

Drive out of Savannah's downtown and you'll find one-of-a-kind marsh views and stunning sunset vistas. Thunderbolt, bordering on Savannah's east side and the Wilmington River, is a lush residential community that's home to historic Bonaventure Cemetery and delicious seafood spots like Tubby's Tank House. Head east on US-80 and discover Wilmington Island, a cozy neighborhood on the Wilmington River. Historic Fort Pulaski and Oatland Island Wildlife Center are nearby.

★ **Fodor's**Choice **Bonaventure Cemetery.** The largest of Savannah's municipal cemeteries, Bonaventure spreads over 160 acres and sits on a bluff above the Wilmington River. Once a plantation, the land became a private cemetery in 1846 and the public cemetery was established in 1907. The scenescape is one of lush natural beauty transposed against the elegant and almost eerie backdrop of lavish marble headstones, monuments, and mausoleums. John Muir reportedly camped at Bonaventure in 1867 on his legendary "thousand-mile walk." Local photographer Jack Leigh, novelist and poet Conrad Aiken, and singer-songwriter Johnny Mercer are among those interred here. ⊠ *330 Greenwich Rd., Thunderbolt* ☎ *912/651–6843* ⊕ *www.bonaventure-historical.org.*

★ **Fodor's**Choice **Fort Pulaski National Monument.** Named for Casi-
FAMILY mir Pulaski, a Polish count and Revolutionary War hero, this must-see sight for Civil War buffs was designed by Napoléon's military engineer and built on Cockspur Island between 1829 and 1847. Robert E. Lee's first assignment after graduating from West Point was as an engineer here. The fort was thought to be impervious to attack, but as weapons advanced, it proved penetrable. During the Civil War, the fort fell after bombardment by newfangled rifled cannons. The restored fortification, operated by the

National Park Service, has moats, drawbridges, massive ramparts, and towering walls. The park has trails and picnic areas. ⊠ *U.S. Hwy. 80* ☎ *912/786–5787* ⊕ *www.nps.gov/fopu* ⊑ *$7.*

FAMILY **Oatland Island Wildlife Center.** A few miles east of the Historic District, this wildlife preserve is home to a variety of animal habitats spread along a 2-mile-long path. Several coastal habitats are represented, including the wetlands that are home to alligators, herons, and cranes. Bobcats, wolves, buffalo, armadillo, and assorted birds of prey are also on exhibit. ■TIP➔ **Be sure to bring comfortable shoes.** ⊠ *711 Sandtown Rd.* ☎ *912/395–1212* ⊕ *www.oatlandisland.org* ⊑ *$5.*

Old Fort Jackson. The oldest standing fort in Georgia was garrisoned in the War of 1812 and was the Confederate headquarters for the river batteries. Surrounded by a tidal moat, the brink fort guards Five Fathom Hole, the 18th-century deep-water port in the Savannah River. Inside you'll see exhibits that highlight the life of a soldier in the 19th century. Battle reenactments, blacksmithing demonstrations, and traditional music programs are among the attractions. ⊠ *1 Fort Jackson Rd.* ☎ *912/232–3945* ⊕ *www.chsgeorgia.org/OFJ* ⊑ *$8.*

TYBEE ISLAND

The Yamacraw Indians originally came to this island in the Atlantic Ocean to hunt and fish, but these days, the island is chock-full of seafood restaurants, chain motels, and souvenir shops—most of which sprang up during the 1950s and haven't changed much since. Fun-loving locals still host big annual parties like fall's Pirate Festival and spring's Beach Bum Parade. Tybee Island's entire expanse of taupe sand is divided into three public beach stretches: North Beach, the Pier and Pavilion, and the South End. Beach activities abound, including swimming, boating, fishing, sea kayaking, and parasailing. Newer water sports have gained popularity, including kiteboarding and stand-up paddleboarding.

Tybee Island Lighthouse and Museum. Considered one of North America's most beautifully renovated lighthouses, the Tybee Light Station has been guiding Savannah River mariners since 1736. It's not the first lighthouse built on this site; the original was built on orders of General James Oglethorpe in 1732. You can walk up 178 steps for amazing views at the top. The lighthouse keeper's cottage houses a small theater showing a video about the lighthouse. The nearby museum is housed in a gun battery constructed for the Spanish-American War. ✉ *30 Meddin Dr., Tybee Island* ☎ *912/786–5801* ⊕ *www.tybeelighthouse.org* ✍ *$9* ⊘ *Closed Tues.*

FAMILY **Tybee Island Marine Science Center.** Don't miss the Tybee Island Marine Science Center's interesting exhibit on Coastal Georgia, which houses local wildlife ranging from Ogeechee corn snakes to American alligators. Schedule one of two guided walks along the beach and marshes if you're interested in the flora and fauna of the Lowcountry. There is also a "Turtle Talk," which consists of a classroom discussion and hands-on workshop. ■TIP→ **Arrive early, as parking near the center can be competitive in the busier months.** ✉ *1509 Strand Ave., Tybee Island* ☎ *912/786–5917* ⊕ *www.tybee-marinescience.org* ✍ *$5; tours $10.*

WHERE TO EAT

Updated
by Anna
Chandler

SOUTHERN CUISINE IS RICH IN tradition, but the dining scene in Savannah is more than just fried chicken and barbecue. Many of the city's restaurants have been exploring locally sourced ingredients as a way to tweak their usual homespun offerings, a change that is now attracting chefs and foodies alike.

Although the farm-to-table trend was first spotted at upscale spots like Cha Bella or Local 11ten, more neighborhood restaurants are now getting in on the action. In the Victorian District, Starland District, and Thomas Square District, places like Atlantic, The Vault Kitchen + Market, and Cotton & Rye serve elegant dishes with local flavor and thoughtful wine pairings. Downtown, take in the star power of The Grey, home of James Beard–winner Chef Mashama Bailey, or Southern food titan Sean Brock's Husk.

The arrival of some new kids on the block doesn't mean the old standbys have ridden off into the sunset just yet. For traditional, exquisitely prepared menus, be sure to visit Elizabeth on 37th or the Olde Pink House, both of which have been pleasing local palates for decades. Or follow the crowds to either Paula Deen's famous Lady & Sons or the ever-popular Mrs. Wilkes' Dining Room (which even President Obama once visited), where you'll find all the fried chicken, collard greens, and mac and cheese you can handle. Or beat the lines at locals-only places like Sisters of the New South on the city's Eastside.

If you're looking for barbecue, several spots throughout Savannah can satisfy your urge for slow-cooked meats of all kind. For lunch, check out Sandfly Bar-B-Q, whose Victorian District outpost slings brisket, pulled pork, and wings in a refurbished railway car. Another popular spot with local meat lovers is Wiley's Championship BBQ, located on nearby Wilmington Island.

That's just a few ideas to get you started. While exploring Savannah, you're sure to find any number of other exciting options as well, whether you're craving noodle bowls or a simple sandwich.

HOURS, PRICES, AND DRESS

Most popular restaurants serve both lunch and dinner, usually to around 9 pm, later on Friday and Saturday night. Sunday brunch is a beloved institution, but be prepared to wait for a table at most of the popular spots.

Best Bets for Savannah Dining

With the many restaurants to choose from, how will you decide where to eat? Fodor's writers and editors have selected their favorite restaurants by price, cuisine, and experience in the Best Bets lists below. The Fodor's Choice properties represent the "best of the best." Peruse our reviews for details about the restaurants.

Fodor's Choice: Back in the Day Bakery, Circa 1875, Elizabeth on 37th, Garibaldi's, Green Truck Pub, Local 11ten, Mrs. Wilkes' Dining Room, Olde Pink House, Wiley's Championship BBQ, Zunzi's

Best Budget Eats: Al Salaam Deli, Back in the Day Bakery, Green Truck Pub, Treylor Park, Vinnie VanGoGo's, Wiley's Championship BBQ, Zunzi's

Best Barbecue: Sandfly Bar-B-Q, Wiley's Championship BBQ

Best Southern Food: The Grey, Elizabeth on 37th, Husk, Mrs. Wilkes' Dining Room, Sisters of the New South, Vic's on the River

Best Brunch: B. Matthews Eatery, Ordinary Pub, The Collins Quarter

Best Lunch: Back in the Day Bakery, Kayak Kafe, Zunzi's, Starland Cafe

Child-Friendly: Crystal Beer Parlor, Green Truck Pub, The Pirates' House, Vinnie VanGoGo's, Zunzi's, The Crab Shack, B&D Burgers

Best for Foodies: The Grey, Husk, Elizabeth on 37th, Cotton & Rye, Green Truck Pub, Local 11ten

Most Romantic: Circa 1875, Elizabeth on 37th, Noble Fare, Olde Pink House

Outdoor Seating: The Wyld Dock Bar, Local 11ten, The Public Kitchen & Bar, B&D Burgers, Vinnie VanGoGo's, Zunzi's

Prices, although on the rise, are lower than in most major cities, especially on either coast.

Some locals and restaurant owners have a laid-back attitude about dressing for a night out. And if you are hitting a River Street tourist restaurant, a small neighborhood eatery, or a barbecue joint, jeans are just fine. However, if you are going to an upscale restaurant, dress in keeping with the environment, especially on weekend nights.

WHAT IT COSTS			
$	$$	$$$	$$$$
Restaurants under $15	$15–$19	$20–$24	over $24

Restaurant prices are for a main course at dinner, not including taxes (7.5% on food, 8.5% tax on liquor).

HISTORIC DISTRICT

$$$$ ✕ **a.lure.** *Modern American.* This simple, sophisticated dining room is smartly designed so there isn't a bad seat in the house. Don't be afraid to fill up on light bites—like the lamb carpaccio with house-made blue-cheese ice cream or the fried green tomatoes paired with American speck ham, pimento cheese and green goddess dressing—and then skip right to dessert: the frozen goat-cheese soufflé is delightful in both flavor and architectural presentation. **Known for:** shrimp and grits; intimate ambience; reimagined Southern fare. $ *Average main: $31* ✉ *309 W. Congress St., City Market* ☎ *912/233–2111* ⊕ *aluresavannah.com* ⊘ *No lunch.*

$ ✕ **B&D Burgers.** *Burger.* Locally owned and operated B&D
FAMILY Burgers is a great bet for a quick, low-key bite to eat with offerings like—tempura-style chicken fingers and the grand assortment of locally themed burgers. The large, two-story dining room is decorated in Lowcountry flair, including faux trophy alligators and nets and buoys, but be encouraged to venture outside; this place has some of the best outdoor dining in the city and the expansive patio is equipped with a video screen for sports events and large umbrellas that protect against the rain and sun. **Known for:** big-screen sports viewing; kid-friendly menu; locations on Broughton Street, Southside, and Pooler. $ *Average main: $11* ✉ *209 W. Congress St., Historic District* ☎ *912/238–8315* ⊕ *bdburgers.net.*

$$ ✕ **B. Matthews Eatery.** *Eclectic.* The freshly updated and expanded kitchen here offers a great menu that ranges from the familiar to the unexpected; it's a favorite brunch spot for locals and tourists. Breakfast is a highlight, while lunch is known for being a great value—most of the well-stuffed sandwiches go for around $9; dinner entrées are more upscale fare that won't break the bank, and the best bets include shrimp and grits and braised short ribs. **Known for:** vibrant brunch and lunch scene; good vegetarian options; unique twist on Southern classics like the fried green tomato and pimento cheese sandwiches or the black-eyed pea cakes served up with Cajun rémoulade. ⑤ *Average main: $19* ✉ *325 E. Bay St., Historic District* ☎ *912/233–1319* ⊕ *www. bmatthewseatery.com* ⊗ *No dinner Sun.*

$ ✕ **Bier Haus.** *German.* This Belgian–German gastropub has made a name for itself with its generous pots of mussels steamed in your choice of beer; the menu offers several vegetarian options as well, including mushrooms and artichokes with polenta. Aside from the food, Bier Haus rightfully boasts about its 25 rotating taps (about 10 are Belgian and 6 are German), plus more than 90 bottled beers. **Known for:** international brews; cozy space; German bites including Schweineschnitzel, a classic German dish consisting of a fried pork cutlet, and sausages made by Ogeechee Meat Market. ⑤ *Average main: $14* ✉ *513 E. Oglethorpe St., Historic District* ☎ *912/349–1167* ⊕ *www.thebierhaus.co.*

★ **Fodor's**Choice ✕ **Cha Bella.** *American.* The first farm-to-table
$$$$ restaurant in Savannah, Cha Bella continues to serve only dishes made with the finest local ingredients, so even if you've been here recently, there may be some surprises. The decor is contemporary and comfortable, but the real dining experience is found outside on the patio during the spring and fall. A seared local red snapper with vegetables and pearl couscous is definitely a highlight. **Known for:** Savannah's first farm-to-table restaurant; a delightful array of cocktails; menu changes regularly based on what's fresh and available. ⑤ *Average main: $27* ✉ *102 E. Broad St., Historic District* ☎ *912/790–7888* ⊕ *www.cha-bella. com* ⊗ *No lunch.*

★ **Fodor's**Choice ✕ **Circa 1875.** *French.* The closest thing you'll
$$$$ find to a Parisian bistro in Savannah, this intimate gastropub offers a menu rich of traditional French dishes; trust the well-trained staff to suggest a wine pairing for your meal. The escargot and pâté make excellent starters before you move on to main dishes like steak frites or cassoulet. Head next door to the bar either for a nightcap, or if you're in the mood for a late-night bite, the kitchen stays open late for orders from the bar. **Known for:** Parisian atmosphere and authentic French cuisine; intimate, romantic space; fantastic mussels steeped in fennel, shallots, and white wine. ⑤ *Average main: $31* ✉ *48 Whitaker St., Historic District* ☎ *912/443–1875* ⊕ *www.circa1875.com* ⊗ *No lunch. Closed Sun.*

$$ ✕ **The Collins Quarter.** *Café.* Modeled after the cozy coffee cafés of Melbourne, Australia, this bustling locale serves espresso, cold brew, and its famous spiced lavender mochas,

Where to Eat in Savannah

a.lure, **4**

Al Salaam Deli, **48**

Atlantic, **42**

B. Matthews Eatery, **16**

B&D Burgers, **6**

Back in the Day Bakery, **38**

Bier Haus, **21**

Black Rabbit, **37**

Brighter Day Natural Foods, **39**

Cha Bella, **20**

Circa 1875, **10**

The Collins Quarter, **24**

Cotton & Rye, **49**

Crystal Beer Parlor, **35**

Desposito's, **52**

Elizabeth on 37th, **44**

Fire Street Food, **29**

The Flying Monk Noodle Bar, **11**

45 Bistro, **22**

Fox & Fig, **30**

Garibaldi Cafe, **3**

Green Truck Neighborhood Pub, **47**

The Grey Market, **5**

The Grey Restaurant, **26**

Gryphon, **32**

Huey's Southern Café, **13**

Husk Savannah, **25**

Kayak Kafe, **50**

The Lady & Sons, **9**

Little Duck Diner, **8**

Local 11ten, **45**

Mrs. Wilkes' Dining Room, **33**

Noble Fare, **34**

Olde Pink House, **15**

The Ordinary Pub, **7**

Pacci Italian Kitchen, **18**

Pirates' House, **19**

The Public Kitchen & Bar, **31**

Sandfly BBQ, **36**

700 Drayton Restaurant, **43**

Sisters of the New South Café, **53**

SoHo South Cafe, **28**

Starland Cafe, **41**

Sushi Zen Savannah, **1**

39 Rue de Jean, **27**

Treylor Park, **14**

The Vault Kitchen and Market, **40**

Vic's on the River, **12**

Vinnie Van Go-Go's, **2**

Wiley's Championship BBQ, **17**

The Wyld Dock Bar, **51**

Yia Yia's Kitchen, **46**

Zunzi's, **23**

Savannah River

River St.
Riverfront Plaza
Factors Walk

13 **17** →
12

E. Bay St.
14 **16** **18**

E. Bryan St.
19

Johnson
Sq.

E. Julian St.
15
Reynolds
Sq.

Warren
Sq.

E. Congress St.

E. Broughton St.
E. Broughton St.
20

22

E. State St.

Wright
Sq.
E. President
23
Oglethorpe
Sq.

Columbia
Sq.
E. President St.

E. York St.

24

E. Oglethorpe Ave.

21

Colonial
Park
Cemetery

Chippewa
Sq.

E. Hull

E. Perry
29

E. Liberty St.
E. Liberty St.

31

30

E. Harris St.

Madison
Sq.
♦
St. John's Episcopal Church

Lafayette
Sq.
E. Macon St.

Troup
Sq.

E. Charlton St.
E. Charlton St.

32

E. Jones St.

Monterey
Sq.

Calhoun
Sq.

E. Taylor St.
L. Wayne St.

Whitefield
Sq.

E. Gordon St.

0
1/4 mile

0
400 meters

51 - 53

Forsyth
Park

E. Gaston Ln.

42 - 46

47 **48**

49

50

41

as well as a curated menu that features favorites like smashed avocado toast at brunch and duck confit, served alongside fingerling potatoes and oyster mushrooms, at dinner. The beer selection includes favorites from craft breweries around the country, and the wines were carefully selected from some of the world's

> **MONEY-SAVING TIPS**
>
> Download the Savannah ePASS (⊕ *savannahepass. com*) for culinary savings during your stay in the Hostess City. You might get a free appetizer or dessert or a discount on your final check.

most unique regions to complement the food. **Known for:** chic café setting; walk-up window service; spiced lavender mochas. $ *Average main: $17* ✉ *151 Bull St., Historic District* ☎ *912/777–4147* ⊕ *thecollinsquarter.com* ☉ *No dinner Mon. and Tues.*

$$ ✕ **Crystal Beer Parlor.** *American.* This former speakeasy has FAMILY been serving hungry locals since 1933, and the back dining rooms are covered in historic newspaper clippings and local ephemera, while those around the bar maintains several of the original highback booths. As you can tell from the decor, this place is a landmark—and that goes for the menu, which includes basics like delicious burgers, wings, sandwiches, and some of the best shrimp salad you'll ever have. **Known for:** historic tavern setting; bustling environment and long lines; the creamy Crystal crab stew. $ *Average main: $15* ✉ *301 W. Jones St., Historic District* ☎ *912/349–1000* ⊕ *www.crystalbeerparlor.com.*

$ ✕ **Fire Street Food.** *Modern Asian.* Restauranteurs Ele and FAMILY Sean Tran brought Asian-style street food to Savannah with their menu that boasts everything from sushi rolls to noodle soups, and some of the best sweet-and-spicy chicken wings in town. Occupying a bright, hypermodern space, this eatery offers an offbeat alternative to the slow-paced Southern Savannah feel. Enjoy a quick meal in the dining room, stop by when you have a late-night craving, or order a few of the small plates to go. **Known for:** bright and modern space; late-night bites; street food staples. $ *Average main: $14* ✉ *13 E. Perry St., Historic District* ☎ *912/234–7776* ⊕ *firestreetfood.com.*

$ ✕ **The Flying Monk Noodle Bar.** *Asian Fusion.* Noodle, rice, and soup dishes from across Asia come together on the eclectic, flavorful menu at the Flying Monk. The well-appointed space and laid-back atmosphere complement the savory dishes. Start with vegetarian-friendly edamame

BEST LOCAL SPECIALTIES

Classic Lowcountry Cuisine. Traditional specialties like shrimp and grits are still menu mainstays at many restaurants, such as the ever-popular Huey's. Variations on she-crab soup abound; there are great ones at the Crystal Beer Parlor or the Olde Pink House, for example. The best ones are made with sinful amounts of butter and heavy cream but are worth the rare indulgence. Although a dish called Lowcountry Boil is more common at cookouts than on restaurant menus, keep an eye out for an opportunity to try it. This tantalizing mix of shrimp, smoked sausage, corn on the cob, and potatoes is boiled in huge pots with plenty of seasoning.

Reinvented Local Favorites. Although Southern cuisine has some of the longest-running food traditions in the country, young chefs are giving a number of the old favorites a new spin. Mashama Bailey of The Grey, received a James Beard award for her take on Port City Southern; for a more casual option, try The Grey Market's traditional meat-and-three Southern lunch counter. At B. Matthews you might find black-eyed-pea cake with Cajun rémoulade or fried-green-tomato sandwiches with oregano aioli. The Olde Pink House serves an innovative shrimp 'n' grits with Andouille sausage and sweet-potato biscuits.

The Freshest Seafood. In most places worth your dining dollars, seafood is fresh off the Lowcountry boats. The most beloved local fruit of the sea is white shrimp, caught just off the shores of Tybee. You'll find them served all sorts of ways: in po'boy sandwiches, deep-fried, and mixed with grits. Keep an eye out for local grouper, red fish, and oysters. Perhaps the tastiest coastal mainstay is the blue crab, which flourishes in the marsh estuaries off the coast.

3

dumplings or the meaty braised pork belly. Move on to the signature Vietnamese pho or Japanese ramen noodle soups. For those interested in a traditional rice dish, the curry can't be beat. **Known for:** authentic Asian fare; quick service; vegetarian-friendly menu. $ *Average main: $9* ⌂ *5 W. Broughton St., Historic District* ☎ *912/232–8888* ⊕ *www.flywiththemonk.com.*

$$$$ ✕ **45 Bistro.** *Modern American.* On the ground floor of the Marshall House, 45 Bistro has some of the best views of Broughton Street from the floor-to-ceiling windows that run the length of the room. Most of the menu abounds with

regional flavors—local crab, wild shrimp, spiced pecans—but standards like the wet-aged rib eye are equally as satisfying, as are the updated old favorites like shrimp and grits married to fried Vidalia onion rings, or the grilled romaine hearts that ignite the exceptional Caesar salad. **Known for:** elevated comfort foods; historic charm; a great steak. ⑤ *Average main: $34* ✉ *Marshall House, 123 E. Broughton St., Historic District* ☎ *912/234–3111* ⊕ *45bistro.com* ⊘ *Closed Sun. No lunch.*

$$ ✕**Fox & Fig.** *Vegetarian.* After gaining a cult following at Foxy Loxy Cafe, proprietor Jen Jenkins has created a haven for vegans, vegetarians, and omnivores with her plant-based menu that features all-day brunch, lunch, and dinner options. Popular items include the Fox Burger (a Beyond Burger with arugula, caramelized onions, and agave-dijon on pretzel bun), milky shakes that use Leopold's coconut cream ice cream, soaked chia porridge, and eggless quiche. **Known for:** vegan eats; house-made ingredients; all-day brunch. ⑤ *Average main: $11* ✉ *321 Habersham St., Historic District* ☎ *912/297–6759* ⊕ *www.foxandfigcafe.com.*

★ Fodor's Choice ✕**Garibaldi Cafe.** *Modern Italian.* This well-appointed restaurant is well known to locals and travelers **$$$$** alike for its contemporary cuisine and well-priced Italian classics. Ask your knowledgeable and professional server to offer wine pairings from the intelligent and global wine cart. **Known for:** elegant and intimate setting; crispy flounder with apricot and shallot sauce; Italian classics. ⑤ *Average main: $27* ✉ *315 W. Congress, Historic District* ☎ *912/232–7118* ⊕ *www.garibaldisavannah.com* ⊘ *No lunch.*

★ Fodor's Choice ✕**The Grey Market.** *Diner.* After the success of The **$$** Grey, a mecca of Port City Southern cuisine, restauranteurs Johno Morisano and Chef Mashama Bailey created this hip bodega-inspired take on a Southern lunch counter. Whether you're looking for a breakfast sandwich, an egg cream, a bottle of wine, or a Band-Aid, the Market has you covered. Grab and go dinners, sandwiches, and salads are great for picnics, and the market shop has everything for the Grey enthusiast from branded mugs to Grey Groceries jars of bread and butter pickles. **Known for:** NYC meets Southern lunch counter vibe; grab and go options; breakfast like the Sizzlin' Smoky Pig (pulled pork, egg, and pepper relish on a roll). ⑤ *Average main: $12* ✉ *109 Jefferson St., Downtown* ☎ *912/201–3924* ⊕ *www.thegreymkt.com.*

★ Fodor's Choice ✕**The Grey Restaurant.** *American.* In a restored **$$$$** Greyhound bus depot, James Beard–winner Chef Mashama Bailey and an impeccable team create gorgeous dishes that fuse Port City Southern cuisine with European inspiration. Whether you're tucked in the more casual diner car or perched in luster of the Art Deco–inspired dining room, service is impeccable, and the ever-changing menu offers sumptuously made mains from water, earth, and sky. **Known for:** impressive collection of accolades; Port City Southern cuisine; reservations recommended. Ⓢ *Average main: $31* ✉ *109 Martin Luther King Jr. Blvd., Downtown* ☎ *912/662–5999* ⊕ *www.thegreyrestaurant.com* ⊗ *Closed Mon.*

3

$ ✕ **Gryphon.** *American.* Shimmering stained glass, stunning woodwork, and magnificent decor make this old-time pharmacy one of the most handsome settings in town. Delectable sandwiches and salads are the main bill of fare, but for more ambitious selections, opt for the ratatouille and shrimp orzo, served with locally caught wild Georgia shrimp. **Known for:** sandwiches and salads; traditional afternoon high tea, with wide selection of teas; menu as groomed as the atmosphere. Ⓢ *Average main: $12* ✉ *337 Bull St., Historic District* ☎ *912/525–5880* ⊕ *www.scad. edu/experience/gryphon* ⊗ *No dinner.*

$$ ✕ **Huey's Southern Café.** *Creole.* As Southern food goes,
FAMILY Huey's is decidedly more New Orleans than Coastal Georgia, but it's not too far from home, as you'll discover with one bite of the sinfully rich beignets served with praline sauce—they are a taste of perfection. Although lunch and dinner items like po'boys and muffaletta accompanied by red beans and rice are delicious, the breakfast and brunch menu is the highlight. **Known for:** kid-friendly menu; people-watching and great views of passing ships; Bloody Marys. Ⓢ *Average main: $18* ✉ *115 E. River St.* ☎ *912/234–7385* ⊕ *hueysontheriver.net.*

★ **Fodor's**Choice ✕ **Husk Savannah.** *Southern.* After transforming
$$$ the Charleston restaurant scene with internationally recognized elevated Southern cuisine crafted from heirloom ingredients, James Beard Award–winning Chef Sean Brock has brought his unique flavor to Savannah. Housed in a restored (and rumored to be haunted) Historic District home, Husk Savannah features an ever-changing menu of coastal Georgia and deep South delights. **Known for:** award-winning chef Sean Brock as its creator; Sunday brunch; classic Southern building with modern decor. Ⓢ *Average main: $22* ✉ *12 W. Oglethorpe Ave., Historic District* ☎ *912/349–2600* ⊕ *www.husksavannah.com* ⊗ *Closed daily 2–5:30.*

$$$ ✕**The Lady & Sons.** *Southern.* Y'all, this is the place that Paula Deen, high priestess of Southern cooking, made famous. There are plenty of crowds these days, but everyone patiently waits to attack the buffet, which is stocked for both lunch and dinner with crispy fried chicken, mashed potatoes, collard greens, lima beans, and other favorites. Peach cobbler and banana pudding round off the offerings. The fried green tomatoes are a great starter, and long-time fans vouch for the crab-cake burger at lunch or chicken potpie or barbecue grouper at dinner. **Known for:** celebrity chef Paula Deen; gut-busting Southern eats; homemade dessert classics like banana pudding. ⑤ *Average main: $24* ✉ *102 W. Congress St., Historic District* ☎ *912/233–2600* ⊕ *www.ladyandsons.com.*

★ Fodor'sChoice ✕**Little Duck Diner.** *Diner.* This enchanting fam-
$$ ily-friendly diner perched on the corner of bustling Ellis
FAMILY Square offers an array of comfy bites all day long. With a full menu of milk shakes and diner favorites like apple pie à la mode and crispy chicken and waffles, a trip to Little Duck's white marble and brass-accented space is a special occasion for all. **Known for:** vintage diner-inspired space with modern touches; comfy eats; lavender "bubble bath" bellinis topped with a rubber ducky. ⑤ *Average main: $12* ✉ *150 W. Julian St., Historic District* ☎ *912/235–6773* ⊕ *www.littleduckdiner.com.*

★ Fodor'sChoice ✕**Mrs. Wilkes' Dining Room.** *Southern.* Folks line
$$$ up to enjoy Mrs. Wilkes' fine Southern fare, which has been
FAMILY served family-style at big tables for decades. Her grand-daughter and great-grandson are keeping it a family affair in more ways than one (kids under 10 eat for half-price), and these days you can expect fried or roasted chicken, beef stew, collard greens, mashed potatoes, macaroni and cheese, sweet-potato soufflé, and corn bread, along with favorites like banana pudding for dessert. **Known for:** Southern cooking served family-style; former President Barack Obama and his entourage had lunch here when he visited Savannah; cash-only policy ($25 pp). ⑤ *Average main: $25* ✉ *107 W. Jones St., Historic District* ☎ *912/232–5997* ⊕ *www.mrswilkes.com* ⊟ *No credit cards* ⊙ *Closed weekends and Jan. No dinner.*

$$$$ ✕**Noble Fare.** *Eclectic.* This eatery's clientele ranges from thirtysomethings celebrating a special occasion to well-heeled older residents who love the elegant atmosphere. The bread service includes honey butter, pistachio pesto, olive oil, and balsamic vinegar for your biscuits, flatbreads, rolls, and focaccia, all of which are artistically presented

on contemporary dishes. A savory meal can produce a chemical need for chocolate, so the molten-lava cake with raspberry sauce and custard ice cream may be a requirement, especially paired with a Zinfandel port. **Known for:** perfectly fresh fish; melt-in-your-mouth honey cured pork chop; prix-fixe tasting menu. ⑤ *Average main: $33* ⊠ *321 Jefferson St., Historic District* ☏ *912/443–3210* ⊕ *www. noblefare.com* ⊗ *No lunch. Closed Sun. and Mon.*

★ **Fodor'sChoice** ✕ **Olde Pink House.** *Southern.* This Georgian
$$$$ mansion was built in 1771 for James Habersham, one of the wealthiest Americans of his time, and the historic atmosphere comes through in the original Georgia pine floors of the tavern, the Venetian chandeliers, and the 18th-century English antiques. The menu is just as classic and Southern, with chicken potpie, shrimp and grits, and sweet-potato biscuits gracing the menu. A lovely bar has curvaceous doors that can be flung open on balmy nights for outdoor seating. **Known for:** exceptional Southern dining; historical ambience; remarkable wine menu. ⑤ *Average main: $27* ⊠ *23 Abercorn St., Historic District* ☏ *912/232–4286* ⊕ *www. plantersinnsavannah.com/the-olde-pink-house-menu* ⊗ *No lunch Sun. and Mon.*

$$ ✕ **The Ordinary Pub.** *American.* Savannah's most-beloved brunch is tucked away in the basement level of bustling Broughton Street's shopping and dining corridor. The neighborhood eatery serves bottomless Baron D'Arignac mimosas, Bloody Marys made with Savannah-based Ghost Coast Distillery vodkas, cold brew coffee-based cocktails with ingredients from local roaster Perc, and a full menu of brunch favorites—don't miss the pork belly doughnut sliders—and gastropub dinner dishes. **Known for:** bottomless mimosas ("togosas" when poured in a portable plastic cup); lively brunch served seven days a week; eclectic pub fare. ⑤ *Average main: $16* ⊠ *217 ½ W. Broughton St., Historic District* ☏ *912/238–5130* ⊕ *www.theordinarypub.com.*

$$$ ✕ **Pacci Italian Kitchen.** *Italian.* Pacci's has the look and taste of a high-end Italian eatery, but with a laid-back and welcoming atmosphere. Guests gather in the beautifully designed dining room or the open-air patio for signature cocktails like the Biarritz or the Negroni before moving on to some of the best charcuterie and crudites platters in the city. Breads, pastas, desserts, and pickled vegetables are all made in-house. **Known for:** farm-fresh ingredients; homemade pastas; thoughtful interior. ⑤ *Average main: $22* ⊠ *Brice Hotel, 601 E. Bay St., Historic District* ☏ *912/233–6002* ⊕ *www.paccisavannah.com.*

SUNDAY BRUNCH

On Sunday, Savannah's churches are packed to the choir loft, so follow the hungry, postservice crowds for some great cuisine. Given the local fishing traditions and the city's proximity to the ocean, it should be no surprise that seafood appears as brunch items more often in these parts than in other parts of the country. Keep an eye out for seafood omelets with hollandaise sauce, or eggs Benedict, served with a crab cake rather than Canadian bacon. Another local staple is shrimp and grits, which you'd be remiss not to try at least once while in town. If you're not a fan of seafood, don't fret: the ever-popular Southern tradition of sausage-gravy-smothered biscuits is a fine way to start the day, and there's always bacon and eggs, if you're not feeling adventurous.

$$$ ✕ **Pirates' House.** *Southern.* A Savannah landmark, this 1753
FAMILY house is steeped in history, including scary tales of trap doors and secret passages leading down to the waterfront that were used to take inebriated patrons out to waiting boats (they'd wake up at sea and be given the choice between working on the boat or swimming several miles back to shore). The lunch buffet has all the Southern standards, but the food is better on the à la carte menu; there's no buffet for dinner, but the dessert menu is worth sticking around for. Its popularity with tour groups has given it a reputation as a tourist trap, but the food is pretty good, with plenty of kid-pleasing choices. **Known for:** fanciful history; Chatham Artillery Punch; busy atmosphere. ⑤ *Average main: $22 ⊠ 20 E. Broad St., Historic District* ☎ *912/233–5757 ⊕ www.thepirateshouse.com.*

$$ ✕ **The Public Kitchen & Bar.** *American.* A prime location at the corner of Liberty and Bull streets, café-style outdoor dining, and a chic bar adorned with an industrial-style chandelier—Public Kitchen & Bar has it all. Despite the upscale atmosphere, the food is approachable and affordable with contemporary classics like shrimp and grits, and mussels steamed with chorizo and leeks. Not hungry? Don't be afraid to belly up to the bar for a finely crafted cocktail or a glass of wine. **Known for:** elevated Southern cuisine; outdoor dining; handsome interior. ⑤ *Average main: $16 ⊠ 1 W. Liberty St., Historic District* ☎ *912/790–9000 ⊕ www.thepublickitchen.com.*

★ Fodor's Choice ✕ **Soho South Cafe.** *Eclectic.* This garage turned $ art gallery turned restaurant features a playful, Southern-inspired menu with a variety of fresh and beautiful salads, soups, and a handful of entrées like the chicken and waffles sandwich or the fried goat cheese salad—both best bets for lunchtime patrons. **Known for:** unique take on Southern lunch, informed by fresh, local ingredients; located in a renovated garage space; signature tomato-basil bisque accompanying the grilled cheese on sourdough with pimento aioli. Ⓢ *Average main: $12* ⊠ *12 W. Liberty St., Historic District* ☎ *912/233–1633* ⊕ *www.sohosouthcafe. com* ⊗ *No dinner.*

$$ ✕ **Sushi Zen Savannah.** *Japanese.* If you've had your fill of Southern cuisine, head to this downstairs spot for award-winning sushi, daily specialty rolls, and grilled meat and noodle dishes. The dining room's simple design and a mix of seating arrangements is only the beginning: the crown jewel is the patio, a wonderful spot to enjoy a pleasant evening, particularly in spring and fall. **Known for:** late-night hours on weekends; intimate space; creative ingredient combinations. Ⓢ *Average main: $17* ⊠ *30 Martin Luther King Jr. Blvd., Historic District* ☎ *912/233–1187* ⊗ *Closed Mon. No lunch.*

$$$ ✕ **39 Rue de Jean.** *French.* Sister to the famous 39 Rue de Jean restaurant in Charleston, Rue de Jean Savannah also draws inspiration from the style of classic French brasseries. The dining room transports you to Paris with high ceilings, a lively bar, and comfortable seating throughout, and the kitchen offers classic dishes like bouillabaisse with shrimp, local fish, clams and garlic in a white wine-saffron tomato broth; braised rabbit; and duck confit. **Known for:** coq au vin; excellent customer service; brasserie style. Ⓢ *Average main: $31* ⊠ *605 W. Oglethorpe Ave.* ☎ *912/721–0595* ⊕ *www.holycityhospitality.com* ⊗ *No lunch.*

$$ ✕ **Treylor Park.** *American.* Expect whimsical takes on low-brow eats at this bustling favorite, where the taco menu alone is a playground of flavor with options like the peppery fried chicken and pancake tacos or the savory shrimp and grits tacos. With all-day breakfast options, an interior that honors the restaurant's camp influences while keeping it hip and modern, and a robust beer and cocktail menu, it's no wonder this is one of Savannah's hot spots. **Known for:** creative takes on comfort food like PB&J chicken wings; late night bites; patio seating. Ⓢ *Average main: $11* ⊠ *225 E. Bay St., Downtown* ☎ *912/495–5557* ⊕ *www. treylorpark.com.*

3

$$$$ ✕ **Vic's on the River.** *Southern.* This upscale Southern charmer is one of the finest spots in town for well-executed Southern delicacies like Savannah Sausage Co. andouille hash and seafood po'boys. The five-story brick building was originally designed by the famous New York architect John Norris as a warehouse in the 19th century and was painstakingly renovated into the elegant space you'll find these days; reserve a window table for great views of the Savannah River. Lunch is popular with local business executives and out-of-towners looking for quick and delicious options. The wine list is nothing short of formidable and suits every palate and price range, and the super-rich praline cheesecake is strongly recommended. Grab a copy of the eatery's cookbook to get a closer look at the kitchen. **Known for:** spectacular views; Sunday brunch; award-winning crawfish beignets. ⑤ *Average main: $26 ✉ 26 E. Bay St., Historic District* ☎ *912/721–1000* ⊕ *www.vicsontheriver.com.*

$ ✕ **Vinnie Van Go-Go's.** *Pizza.* With a secret dough recipe and
FAMILY   a homemade sauce, Vinnie's is critically acclaimed by pizza and calzone enthusiasts from around the Southeast. Lots of visitors get a kick out of watching the cooks throw the dough in the air in the big open kitchen, but there are only a few tables inside, along with a long stretch of stools at the bar; the heart of the restaurant is its plentiful outdoor seating, great for people-watching. Because of its prime City Market location, the wait for a table can be an hour or more, but you'll understand why with one bite of your pie. **Known for:** outdoor seating; bustling, casual dining; long waits and cash-only policy. ⑤ *Average main: $14 ✉ 317 W. Bryan St., City Market* ☎ *912/233–6394* ⊕ *www.vinnievangogo.com* ⊟ *No credit cards* ⊘ *No lunch Mon.–Thurs.*

$ ✕ **Zunzi's.** *South African.* The line out the door is testament to the yummy flavors found on a menu filled with South African, Dutch, Italian, and Swiss influences. Sandwiches are king—there are build your own options as well as a set menu—and there's a respectable selection of vegetarian options, including the vegetarian curry, which is especially delightful when washed down with Zunzi's unique sweet tea. **Known for:** takeout; Conquistador sandwich (French bread piled high with grilled chicken and the signature sauce); vegetarian options. ⑤ *Average main: $9 ✉ 108 E. York St., Historic District* ☎ *912/443–9555* ⊕ *zunzis.com.*

VICTORIAN DISTRICT AND EASTSIDE

$ × **The Black Rabbit.** *American.* On bustling Barnard Street in the Victorian District, this new café and bar serves up affordable, scrumptious sandwiches and creatively crafted cocktails in a small, intimate space. With a name inspired by decades-old artwork on the building's garage door, The Black Rabbit is a concept from seasoned Savannah restauranteurs who know how to make unforgettable food at unbeatable prices. **Known for:** cozy space; late-night bites like the Three Piggies sandwich (Spam, pit ham, and sliced pork shoulder); modern luncheonette vibes. ⑤ *Average main: $10* ⌂ *1215 Barnard St.* ☎ *912/200–4940* ⊕ *www. blackrabbitsav.com* ⊘ *Closed Sun.*

$ × **Brighter Day Natural Foods.** *Deli.* This deli and juice bar is one of Savannah's best-kept secrets offering custom made organic sandwiches with meat, vegetarian, and vegan options, as well as side dishes, salads, and cakes made right on the premises. This grocery store offers one of the city's best take-out lunches, and its location at the southern end of Forsyth Park makes it the perfect place to put together a picnic. **Known for:** baked cheese and avocado sandwich or stuffed grape leaves; walk-up window 11–4; organic juices, smoothies, and wheatgrass shots. ⑤ *Average main: $8* ⌂ *1102 Bull St.* ☎ *912/236–4703* ⊕ *brighterdayfoods.com.*

★ **Fodor's**Choice × **Local 11ten.** *Modern American.* This stark, minimalist place features an upbeat and contemporary menu that draws young chefs on their nights off. Seasonally driven, the menu is continually changing depending on the local harvest and the chef's vision, but they are usually perfectly prepared and presented; when available, the fried oyster salad, charcuterie selection, and venison medallions are highly recommended, as are Local's celebrated scallops. With dessert, take in the fine-art installations on the walls, which rotate regularly to feature the best local talent. **Known for:** seasonal menu with farm-sourced ingredients; sea scallops over black rice; open-air rooftop bar. ⑤ *Average main: $33* ⌂ *1110 Bull St.* ☎ *912/790–9000* ⊕ *www. local11ten.com* ⊘ *No lunch.*

$$$$

$ × **Sandfly Bar-B-Q.** *Barbecue.* The Victorian District outpost of this Memphis-born, Savannah-bred BBQ spot slings brisket, pulled pork, and wings in a refurbished railway car. **Known for:** Hog Wild Platter (pork, brisket, ¼ chicken, sausage, 2 ribs, 2 sides, 2 pieces of Texas toast); open until they run out of BBQ; diner atmosphere in a streamliner.

3

PORT CITY SOUTHERN

Savannah's culinary scene warmly embraces Southern comforts, modern culinary creativity, and, perhaps most important, the Atlantic Ocean's bounty. Sweet Georgia shrimp, perfectly salty Lowcountry oysters, and steamed blue crabs are welcome staples on a Savannah table. James Beard award–winner chef Mashama Bailey of Savannah's The Grey calls the Hostess City's flavor "Port City Southern," an elevated take on Southern comforts with an emphasis on locally sourced ingredients and a love of fresh seafood. The Grey might be the hottest spot to experience Port City Southern—particularly with Bailey's recent appearance on Netflix's *Chef's Table*—but many local establishments combine carefully selected ingredients with age-old tradition in the Savannah area.

⑤ *Average main: $15* ⊠ *1220 Barnard St.* ☎ *912/335–8058* ⊕ *www.sandflybbq.com* ⊘ *Closed Sun.*

$$$$ ✕**700 Drayton Restaurant.** *American.* With its splashy interior, this is a one-of-a-kind spot in Savannah whether you're looking for a power lunch or a romantic dinner. The former Kayton Mansion was converted into a lounge and restaurant that pairs fine dining with eccentric touches like Versace leopard-print chairs. Breakfast is served daily, and Sunday brunch is nice for special occasions. **Known for:** flawless she-crab bisque; elegant interiors; sumptuous appetizers like cooked-to-perfection Sapelo Island clams. ⑤ *Average main: $29* ⊠ *Mansion on Forsyth Street, 700 Drayton St.* ☎ *912/721–5002* ⊕ *700drayton.com.*

STARLAND DISTRICT, THOMAS SQUARE, AND MIDTOWN

$ ✕**Al Salaam Deli.** *Middle Eastern.* If your tastebuds are bored with the same old thing, head to one of Savannah's few restaurants specializing in Middle Eastern fare. Owned and operated by a husband and wife team, Al Salaam is celebrated for its moist and authentic falafel, spit-roasted lamb, and platters with hummus or baba ganoush. Take time to look around the small space, enticingly papered over with vintage covers of *National Geographic* and depicting cultures from the world over. **Known for:** authentic falafel; plentiful food and low prices; takeout options.

Ⓢ *Average main: $9* ✉ *2311 Habersham St., Thomas Square* ☎ *912/447–0400* ☾ *Closed Sun.*

★ Fodor'sChoice ✕ **Atlantic.** *American.* In a restored gas station on
$$ busy Victory Drive, extraordinary service and an innovative menu of fresh, seasonal fare has made Atlantic a cherished neighborhood staple. The dishes are small and meant to be shared, so order several to fully explore all of the local flavors. The dinner menu offers cool bites, warm bites, small plates and big plates and changes often, as does the thoughtful craft cocktail list. **Known for:** lively interior; patio dining; standout wine list. Ⓢ *Average main: $15* ✉ *102 E. Victory Dr., Thomas Square* ☎ *912/417–8887* ⊕ *www. atlanticsavannah.com* ☾ *Closed Sun. No lunch.*

★ Fodor'sChoice ✕ **Back in the Day Bakery.** *Bakery.* From the folksy
$ artwork to the sweet splashes of pastels to the banners hanging from the ceiling, this corner bakery evokes a spirit of days gone by. A great place to start your day with a cup of coffee and a pastry, Back in the Day also serves fresh and yummy lunch selections that includes a good variety of both meaty and vegetarian sandwiches. A trip to this cheerful café will undoubtedly remind you, as the slogan goes, to "Slow down and taste the sweet life." **Known for:** cases of delicious goodies including the city's most sinful cupcakes; standout lunch menu that features sandwiches on crusty, homemade bread; cheery vintage interior. Ⓢ *Average main: $7* ✉ *2403 Bull St.* ☎ *912/495–9292* ⊕ *backinthedaybakery. com* ☾ *Closed Mon.–Wed. No dinner.*

★ Fodor'sChoice ✕ **Cotton & Rye.** *American.* Just beyond down-
$$$ town's hustle and bustle sits one of Savannah's finest supper experiences. A regular winner of local culinary accolades, including awards for its gluten-free options, Cotton & Rye serves Southern comforts with elegance and unrivaled customer service. It's a cozy and romantic spot, where regulars come for the fried chicken thighs and stay for the chocolate buttermilk pie. **Known for:** comfortable elegance; breads, sausages, and pâtés made from scratch; nearly every item on the menu can be made gluten-free. Ⓢ *Average main: $18* ✉ *1801 Habersham St., Thomas Square* ☎ *912/777–6286* ⊕ *www.cottonandrye.com* ☾ *Closed Sun. No lunch.*

★ Fodor'sChoice ✕ **Elizabeth on 37th.** *Southern.* This elegant turn-
$$$$ of-the-20th-century mansion has been feeding regional specialties to Savannah's upper crust for decades. Chef Kelly Yambor has helmed the kitchen since 1996, and she masters dishes like Georgia shrimp and Savannah red rice, and the double cut Berkshire pork chop with apple-cabbage slaw. Splurge for the chef's seven-course tasting menu—you won't

regret it. Don't be afraid to ask for wine recommendations, because the wine cellar is massive and the staff is knowledgeable. As might be imagined, the service is impeccable. **Known for:** impressive wine list; top fine-dining experience in town; seven-course tasting menu option. $ *Average main: $35* ⊠ *105 E. 37th St., Thomas Square* ☎ *912/236–5547* ⊕ *www.elizabethon37th.net* ⊘ *No lunch.*

★ Fodor'sChoice ✕ **Green Truck Neighborhood Pub.** *Burger.* Serving one of the best burgers in the state, this casual haunt draws diners from far and wide for its grass-fed beef; vegetarians find satisfaction with the hearty meatless patties. Everything from the coffee to the produce is locally sourced, and even the ketchup is made in-house. **Known for:** great beer selection; homemade ketchup and pimento cheese; big crowds and long waits. $ *Average main: $12* ⊠ *2430 Habersham St., Thomas Square* ☎ *912/234–5885* ⊕ *www. greentruckpub.com* ⊘ *Closed Sun.*

$

FAMILY

$$ ✕ **Starland Cafe.** *Café.* This neighborhood favorite has been serving one of Savannah's best lunches for years. Whether it's a fresh pressed panini like the vegetarian Greek asparagus panini (brimming with crispy asparagus, hummus, marinated artichokes feta, tomato, pesto, and house aioli) or the generously portioned Kitchen Sink salad (dates, raisins, artichokes, apples, grapes, crunchy rice noodles, tomatoes, and onion), it's hard to go wrong with a menu that prioritizes freshness and locally sourced greens. **Known for:** bustling weekday lunch crowd; famous tomato Thai soup; iced Earl Grey tea. $ *Average main: $16* ⊠ *11 E. 41st St. , between Bull and Drayton Sts.* ☎ *912/443–9355* ⊕ *www. starlanddining.com* ⊘ *No dinner. Closed Sun.*

$$ ✕ **The Vault Kitchen and Market.** *Asian Fusion.* In the heart of the hip Starland District, this former bank features a varied menu of Asian fusion and sushi delights. The bright and bustling space, which honors its past in clever design choices, welcomes visitors with flavors from Laos, Japan, and beyond, including melt-in-your-mouth miso salmon. With a main, cocktail, and sushi menu, it's a great place for a business lunch or date night. **Known for:** industrial chic interior; chicken clay pot with Thai green eggplant and rice swimming in curry, herbs, Thai chili and ginger; unique sushi rolls. $ *Average main: $15* ⊠ *2112 Bull St.* ☎ *912/201–1950* ⊕ *www.thevaultkitchen.com.*

CLOSE UP

Cooking School

Chef Darin's Kitchen Table. After making a name for himself at the Mansion on Forsyth Park, Chef Darin created his own cooking school in 2015 with hands-on classes for cooks of all levels. The state-of-the-art facility includes a kitchen stocked with five KitchenAid dual-fuel ranges and a double wall oven as well as Savannah's only local kitchen shop. Class subjects range from Lowcountry comfort food to Pan Asian cuisine, and it's easy to follow every step thanks to a 55" monitor with a remote control camera right in the kitchen. ⊠ *2514 Abercorn St. , Suite 140, Thomas Square* ☎ *912/704–6882* ⊕ *www.chefdarin.com* 🍽 *From $90* ☟ *Closed Sun. and Mon.*

MOON RIVER DISTRICT

★ **Fodor'sChoice** ✕ **The Wyld Dock Bar.** *Seafood.* Formerly a yacht
$$ club and dock bar, the newest iteration of this waterfront dining experience brings a modern feel to a beautifully weathered space. Tuck into local shrimp and fish, and don't forget an order of the fried Brussels sprouts—or just come for the "painkiller" slushie and the sunset views. **Known for:** unparalleled marsh views; outdoor seating; local seafood. ⑤ *Average main: $11* ⊠ *2740 Livingston Ave.* ☎ *912/692–1219* ⊕ *www.thewylddockbar.com* ☟ *Closed Mon.*

SOUTHSIDE, GATEWAY, AND GREATER SAVANNAH

$ ✕ **Kayak Kafe.** *Vegetarian.* This palm-shaded eatery is hands down the best spot in town for vegetarian and vegan options, but there's also more than enough on the menu to keep a meat eater happy—consider the fried chicken tacos or the chicken and goat cheese enchiladas. If you have your mind on a cocktail, don't miss the Palm (made with muddled cucumber) or the Hot Derby (with spicy ginger ale from just over the South Carolina border). There's ample parking and a screen where you can watch the big game. **Known for:** hearty salads; excellent brunch; outdoor seating. ⑤ *Average main: $10* ⊠ *5002 Paulsen St., Southside* ☎ *912/349–4371* ⊕ *www.eatkayak.com.*

$ ✕ **Yia Yia's Kitchen.** *Greek.* This is the real deal, an authentic Greek eatery and bakery where grandmother's recipes

INTERNATIONAL EATS

Savannah's food offerings run deeper than just traditional Southern cooking. If it's the islands you crave, head to the Southside of Savannah for a meal at **Sweet Spice** (*5515 Waters Ave., 912/335–8146* ⊕ *www.sweetspicerestaurant.com*). They serve up traditional favorites like jerk chicken and curried goat. For more exotic Korean flavors, make your way to **Kim Chi II** (*149 E. Montgomery Cross Rd., 912/920–7273*). Try the fiery *kimchi banchan* or the bubbling-hot pork-and-tofu stew.

inspired the menu. Most everything is made on the premises and perfectly blends the flavors of the Mediterranean; house favorites include Greek salads, savory spanakopita (spinach pie), and meat or vegetarian dolmades (stuffed grape leaves). **Known for:** tempting dessert case featuring gooey baklava or creamy tiramisu; take-out items great for picnics; neighborhood location. ⑤ *Average main: $10* ✉ *3113 Habersham St., Southside* ☎ *912/200–3796* ⊕ *www. yiayiasav.com* ⊘ *No dinner on weekends.*

THE ISLANDS AND THUNDERBOLT

$ ✕**Desposito's.** *Seafood.* This place is about as low key as it
FAMILY gets, as evidenced by the neon beer signs on the walls and the day-old newspapers doubling as tablecloths. Located just across the bridge from Savannah, Desposito's has been serving up cold beer and fresh fish for decades and the no-nonsense menu offers a small but tempting variety of seafood, as well as options for landlubbers. **Known for:** casual atmosphere; tucked-away location; great place to bring kids. ⑤ *Average main: $9* ✉ *3501 Marye St., Whitemarsh Island* ☎ *912/897–9963* ⊘ *Closed Sun. and Mon.*

$ ✕**Sisters of the New South Café.** *Southern.* Some of the best Southern food in Savannah can be found at the original Sisters of the New South Café (there are additional locations in Atlanta). Favorites at this family-run spot include smothered shrimp over rice, slow-cooked oxtails, and homemade desserts like gooey peach cobbler, decadent red velvet cake with cream-cheese frosting, and tangy Key lime pie. **Known for:** breakfast and lunch specials; generous portions; cafeteria-style service. ⑤ *Average main: $10* ✉ *2605 Skidaway Rd., Thunderbolt* ☎ *912/335–2761* ⊕ *www.thesistersofthenewsouth.com.*

★ **Fodor's**Choice ✕ **Wiley's Championship BBQ.** *Barbecue.* Tucked
$ away in a strip mall on the way out to Tybee Island, this highlight of the local BBQ scene closes early if they run out of barbecue. The small space is intimate and friendly and the staff is like long-lost family, but there are only a few tables, so you may have to choose between waiting for a seat and grabbing something to go. **Known for:** slow-cooked BBQ staples; BBQ sampler feeds two people and lets you sample just about everything they make; Extra-Tingly Better Than Sex BBQ sauce. ⑤ *Average main: $14* ✉ *4700 U.S. 80 E, Wilmington Island* ☎ *912/201–3259* ⊕ *www.wileyschampionshipbbq.com* ⊘ *Closed Sun. and daily 3–5.*

TYBEE ISLAND

$$ ✕ **A-J's.** *Seafood.* This island bar and grill resembles a fish camp that was expanded time and time again to accommodate its growing clientele. Colorful and laid back, the ambience is characteristic of Tybee Island itself, which perhaps explains why it is a favorite among locals, and the food, mostly fresh seafood, is simple and delicious. **Known for:** spacious patio overlooking the marsh; great spot to watch the sunset; live entertainment Friday–Sunday. ⑤ *Average main: $17* ✉ *1315 Chatham Ave., Tybee Island* ☎ *912/786–9533* ⊕ *ajsdocksidetybee.com.*

$$ ✕ **Bubba Gumbo's.** *Seafood.* Watch boats pass and the sun set
FAMILY over Lazaretto Creek while enjoying fried oysters, steamed shrimp, hush puppies, and Lowcountry boil. A laid-back beach bum vibe welcomes boaters, local surfers, and visitors alike inside an unfussy dining room or on the ample porch. **Known for:** scenic view; casual atmosphere; fresh-caught seafood. ⑤ *Average main: $10* ✉ *1 Old Tybee Rd., Tybee Island* ☎ *912/786–4445* ⊕ *www.tybeebubbags.com* ⊘ *No lunch Sun.–Thurs.*

$$ ✕ **The Crab Shack.** *Seafood.* "Where the elite eat in their bare
FAMILY feet" is the motto of this laid-back eatery tucked away on a side street just over the bridge to Tybee Island. The beer is cold, the vibe is relaxed, and items like the Lowcountry boil—a huge plate of shrimp, corn on the cob, and smoked sausage—are delicious. Out front is a large pool filled with baby alligators that is a huge hit with kids—a good way to

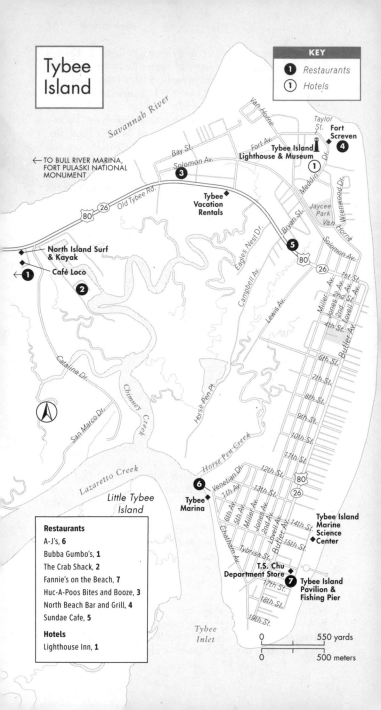

Tybee Island

KEY
1 *Restaurants*
(1) *Hotels*

Savannah River

← TO BULL RIVER MARINA,
FORT PULASKI NATIONAL
MONUMENT

Van Horne

Taylor
St.

4 Fort
Screven

Fort Av.

Bay St.

Tybee Island
Lighthouse & Museum

Solomon Av.

Meddin Dr.

3

Wrenwood Dr.

Tybee
Vacation
Rentals

Jaycee
Park

Van
Horne

Old Tybee Rd.

80 26

Bryan St.

Solomon Av.

North Island Surf
& Kayak

5

80

26

Café Loco
1

Eagles Nest Dr.

1st St.

2

Campbell Av.

Miller Av.

Jones Av.

2nd Av.
2nd St.

Lovell Av.

Butler Av.

Lewis Av.

4th St.

6th St.

Catalina Dr.

7th St.

8th St.

Chimney Creek

San Marco Dr.

9th St.

Horse Pen Pt.

10th St.

11th St.

Horse Pen Creek

12th St.

Lazaretto Creek

6

Venetian Dr.

13th St.

7th Av.

80

26

Little Tybee
Island

Tybee
Marina

6th Av.

5th Av.

Miller Av.

Jones Av.

2nd Av.

14th St.

Lovell Av.

Butler Av.

Tybee Island
Marine
Science
Center

Chatham Av.

15th St.

Tybrisa St.

T.S. Chu
Department Store

7

Tybee Island
Pavilion &
Fishing Pier

16th St.

17th St.

18th St.

19th St.

Tybee
Inlet

0		550 yards

0		500 meters

Restaurants
A-J's, **6**

Bubba Gumbo's, **1**

The Crab Shack, **2**

Fannie's on the Beach, **7**

Huc-A-Poos Bites and Booze, **3**

North Beach Bar and Grill, **4**

Sundae Cafe, **5**

Hotels
Lighthouse Inn, **1**

keep them entertained if there's a wait for tables, which is possible on weekends when the weather's nice. Just inside is a huge patio lit with tiki torches and packed with picnic tables. Seating is available in screened-in dining areas if there's rain or sand gnats. **Known for:** scenic views; family-friendly environment; resident felines and alligators. Ⓢ *Average main: $15* ✉ *40 Estill Hammock Rd., Tybee Island* ☎ *912/786–9857* ⊕ *www.thecrabshack.com.*

$ ✕ **Fannie's on the Beach.** *Seafood.* A great place to grab a bite after a long day power-lounging on the beach, this beachside eatery is a favorite with locals and visitors alike. The menu lists simple favorites like sandwiches, burgers, and fried seafood, but all are prepared exceedingly well. The pizza menu includes some interesting choices, including pies topped with salmon or scallops and bacon. **Known for:** great views of the ocean from the third-story deck; live music Wednesday to Saturday; creative pizzas. Ⓢ *Average main: $13* ✉ *1613 Strand Ave., Tybee Island* ☎ *912/786–6109* ⊕ *www.fanniesonthebeach.com.*

★ **Fodor'sChoice** ✕ **Huc-A-Poos Bites and Booze.** *American.* Drink
$ and eat like the locals do at this charming, laid-back spot.
FAMILY With walls covered in vintage signs, records, and various trash and treasure, guests enjoy a great breeze on a large porch or in the screened-in restaurant as they tuck into slices or 18-inch stone baked pies loaded with tantalizing ingredients and unique combinations; the beer is ice-cold and best enjoyed in pitchers, and the prices can't be beat. **Known for:** authentic island relaxation; live music on the weekends; lively game nights during college football season. Ⓢ *Average main: $15* ✉ *Huc-A-Poos, 1213 E. Hwy. 80, Tybee Island* ☎ *912/786–5900* ⊕ *www.hucapoos.com.*

$$ ✕ **North Beach Bar and Grill.** *Seafood.* Between the historic
FAMILY Tybee Island Lighthouse and North Beach lies one of the island's most colorful, Caribbean-inspired eateries. The menus feature local and sustainable seafood, including delectable crab cakes and the fresh citrus shrimp salad, along with lots of family-friendly options. Find live music on the large porch on some nights, or grab a seat at the bar for a local beer or frosty mixed drink. **Known for:** laid-back patio seating; seafood fritters; beachside convenience. Ⓢ *Average main: $13* ✉ *33 Meddin Dr., Tybee Island* ☎ *912/786–4442* ⊕ *www.northbeachbarandgrill. net* ⊗ *Closed Tues.*

★ Fodor'sChoice ✕ **Sundae Cafe.** *American.* Tucked into an unassuming strip mall off the main drag on Tybee Island, this gourmet restaurant is a diamond in the rough. Locals and tourists alike enjoy the diverse menu, fresh seafood, and brilliant food combinations—don't miss the unique seafood "cheesecake" starter, consisting of shrimp and crabmeat over greens with a hint of gouda. For lunch, the rich fried green tomato BLT can stop your heart (in more ways than one!), while the pork chops are always a sure bet at dinner. **Known for:** generous portions at reasonable prices; tucked-away location; reservations recommended. ⑤ *Average main: $19* ✉ *304 1st St., Tybee Island* ☎ *912/786–7694* ⊕ *www.sundaecafe.com* ⊘ *Closed Sun.*

$$
$$

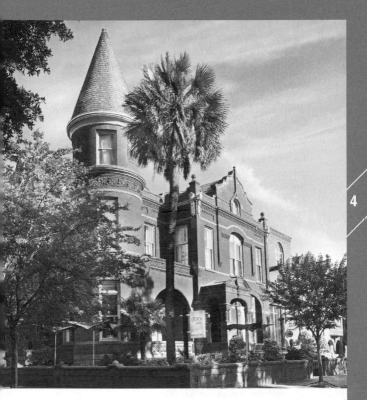

WHERE TO STAY

Updated
by Anna
Chandler

THE HOSTESS CITY OPENS ITS doors every year to millions of visitors who are drawn to its historic and vibrant downtown. Because the majority of attractions are within the Historic District, most of the city's best hotels are there, too. Many are within easy walking distance of the city's premier restaurants and historic sites. In terms of accommodations, Savannah is best known for its many inns and B&Bs, which have moved into the stately antebellum mansions, renovated cotton warehouses, and myriad other historic buildings stretching from the river out to the Victorian neighborhoods in the vicinity of Forsyth Park. Most are beautifully restored with the requisite high ceilings, ornate carved millwork, claw-foot tubs, and other quaint touches. Some stay in close touch with the past and do not offer televisions or telephones; others have mixed in the modern luxuries that many travelers have grown accustomed to, including flat-screen TVs, Wi-Fi, and upscale bath amenities. Often, Southern hospitality is served up in the form of evening wine-and-cheese socials, decadent breakfasts, and pralines at turndown service.

A flush of newer boutique hotels has shaken some of the dust out of Savannah's lodging scene and raised the bar for competing properties. Properties like Perry Lane Hotel, the Brice, and the luxurious Mansion on Forsyth Park would be at home in a much larger city, but all have figured out how to introduce a sleek, cosmopolitan edge without bulldozing over Savannah's charm.

HOTEL PRICES

The central location and relatively high standards of quality in Savannah's Historic District hotels do drive up room rates, especially during peak seasons, holidays, and special events like St. Patrick's Day. The number of hotel rooms has more than doubled in the past 15 years, and occupancy rates have grown accordingly, even in the former slow season from September through January. October is another relatively busy time thanks to the pleasant temperatures and packed events calendar.

You will sometimes save by booking online or purchasing a package deal. Look for good last-minute deals when bookings are light. These are often available in late summer, when the heat and humidity are at their highest. If you're on a tight budget, there are plenty of nice, new, midrange options from trusted hotel chains in less traveled but conveniently located areas a short drive from downtown,

Best Bets for Savannah Lodging

We offer a selective listing of quality lodging experiences in every price range, from a city's best budget motel to its most sophisticated luxury hotel. Here we've compiled our top recommendations by price and experience. The very best properties—those that provide a particularly remarkable experience—are designated with the Fodor's Choice logo.

Fodor's Choice: Andaz, Cotton Sail, Gastonian, Hamilton-Turner Inn, Kehoe House, Lighthouse Inn, Mansion on Forsyth Park, Marshall House, The Kimpton Brice, Westin Savannah Harbor Golf Resort & Spa

Best Budget Stay: Holiday Inn Express Historic District, Savannah Bed & Breakfast Inn, Thunderbird Inn

Best Celebrity Retreat: Hamilton-Turner Inn, Mansion on Forsyth Park, The Marshall House

Best Hotel Bars: Andaz, Cotton Sail, The Kimpton Brice, The Marshall House

Best for Romance: Gastonian, Hamilton-Turner Inn, Kehoe House, Mansion on Forsyth Park

Best B&Bs: Ballastone Inn, Dresser Palmer House, Foley House Inn, Gastonian, Hamilton-Turner Inn, Kehoe House

Best Pool: Holiday Inn Express Historic District, Mansion on Forsyth Park, Westin Savannah Harbor Golf Resort & Spa

Best Views: Cotton Sail, The Marshall House, Westin Savannah Harbor Golf Resort & Spa

Pet-Friendly: East Bay Inn, Hampton Inn, The Kimpton Brice, Olde Harbour Inn, Westin Savannah Harbor Golf Resort & Spa

Best Interior Design: Andaz, Cotton Sail, Dresser Palmer House, Hamilton-Turner Inn, Kehoe House, The Kimpton Brice, Perry Lane Hotel

Best Location: Andaz, Cotton Sail, Foley House Inn, Hotel Indigo, Mansion on Forsyth Park

4

including midtown and the airport. Just be aware that what you are gaining in affordability you will often be losing in convenience and historic charm.

WHAT IT COSTS			
$	$$	$$$	$$$$
Hotels	Under $150	$151–$200	$201–$250	over $250

Prices for two people in a standard double room in high season.

HISTORIC DISTRICT

$$$$ ⌧ **The Alida Hotel.** *Hotel.* A new addition to Savannah's Riverfront, the Alida collaborated with the Savannah College of Art and Design to create the industrial-meets-mid-century-modern vibe that's peppered with vibrant original, local artwork. **Pros:** very chic with great natural light; attentive staff; local/artisanal details feel special. **Cons:** several floors will lack a view once the new Kessler hotel is built in front of Alida (currently under construction); Williamson Street gets very busy and rowdy with partiers at night; no in-room coffee (though available on request). ⑤ *Rooms from: $288* ✉ *412 Williamson St., Historic District* ☎ *912/715–7000* ⊕ *www.thealidahotel.com* ⌦ *194 rooms* ⑩ *No meals.*

$$$$ ⌧ **Andaz Savannah.** *Hotel.* The interiors at the Andaz make quite a statement: The exposed-brick walls in the spacious lobby are offset by cozy, nested seating areas. **Pros:** concierge with extensive insider knowledge; excellent location overlooking Ellis Square, two blocks from the river; cosmopolitan rooftop pool. **Cons:** sounds of revelers on Congress Street can sometimes be heard in rooms; no free parking; conference spaces don't match the designer appeal of the rest of the hotel. ⑤ *Rooms from: $279* ✉ *Ellis Square, 14 Barnard St., Historic District* ✛ *At Barnard and Bryan Sts. on Ellis Square* ☎ *912/233–2116* ⊕ *savannah.andaz.hyatt. com* ⌦ *151 rooms* ⑩ *No meals.*

$$ ⌧ **Azalea Inn & Villas.** *B&B/Inn.* Expect a hospitable ambience, a wonderful breakfast, and afternoon wine service at this 1889 mansion built for a Cotton Exchange tycoon. **Pros:** rooms exude romance and luxury; baked goods are put out during the day; this is one of the few local B&Bs with a pool. **Cons:** just outside the heart of the Historic District, it's a bit of a walk to many attractions; less expensive rooms are small; the carriage house is not as distinctive. ⑤ *Rooms from: $179* ✉ *217 E. Huntingdon St., Historic District* ☎ *912/236–6080, 800/582–3823* ⊕ *www.azaleainn. com* ⌦ *10 rooms, 3 villas* ⑩ *Free Breakfast.*

$$ ⌧ **Ballastone Inn.** *B&B/Inn.* Step back into the Victorian era at this sumptuous inn on the National Register of Historic Places, which features fine antiques and reproductions, luxurious scented linens and down blankets on canopied beds; and a collection of original framed prints from *Harper's* scattered throughout. **Pros:** excellent location; romantic atmosphere; magnificently appointed suites. **Cons:** limited off-street parking; busy downtown area can be noisy. ⑤ *Rooms from: $329* ✉ *14 E. Oglethorpe Ave.,*

Historic District ☎ *912/236–1484, 800/822–4553* ⊕ *www. ballastone.com* ➬ *16 rooms* ⏹ *Free Breakfast.*

$$$$ ⌂ **The Bohemian.** *Hotel.* Giving you easy access to the hustle and bustle of River Street, this boutique hotel is a much-needed addition to the hotel landscape—instead of the Victorian decor that's so prevalent in Savannah; a stay at the Bohemian is like settling into a gentleman's study in a regal English manse. **Pros:** river-view rooms offer lovely vistas; pets are allowed for a nonrefundable fee of $100; access to spa at the Mansion on Forsyth Park. **Cons:** decor is a little over-the-top; the rooftop lounge stays open late and the noise can sometimes be heard in guest rooms; not very kid-friendly. ⑤ *Rooms from: $250* ⊠ *102 W. Bay St., Historic District* ☎ *912/721–3800, 888/213–4024* ⊕ *www. kesslercollection.com/bohemian-savannah* ➬ *75 rooms* ⏹ *No meals.*

$$$ ⌂ **Cotton Sail Hotel.** *Hotel.* A part of the Tapestry Collection by Hilton, this establishment is perched over River Street and offers expansive views of the Savannah River. **Pros:** hints of period charm; great location; rooftop bar is a great place to meet locals and out-of-towners. **Cons:** bar gets busy on the weekends, which can mean noise; not as historic as other properties; valet parking is pricey. ⑤ *Rooms from: $224* ⊠ *126 W. Bay St., Historic District* ☎ *912/200–3700* ⊕ *www.thecottonsailhotel.com* ➬ *56 rooms* ⏹ *No meals.*

$$ ⌂ **The DeSoto.** *Hotel.* Expect tasteful contemporary furnishings at this 15-story property with a rooftop pool, multiple dining options, and a downtown location in the heart of a thriving shopping and dining neighborhood. **Pros:** overlooking Madison Square; nice skyline views from the upper floors; complimentary Wi-Fi. **Cons:** on-street parking or pricey valet; small renovations are still in progress which can create inconveniences; no refrigerator in room. ⑤ *Rooms from: $185* ⊠ *15 E. Liberty St., Historic District* ☎ *912/232–9000* ⊕ *www.thedesotosavannah.com* ➬ *251 rooms* ⏹ *No meals.*

$$ ⌂ **The Dresser Palmer House.** *B&B/Inn.* This rambling Italianate town house from the late 19th century is a standout for its ornate exterior, relaxing front porch, and comfortable ambience. **Pros:** two back gardens with fountains are lovely; evening social offers wine, cheese, and guest camaraderie; one room is wheelchair accessible. **Cons:** lacks the privacy of a large property; just off the beaten path allows for quiet at night but longer walks to central areas; lobby decor could use refreshing. ⑤ *Rooms from: $179* ⊠ *211 E. Gaston St., Historic District* ☎ *912/238–3294, 800/671–0716* ⊕ *www.dresser-*

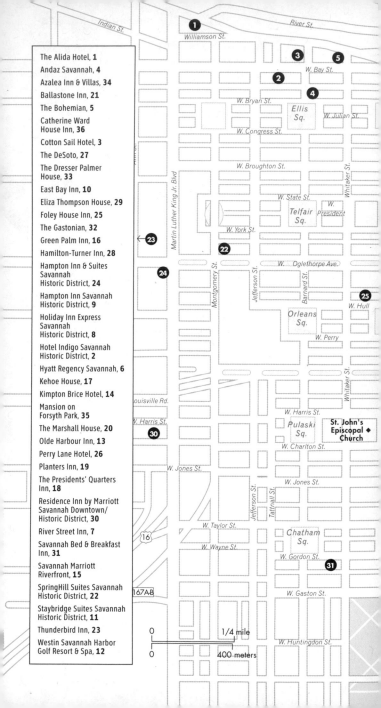

Where to Stay in Savannah

palmerhouse.com ⇔ *16 rooms* ❍ *Free Breakfast.*

$$ ▨ **East Bay Inn.** *B&B/Inn.* Once a series of cotton warehouses and factory offices that were built in 1852, this charming, pet-friendly inn has a handsome brick exterior, hunter-green shutters and awnings, and soaring 12- to 18-foot ceilings adorned with intricate crown molding. **Pros:** hospitality and service get very high marks; nightly turn-down service; routinely offer free tour tickets to guests.

> **BREAKFAST INCLUDED**
>
> When you are trying to decide on what kind of accommodation to reserve in Savannah, consider that B&Bs include breakfast (sometimes a lavish one), complimentary wine and cheese nightly, and even free bottled water. Hotels, particularly the major ones, usually do not even give you a bottle of water.

Cons: not enough parking spaces for the number of rooms; hallways and bathrooms are not as wonderful as the rooms. ⓢ *Rooms from: $139* ⌗ *225 E. Bay St., Historic District* ☎ *912/238–1225, 800/500–1225* ⊕ *www.eastbayinn.com* ⇔ *28 rooms* ❍ *Free Breakfast.*

$$ ▨ **Eliza Thompson House.** *B&B/Inn.* Afternoon wine, cheese, and appetizers and luscious evening desserts and sherry are served in the atmospheric main parlor of this fine town house built by Eliza Thompson's loving husband, Joseph, for their family in 1847. **Pros:** on one of Savannah's most beautiful streets; in a lively residential neighborhood; flat-screen TVs in every room. **Cons:** must purchase parking passes; breakfast can be hit or miss; some of the back rooms are small. ⓢ *Rooms from: $159* ⌗ *5 W. Jones St., Historic District* ☎ *912/236–3620, 800/348–9378* ⊕ *www.elizathompsonhouse.com* ⇔ *25 rooms* ❍ *Free Breakfast.*

$$$ ▨ **Foley House Inn.** *B&B/Inn.* In the center of the Historic District, this elegant inn is made up of two town houses built 50 years apart. **Pros:** gorgeous architecture and decor; luxury bath products; complimentary wine and hors d'oeuvres served in the evening. **Cons:** old pipes can make for slow drainage; fee for parking pass; no elevator. ⓢ *Rooms from: $259* ⌗ *14 W. Hull St., Historic District* ☎ *912/232–6622, 800/647–3708* ⊕ *www.foleyinn.com* ⇔ *19 rooms* ❍ *Free Breakfast.*

★ **Fodor'sChoice** ▨ **The Gastonian.** *B&B/Inn.* Guest rooms—many
$$$$ of which are exceptionally spacious—in this atmospheric Italianate inn dating from 1868 all have fireplaces and are decorated with a mix of funky finds and antiques from

SAVANNAH LODGING TIPS

■ **Do Your Research.** Don't hesitate to call the innkeepers and chat; you'll quickly gauge their attitude and sense of hospitality. And know the parking situation; many of these B&Bs provide only on-street parking, which can be tricky on busy weekends; though they usually pay for your parking pass, you still have to move the car on days when the streets need to be cleaned.

■ **Know What Historic Really Means.** Among the negatives can be antique beds, albeit beautifully canopied, that are short, not even as big as today's doubles. If you are tall or are used to a California King, this could be a definite issue. Rooms can be small, especially if they were originally backrooms meant for children or servants; rooms below street level—often called garden or courtyard rooms—can be damp. Windows aren't usually soundproof, and some squares are noisy in the morning or late at night, depending on the proximity to bars. Many B&Bs in old homes require patrons to share bathrooms.

■ **Savannah Has Hotels, Too.** Full-service hotels such as Hyatt Regency, Marriott, and Westin—as well as several boutique hotels—may be more appealing to visitors who actually prefer a larger, more anonymous property, or at least one with an elevator or swimming pool.

■ **Don't Forget the Chains.** Mid-range chain hotels and motels that normally would not excite or even interest you can be surprisingly appealing in Savannah. Some in the Historic District are creatively renovated historic structures. If you can't afford to stay downtown, you'll find many mid-range chains in midtown and the Southside (still less than 7 miles from downtown), as well as near the airport. The farther out you go, the less expensive your lodging will be.

the Georgian and Regency periods. **Pros:** cordial and caring staff; hot breakfast is hard to beat; afternoon tea and wine and cheese at night. **Cons:** accommodations on the third floor are a climb; some of the furnishings are less than regal; plumbing is old and sometimes problematic. ⑤ *Rooms from: $279* ✉ *220 E. Gaston St., Historic District* ☎ *912/232–2869, 800/322–6603* ⊕ *www.gastonian.com* ⇘ *17 rooms* ⑩ *Free Breakfast.*

$$ ▨ **Green Palm Inn.** *B&B/Inn.* This gingerbread inn built in 1897 is a pleasing little discovery with its spacious, high-ceilinged, and elegantly furnished cottage-style rooms inspired by Savannah's British Colonial heritage. **Pros:** innkeeper is knowledgeable about Savannah's history; quiet location with a garden patio; affordable rates. **Cons:** with only four guest rooms, it might be too intimate for some; location on the eastern edge of the Historic District isn't as convenient as other hotels; designated guest parking is limited. Ⓢ *Rooms from: $191* ✉ *548 E. President St., Historic District* ☎ *912/447–8901, 912/447–8901* ⊕ *www. greenpalminn.com* ⤳ *4 suites* ⦿ *Free Breakfast.*

★ Fodor's Choice ⛆ **Hamilton-Turner Inn.** *B&B/Inn.* With bathrooms
$$$ the size of New York City apartments, this French Empire mansion is celebrated, if not in song, certainly in story, and certainly has a "wow" effect, especially the rooms that front Lafayette Square. **Pros:** wonderfully furnished rooms; breakfast is a treat with baked items such as scones and hot entrées like perfect eggs Benedict; long and interesting history. **Cons:** sedate atmosphere won't appeal to everyone; no guest elevator (except for accessible Room 201); street parking only. Ⓢ *Rooms from: $259* ✉ *330 Abercorn St., Historic District* ☎ *912/233–1833* ⊕ *www.hamilton-turnerinn.com* ⤳ *18 rooms* ⦿ *Free Breakfast.*

$ ⛆ **Hampton Inn & Suites Savannah Historic District.** *Hotel.* The rooms and suites at this well-known chain hotel are a remarkably good value for Savannah's Historic District. **Pros:** spacious accommodations; continental breakfast with plenty of hot options; suites start at only $10 more than a standard room. **Cons:** avoid the suite next to the noisy boiler; charge for parking; noise from nearby traffic. Ⓢ *Rooms from: $204* ✉ *603 W. Oglethorpe Ave., Historic District* ☎ *912/721–1600, 800/426–7866* ⊕ *www.hamptoninn.com* ⤳ *154 rooms* ⦿ *Free Breakfast.*

$$ ⛆ **Hampton Inn Savannah Historic District.** *Hotel.* Located directly across the street from Factors Walk, this former cotton warehouse has antique heart-pine floors that extend the length of the lobby. **Pros:** cushy bedding and duvets; friendly staff; very child-friendly. **Cons:** pool and deck are not high enough for river views; street noise is to be expected; pricey valet parking. Ⓢ *Rooms from: $159* ✉ *201 E. Bay St., Historic District* ☎ *912/231–9700, 912/231–9700* ⊕ *hamptoninn3.hilton.com* ⤳ *144 rooms* ⦿ *Free Breakfast.*

$ ⛆ **Holiday Inn Express Savannah-Historic District.** *Hotel.* Since
FAMILY all buildings in the Historic District must conform to the local charm, Holiday Inn went all-out, creating a handsome interior design in the public spaces, with tasteful animal-print settees, leather club chairs, fireplaces, and classy

Savannah's Spooky Stays

In 2003 the American Institute of Paranormal Psychology christened Savannah the "most haunted city in America." And there have been countless reports of run-ins with spirits and specters in Savannah's many inns and B&Bs.

Some adventurous travelers even request haunted rooms, and you'll find that many properties wear their supernatural reputations like badges of honor. The East Bay Inn, for instance, lovingly refers to their resident ghost, Charlie, like a harmless extended houseguest.

You might occasionally hear the wooden floorboards squeaking; is it Charlie pacing the halls or a 200-year-old building settling in for the night?

At the Eliza Thompson House visitors have reported doors spontaneously locking and ghostly figures appearing in guest rooms. The Marshall House and Olde Harbour Inn also proudly tout their resident ghosts. Whether you consider it a selling point or a deterrent may depend on how superstitious you are, but don't say you haven't been warned.

4

---

chandeliers. **Pros:** impressive Wi-Fi throughout; sound-proof rooms; on-site fitness center. **Cons:** rates are higher than at most similar properties; could use some updates. ⑤ *Rooms from: $121* ✉ *199 E. Bay St., Historic District* ☎ *912/231–9000, 877/834–3613* ⊕ *www.savannahlodging.com* ⏎ *146 rooms* ⑩ *Free Breakfast.*

$$ ⏇ **Hotel Indigo Savannah Historic District.** *Hotel.* Mere steps from Ellis Square and City Market, this historic building was once a dry goods storage house. **Pros:** great location; renovated in 2015; helpful staff. **Cons:** decor lacks the warmth of many other downtown hotels; nearby Bay Street is noisy; no pool. ⑤ *Rooms from: $127* ✉ *201 W. Bay St., Historic District* ✛ *Between Ellis Square and Bay St.* ☎ *877/859–5095* ⊕ *www.hotelindigosavannah.com* ⏎ *309 rooms* ⑩ *No meals.*

$$ ⏇ **Hyatt Regency Savannah.** *Hotel.* A study in modernity amid the history of River and Bay streets, the seven-story Hyatt Regency Savannah has marble floors, glass elevators, and a towering atrium. **Pros:** modern decor; comfortable bedding; views from everywhere including the heated pool and lounge. **Cons:** valet parking is very expensive; many large groups; views don't come cheap. ⑤ *Rooms from: $169* ✉ *2 W. Bay St., Historic District* ☎ *912/238–1234, 866/899–8039* ⊕ *www.hyatt.com* ⏎ *351 rooms* ⑩ *No meals.*

★ Fodor'sChoice ⌂ **Kehoe House.** *B&B/Inn.* Known for its remark-
$$$$ ably friendly and attentive staff, this handsomely appointed
house, dating from the 1890s, was originally the family
manse of William Kehoe, a prominent Savannah businessman. **Pros:** romantic, photo-worthy setting; the two elevators are a rarity in a B&B; great, filling Southern breakfasts.
Cons: a few rooms have the sink and shower in the room;
soundproofing in guest rooms could be better; in-room
fireplaces don't work. Ⓢ *Rooms from: $251* ⌂ *123 Haber-
sham St., Historic District* ☎ *912/232–1020, 800/820–1020*
⊕ *www.kehoehouse.com* ⌂ *13 rooms* ⓘⓞⓘ *Free Breakfast.*

★ Fodor'sChoice ⌂ **The Kimpton Brice Hotel.** *Hotel.* No detail was
$$$ spared when they made a boutique hotel out of this 1860s
warehouse, which later served as a Coca-Cola bottling plant
and then a livery stable. **Pros:** staff is genuinely warm and
helpful; artistic design mixed with old Southern touches;
great view of the secret garden from many of the second
floor rooms. **Cons:** neighboring Bay Street can be loud; no
free parking; given it's in a historic building, the rooms are
smaller than one might expect for the price. Ⓢ *Rooms from:*
$224 ⌂ *601 E. Bay St., Historic District* ☎ *912/238–1200*
⊕ *www.bricehotel.com* ⌂ *145 rooms* ⓘⓞⓘ *No meals.*

★ Fodor'sChoice ⌂ **The Marshall House.** *B&B/Inn.* With original
$$$$ pine floors, handsome woodwork, and exposed brick, this hotel
provides the charm and intimacy of a B&B. **Pros:** great location
near stores and restaurants; exceptional restaurant; balconies
offer great bird's-eye views of Broughton Street. **Cons:** no free
parking; floors show their age in places; the sounds of bustling
Broughton Street can be noisy. Ⓢ *Rooms from: $259* ⌂ *123
E. Broughton St., Historic District* ☎ *912/644–7896* ⊕ *www.
marshallhouse.com* ⌂ *68 rooms* ⓘⓞⓘ *No meals.*

$$$ ⌂ **Olde Harbour Inn.** *B&B/Inn.* Dating from 1892, this pet-
friendly riverfront lodging tries hard to please even if it
doesn't always hit the heights; nevertheless, it's a good
option for those who want to be near the action of River
Street. **Pros:** hearty breakfast menu; welcomes families and
pets; all suites have views of river. **Cons:** not luxurious; location has some negatives, including hard-partying crowds
and late-night noise. Ⓢ *Rooms from: $215* ⌂ *508 E. Factors
Walk, Historic District* ☎ *912/234–4100, 800/553–6533*
⊕ *www.oldeharbourinn.com* ⌂ *24 rooms* ⓘⓞⓘ *Free Breakfast.*

★ Fodor'sChoice ⌂ **Perry Lane Hotel.** *Hotel.* Luxurious and artful
$$$ with an edge, the new Perry Lane Hotel raises the bar for
upscale accommodations in Savannah. **Pros:** beautiful and
chic; staff goes above and beyond; a favorite spot for locals
and tourists alike. **Cons:** in a high-traffic area that can be

noisy; due to its newness, Peregrin rooftop bar is usually very, very packed; no coffeemakers in rooms; $30 daily Destination Amenity Fee. ⑤ *Rooms from: $226* ✉ *256 E. Perry St., Historic District* ☎ *912/244–9140* ⊕ *perrylanehotel.com* ⬂ *179 rooms* ⦿ *No meals.*

$$ ⑃ **Planters Inn.** *Hotel.* A Savannah landmark, the Planters Inn makes sure its guests mix and mingle—the evening wine-and-cheese reception is a house party where the concierge introduces fellow guests, a good cross-section of leisure and business travelers, many of whom are repeats. **Pros:** management and staff truly make you feel at home; great architectural details in the lobby; convenient location near the Olde Pink House, where the kitchen provides for room service. **Cons:** decor and bathrooms could benefit from an update; breakfast could be improved; smaller rooms due to historic nature. ⑤ *Rooms from: $159* ✉ *29 Abercorn St., Historic District* ☎ *912/232–5678, 800/554–1187* ⊕ *www.plantersinnsavannah.com* ⬂ *60 rooms* ⦿ *Free Breakfast.*

$$$ ⑃ **The Presidents' Quarters Inn.** *B&B/Inn.* You'll be impressed even before you enter this lovely historic inn, which has an exterior courtyard so beautiful and inviting that it's popular for wedding receptions. **Pros:** central-but-quiet location; private parking and some private entrances; romantic atmosphere. **Cons:** inn books up fast in spite of ghost rumors; some might not like the contemporary carpeted floors in guest rooms; ground floor rooms are at street level, which can be noisy. ⑤ *Rooms from: $189* ✉ *225 E. President St., Historic District* ☎ *912/233–1600, 800/233–1776* ⊕ *www.presidentsquarters.com* ⬂ *16 rooms* ⦿ *Free Breakfast.*

$$$ ⑃ **Residence Inn by Marriott Savannah Downtown/Historic District.** *Hotel.* Some of the architecture at this reasonably priced lodging re-creates the 19th-century cottages that were used to house executives of the Central of Georgia Railroad. **Pros:** outdoor pool; complimentary hot breakfast; Wi-Fi throughout the hotel. **Cons:** location on the western edge of Historic District isn't the best; looks and feels like a chain hotel; parking for a fee. ⑤ *Rooms from: $177* ✉ *500 W. Charlton St., Historic District* ☎ *912/233–9996* ⊕ *www.marriott.com* ⬂ *109 rooms* ⦿ *Free Breakfast.*

$$$ ⑃ **River Street Inn.** *Hotel.* Housed in a five-story converted warehouse, this 1817 lodging has a harbor-from-yesteryear theme, with nautical murals and model schooners. **Pros:** fitness center; fifth-floor library; complimentary wine and hors d'oeuvres are laid out almost every evening. **Cons:** could use a renovation; no private parking (city garage across the street); beware of the wildly uneven floors. ⑤ *Rooms from:*

4

$235 ⊠ 124 E. Bay St., Historic District ☎ 912/234–6400 ⊕ www.riverstreetinn.com ⇨ 87 rooms ⓄNo meals.

$ ⚏ **Savannah Bed & Breakfast Inn.** *B&B/Inn.* The rooms at this restored 1853 Federal-style row house on historic Gordon Row near Chatham Square aren't quite as luxe as some of Savannah's finer B&Bs, but they are handsomely appointed and retain many elements of the home's original charm, such as beamed ceilings and exposed-brick walls. **Pros:** cottages with kitchens are particularly well priced; free on-street parking; friendly for families. **Cons:** 20-minute walk to the river; front desk not staffed after 9 pm. *⑤ Rooms from: $159 ⊠ 117 W. Gordon St., Historic District ☎ 912/238–0518 ⊕ www.savannahbnb.com ⇨ 30 rooms, 4 cottages, 2 townhomes ⓄFree Breakfast.*

$$ ⚏ **Savannah Marriott Riverfront.** *Hotel.* One of the city's few high-rise hotels—and the major anchor of the east end of the River Street area—the Savannah Marriott Riverfront delivers the professional management demanded by business travelers while offering some of the resort amenities that vacationers crave. **Pros:** views from the balconies of the riverfront rooms are truly magical at night; indoor and outdoor pools; great spa. **Cons:** conventions often dominate the main floor, limiting access to the indoor pool; a fair walk to the hot spots up on River Street; pedicabs can't come here on the cobblestones. *⑤ Rooms from: $179 ⊠ 100 General McIntosh Blvd., Historic District ☎ 912/233–7722, 800/285–0398 ⊕ www.marriott.com ⇨ 387 rooms ⓄNo meals.*

$ ⚏ **SpringHill Suites by Marriott Savannah Downtown/Historic District.** *Hotel.* Holding its own beside any of the city's boutique hotels, the SpringHill Suites has a lobby that's a study in sleek, contemporary design, with earthy wood elements contrasting with pops of color and ultramodern light fixtures. **Pros:** suites include refrigerators and microwaves; on-site gym; free Wi-Fi and hot buffet breakfast. **Cons:** some bathrooms are small and stark; parking is pricey. *⑤ Rooms from: $139 ⊠ 150 Montgomery St., Historic District ☎ 912/629–5300 ⊕ www.marriott.com ⇨ 160 rooms ⓄFree Breakfast.*

$ ⚏ **Staybridge Suites Savannah Historic District.** *Hotel.* Located in a historic building, the Staybridge Suites has a perfect downtown location. **Pros:** breakfast and social hour treats included in stay; parking included in hotel fee; in the heart of everything. **Cons:** $100 pet fee may seem excessive to some; due to historic building, suites are smaller than newer builds; Bay Street is a thoroughfare and can be noisy with revelers and traffic. *⑤ Rooms from: $128 ⊠ 301 E. Bay St.,*

Historic District ☎ *912/721–9000* ⊕ *www.staybridgesuites. com* ⇔ *104 rooms* ⏐◯⏐ *Free Breakfast.*

$ ☎**Thunderbird Inn.** *Hotel.* A stay in this motor lodge will transport you back to the 1960s with hot popcorn awaiting your arrival, white leather chairs in the rooms, and Moon Pies on your pillow with the complimentary turndown, but it offers all the modern amenities of standard brand hotels—flat-screen TVs, fridges, coffeepots—at a highly competitive rate for this part of town. **Pros:** free parking; hip furnishings; great location. **Cons:** as far as the towels go, you get what you pay for; traffic noise can be a little loud. ⑤*Rooms from: $98* ✉ *611 W. Oglethorpe Ave., Historic District* ☎ *912/232–2661, 866/324–2661* ⊕ *www.thethunderbirdinn.com* ⇔ *42 rooms* ⏐◯⏐ *No meals.*

★ **Fodor's**Choice ☎**Westin Savannah Harbor Golf Resort & Spa.**

$$$ *Resort.* Within its own fiefdom, this high-rise property FAMILY with more resort amenities than any other property in the area—including tennis courts, a full-service spa, and a golf course—presides over Hutchinson Island, five minutes by water taxi from River Street and just a short drive over the Talmadge Bridge. **Pros:** heated outdoor pool boasts a great view of River Street; dreamy bedding; great children's program. **Cons:** you are close, but still removed, from downtown; lacks atmosphere; an expensive and annoying resort fee. ⑤*Rooms from: $249* ✉ *1 Resort Dr., Hutchinson Island* ☎ *912/201–2000* ⊕ *www.westinsavannah.com* ⇔ *403 rooms* ⏐◯⏐ *No meals.*

VICTORIAN DISTRICT

$$ ☎**Catherine Ward House Inn.** *B&B/Inn.* Elegance meets comfort at this bed-and-breakfast, applauded for warm and inviting touches like soft music, cozy lighting, and crackling fires in period fireplaces. **Pros:** rooms have antique mantels and fireplaces, some of which work; some rooms have two-person whirlpool tubs; tasty breakfasts. **Cons:** less expensive rooms are small; carriage-house rooms are not as atmospheric as the main house; two-night minimum usually required for weekends. ⑤*Rooms from: $199* ✉ *118 E. Waldburg St.* ☎ *912/234–8564, 800/327–4270* ⊕ *www. catherinewardhouseinn.com* ⇔ *9 rooms* ⏐◯⏐ *Free Breakfast.*

★ **Fodor's**Choice ☎**Mansion on Forsyth Park.** *Hotel.* Sitting on the

$$$$ edge of Forsyth Park, this Marriott Autograph Collection property has dramatic design, opulent interiors with a contemporary edge, and a magnificently diverse collection of some 400 pieces of American and European art, all of

A SIDE OF TYBEE ALMOST GONE

You may hear some wild stories about Tybee Island: that it is a veritable Margaritaville, a kitschy resort area right out of the 1950s, or a hideout for eccentric beach bums. All the rumors are true, but that doesn't mean the island hasn't changed some over the years. If you want to keep in the traditional Tybee vibe, check out

Mermaid Cottages (⊕ www.mermaidcottages.com), which rents a variety of funky, colorful bungalows—with names like the Crabby Pirate and the Pink Flamingo. They are a trip back to nostalgic beach communities of old and a fun way to experience the pleasures of life on the island.

which create a one-of-a-kind experience—sophisticated, chic, and artsy only begin to describe it. **Pros:** stimulating environment transports you from the workaday world; full-service spa; complimentary shuttle to River Street. **Cons:** very pricey; some of the art from the early 1970s is not appealing; location is a good walk from central downtown of Broughton Street, Bay Street, and so on. Ⓢ *Rooms from: $251* ⊠ *700 Drayton St.* ☎ *912/238–5158* ⊕ *www.kesslercollection.com/mansion* ⇴ *125 rooms* ⓄⒾ *No meals.*

TYBEE ISLAND

- ★ Fodor's Choice ⚏ **Lighthouse Inn.** *B&B/Inn.* This yellow-and-
$$$ white frame house is a quiet getaway, a place to unplug and renew, to sit on the front porch and make the rocker creak while watching the sun drop. **Pros:** lovely breakfast entrées; charming claw-foot tubs in the vintage baths; just minutes from a magnificent beach and the Tybee Island Lighthouse. **Cons:** no water views; it is a relatively small, close environment; house rules are strictly enforced. Ⓢ *Rooms from: $209* ⊠ *16 Meddin Dr., Tybee Island* ☎ *912/786–0901, 866/786–0901* ⊕ *www.tybeebb.com* ⇴ *3 rooms* ⓄⒾ *Free Breakfast.*

- $ ⚏ **Tybee Vacation Rentals.** *Rental.* If renting a five-star beach house, a pastel island cottage, or a waterfront condo in a complex with a pool and tennis courts is your coastal-Georgia dream stay, check out Tybee Vacation Rentals. **Pros:** a variety of accommodations available; perfect for self-catering; pool and tennis courts in complex. **Cons:** two-night minimum; properties fill up fast. Ⓢ *Rooms from: $129* ⊠ *1010 Hwy. 80 E, Tybee Island* ☎ *912/786–5853, 855/651–1840* ⊕ *www.tybeevacationrentals.com* ⇴ *10-plus properties.*

NIGHTLIFE AND PERFORMING ARTS

Updated
by Anna
Chandler

THERE'S NO SHORTAGE OF ENTERTAINMENT in the Hostess City, whether you're looking for a live band, a crowded dance floor, or any number of more laid-back options. Plus, you can carry alcoholic beverages with you on the street, adding a festive touch to life after dark.

Congress Street and River Street have the highest concentrations of bars with live music, especially if you're looking for rock, heavy metal, or the blues. Many of the most popular dance clubs are scattered across the same area. If you're in the mood for something more sedate, there are plenty of chic enclaves known for their creative cocktails and cozy nooks that encourage intimate conversation. But just because the city enjoys its liquor doesn't mean that there's nothing going on for those who'd rather not imbibe. There are coffee shops that serve up live music and film screenings, as well as arts venues offering theater, films, and comedy.

NIGHTLIFE

THE HISTORIC DISTRICT

BARS AND NIGHTCLUBS

Artillery. One of Savannah's most beautiful bars, Artillery is housed in a historic landmark built by a volunteer militia group of mounted rangers in 1896. Now, Daniel Reed Hospitality embraces 18th-century-style and modern design elements in its sumptuously restored space. Settle in and buzz a waiter with the push of a call button to order from the expansive wine list, the classic cocktail menu (they make an excellent Manhattan), or the contemporary cocktail selection (Bit of a Pickle is an unusually delicious choice with gin, lemon, white balsamic vinegar, cucumber, dill and cracked pepper.) Expert drinks and great conversation are champion here, and proper attire is a must (no cut-offs, tank tops; flip-flops strongly discouraged; no hats)—and make sure you silence your phone once inside. ⊠ *307 Bull St., Historic District* ⊕ *www.artillerybar.com.*

Barrelhouse South. In the center of Congress Street's bustling nightlife scene, Barrelhouse South offers live music most nights of the week. Packed on the weekends with an enthused mix of bohemian and professional twenty- to thirtysomethings, the crowds dance the night away to bands playing covers and originals that range from funk and R&B to rock. Shoot a round of pool at the second bar in the basement. ✉ *125 W. Congress St., Historic District* ✛ *Off Ellis Square on Congress St.* ☎ *912/662–5576.*

★ **Fodor'sChoice Circa 1875.** In a beautifully renovated space with pressed-tin ceilings and a gorgeous antique bar, this is the place to come for a bottle of wine or champagne by the glass. Recordings of jazz legends like Billie Holiday or Django Reinhardt are usually the soundtrack, and the bar area is filled with tucked-away nooks for couples on a date. The gastropub next door offers a full menu of French fare that can also be ordered late into the night. The gourmet burgers and the mussels are highly recommended. ✉ *48 Whitaker St., Historic District* ☎ *912/443–1875* ⊕ *www. circa1875.com* ☾ *Closed Sun.*

Club One. Savannah's mainstay gay bar offers three levels of fun: drag shows and occasional burlesque and theatre productions upstairs; dance parties on the main floor; and a relaxing spot for conversation or karaoke in the basement bar. Although the decor is a little tacky, the scene is wildly fun when the lights go down and the music starts. ✉ *1 Jefferson St., Historic District* ☎ *912/232–0200* ⊕ *www. clubone-online.com.*

Congress Street Social Club. Part sports bar, part music venue, the Congress Street Social Club is always jam-packed on weekend nights. Enjoy drinks and street eats right off the grill on the patio, dance to live music or a DJ inside, or play a round of pool in Social's basement. For a more laid-back experience, stop by on a weekend afternoon for nibbles, beer, and dogspotting on the patio. ✉ *411 W. Congress St., Historic District* ☎ *912/238–1985* ⊕ *congressstreet-socialclub.com.*

Kevin Barry's Irish Pub. One of the city's most venerable drinking establishments, Kevin Barry's Irish Pub has a friendly vibe, a full menu, and traditional Irish music seven days a week. This is one of the most authentic pubs you'll find this side of the Atlantic, making it a great place to be on St. Patrick's Day; the second floor Hall of Heroes, a monument to the military, makes it a popular stop for servicemen and women. Dig into Irish-inspired eats, like Guinness braised brisket or the corned beef Cuban sandwich, on the lunch and dinner menu. ✉ *114 W. River St., Historic District* ☎ *912/233–9626* ⊕ *www.kevinbarrys.com.*

5

★ **Fodor's**Choice **Lulu's Chocolate Bar.** This laid-back spot invites you to indulge your sweet tooth. Walking through the door, you're immediately greeted by a dessert case full of freshly baked specialties—try some of the homemade truffles. The menu also includes a spectacular list of specialty drinks, including champagne cocktails, chocolate martinis, and a modest selection of beer and wines. Warm up with an Irish coffee or the truly divine "drinkable chocolate," an especially fulfilling twist on hot chocolate. ⊠ *42 Martin Luther King Jr. Blvd., Historic District* ☎ *912/480–4564* ⊕ *www.luluschocolatebar.com.*

Molly MacPherson's Scottish Pub & Grill. This Scottish pub is a must for Scotch lovers, who'll find a selection of more than 100 single malts. Well-prepared Scottish and American specialties include bangers and mash and fish-and-chips. Local rock bands and singer-songwriters perform Thursday, Friday, and Saturday night. Stop by the original location near City Market or venture out to Molly's Richmond Hill and Pooler outposts. ⊠ *311 W. Congress St., Historic District* ☎ *912/239–9600* ⊕ *macphersonspub.com.*

FAMILY **Moon River Brewing Company & Beer Garden.** Savannah's first microbrewery, Moon River occupies a historic building that once served as a hotel, as well as a lumber and coal warehouse. The adjacent outdoor beer garden is known for great people-watching, live music, and breezes off the nearby river. Check out the amazing variety of handcrafted lagers, ales, and wheat beers, compliments of award-winning brewmaster John Pinkerton. Pinkerton monitors the large steel vats of beer, which you can see through the glass partition. Soak up the first few rounds with a good variety of pub food. ⊠ *21 W. Bay St., Historic District* ☎ *912/447–0943* ⊕ *www.moonriverbrewing.com.*

The Original Pinkie Masters. This dive bar's biggest claim to fame was that Georgia's own Jimmy Carter stood up on the bar to announce his bid for the presidency. The people are friendly, the drinks are cheap, the analog jukebox is loaded with an unexpected mix of soul, R&B, and punk, and the vibe is laid-back with zero frills. ⊠ *318 Drayton St., Historic District* ☎ *912/999–7106* ⊕ *www.theoriginal-savannah.com* ⊙ *Closed Sun.*

★ **Fodor's**Choice **Peregrin.** Perched on top of Perry Lane Hotel, Peregrin offers the best view of the city's church steeples and architectural details on a lush, colorful patio. Revelers can play cornhole while sipping Frozé (frozen rosé) or the

NIGHTLIFE TIPS

■ **Drinking on the Street Is Allowed.** You can take your drink out onto the street, but it has to be in a plastic cup—no cans or bottles. Barkeeps and door staff usually have a supply of plastic cups on hand, known locally as "to-go cups." As long as your drink is less than 16 ounces and you're somewhere north of Jones Street, then it's perfectly legal to stroll around.

■ **Celebrate on Sunday morning.** To abide with the state's blue laws, most bars and clubs are closed on Sunday. There are a few exceptions, because some places that serve food remain open, but the choices are slim compared with Friday and Saturday nights. Thanks to the "Brunch Bill" passed in 2018, restaurants can now serve alcohol before 12:30 pm, so locals enjoy morning revelry with mimosas and bloody marys over breakfast.

■ **Try a Pub Crawl.** The same way taking a tour during the day will help you get your bearings, there are plenty of tours geared toward the nightlife. Several companies offer haunted pub crawls and other "spirited" walking tours to acquaint you with some local "haunts." It can be both entertaining and a good way to find places you might want to revisit on subsequent nights.

■ **No Smoking in Bars.** After heated discussions between elected officials and bar owners, the city banned smoking in bars in 2010. There are still a few places where smokers can get their fix, including a handful of open-air patios, but don't light up inside or within 10 feet of the front door.

■ **See What's Brewing.** Local breweries like Southbound and Service Brewing Co. have popped up in recent years. They offer tours of their facilities, where a tasty array of craft beers are brewed onsite and ripe for the sipping. You can also try a locally made craft spirit at Ghost Coast Distillery or take a tour to learn about the history of liquor in Savannah.

5

Planter's Punch. Wine lovers will revel in the curated menu, and there's a small array of bites like dill pickle dip and crab and shrimp lettuce wraps if you're feeling peckish. ✉ *Perry Lane Hotel, 256 East Perry St., Historic District* ✛ *Between Parker's Urban Gourmet and Green Fire Pizza* ☎ *912/559–8365* ⊕ *www.peregrinsavannah.com.*

★ **Fodor's** Choice **Planters Tavern.** Lighted by flickering candles, this tavern in the basement of the Olde Pink House is one of Savannah's most romantic late-night spots. There's a talented piano player setting the mood, two stone fireplaces, and an array of fox-hunt memorabilia. The upstairs menu is available, with the same quality of service but a slightly less formal approach. ■ TIP→ **The handful of tables fill up fast, but the staff will serve you wherever you find a spot.** ⊠ *23 Abercorn St., garden level, Historic District* ☎ *912/232–4286.*

Savannah Smiles. Reminiscent of an old roadside honky tonk, Savannah Smiles features dueling piano players that take requests via napkins, and a tip will get your song bumped up in the playlist. Patrons are encouraged to participate in the onstage antics. The kitchen is open late. ⊠ *314 Williamson St., Historic District* ☎ *912/527–6453* ⊕ *www.savannahsmilesduelingpianos.com* ⊙ *Closed Sun.–Tues.*

The Wayward. The Perry Lane Hotel's take on an elevated dive bar, the Wayward combines grimy punk aesthetics with sleek, modern design touches like a salon-style gallery wall with paintings of Bill Murray and a vintage motorcycle hanging over the bar. Order a boilermaker, enjoy some free popcorn, and play a around of pinball in the small arcade. ⊠ *Perry Lane Hotel, 257 E. Perry St., Historic District* ☎ *912/559–8362* ⊕ *www.waywardsavannah.com.*

COFFEEHOUSES

★ **Fodor'sChoice The Coffee Fox.** The newest addition to the local coffeehouse scene, the Coffee Fox is downtown's answer to Foxy Loxy. Specializing in locally roasted Perc coffee, homemade baked goods, and craft beers, the Coffee Fox is a great stop whether you're on the run or looking to perch. The cold brew will win the hearts of coffee aficionados in the hot summer months. The popular Mexican Mocha is a sweet and spicy twist on the traditional mocha featuring local chocolatier Adam Turoni's dark chocolate. For an unusual pairing, try the Eye Opener, a mole porter by Second Self paired with a double shot of espresso. ⊠ *102 W. Broughton St., Downtown* ☎ *912/401–0399* ⊕ *thecoffeefox.com.*

★ **Fodor'sChoice Foxy Loxy.** A little south of Downtown Savannah, this charming coffeehouse and café provides the cozy comfort lacking in many other Savannah coffee shops. Purveying a variety of coffee drinks—many made with locally roasted Perc Coffee—craft beers, and wine, Foxy Loxy is a staple in the lives of loyal customers of all ages. Try delicious baked treats like kolaches or bourbon bacon brownies. Don't forget to admire the decor and the rotating printmaking exhibits. On Friday night, cozy up by the fire pits in the courtyard with a half-price bottle of wine or a s'mores kit. Leashed pets are welcome in the expansive outdoor space. ✉ *1919 Bull St., Historic District* ☎ *912/401–0543* ⊕ *www.foxyloxycafe.com.*

Gallery Espresso. This long-established coffee haunt and art enclave features a steady rotation of local artists. The staff can be curt, but it is a real neighborhood joint and a popular destination for art students. The comfortable vintage couches and chairs are a great place to curl up with a book. ✉ *234 Bull St., Historic District* ☎ *912/233–5348* ⊕ *www. galleryespresso.com.*

Sentient Bean. On the southern edge of Forsyth Park, this hangout was one of Savannah's best-kept secrets until it was written up by the *New York Times.* It is a favorite gathering spot for locals of all stripes, who swarm by its welcoming atmosphere and organic fare. The Bean offers a small but delectable menu of breakfast and lunch options, along with a variety of fair-trade coffees, teas, and smoothies. In the evening, customers can enjoy poetry readings, film screenings, and live music over a beer or glass of wine at happy-hour prices. ✉ *13 E. Park Ave., Historic District* ☎ *912/232–4447* ⊕ *www.sentientbean.com.*

LIVE MUSIC CLUBS

Alley Cat Lounge. Although tucked away down an alley (or "lane," as they're properly known in Savannah), Alley Cat is a hot spot among local young professionals and service industry workers, beloved for its elegant interior, lengthy newspaper-style menu, and a rotating array of lovingly made craft cocktails. Tiki drinks are a frequent favorite—or a customary shot of Fernet Branca. ✉ *207 W. Broughton St., Downtown* ✚ *In alley between State St. and Broughton St.* ☎ *912/677–0548* ⊕ *www.alleycatsavannah.com.*

Casimir's Lounge. This sleek nightspot regularly features live jazz, blues, and acoustic stylings. The decor is luxe, perhaps even a bit over-the-top. There's a great balcony on the side where you can have a drink while enjoying a view of the park. The mussels and burgers are highly recommended. ✉ *Mansion on Forsyth Park, 700 Drayton St., Historic District* ☎ *912/721–5002* ⊕ *www.mansiononforsythpark. com* ☺ *Closed Sun.–Tues.*

Jazz'd Tapas Bar. This chic subterranean venue attracts a crowd of young professionals and visitors who belly up to the industrial-style bar for some of Savannah's best martinis. Local jazz and blues artists perform Tuesday through Sunday. The nicely presented tapas are tasty and easy on the budget. ✉ *52 Barnard St., Historic District* ☎ *912/236–7777* ⊕ *jazzdtapasbar.com.*

The Jinx. There's live music almost every night of the week at the Jinx. Weekends could feature anything from heavy metal or punk to outlaw country. The house special is a Pabst Blue Ribbon and a shot of Wild Turkey 101. Tuesday is the hugely popular hip-hop night, and Saturday happy hour regularly features the Jinx's house band playing country classics and original songs. If you like tattoos, you will see some of the best in the city. ✉ *127 W. Congress St., Historic District* ☎ *912/236–2281* ⊘ *Closed Sun.*

The Warehouse. An old-school dive bar that claims to have "the coldest beer in town," the Warehouse's River Street location means more tourists than locals. The service is friendly, and lots of different local bands play everything from original rock and country to classic covers. The kitchen serves deep-fried fare like chicken fingers, fried pickles, and gator bites if you get a hankering for something to snack on. ✉ *18 E. River St., Historic District* ☎ *912/234–6003* ⊕ *thewarehousebarandgrille.com.*

THE STARLAND DISTRICT, THOMAS SQUARE, AND MIDTOWN

BARS AND NIGHTCLUBS

Lone Wolf Lounge. In the heart of Savannah's Thomas Square District, the Lone Wolf Lounge offers the warm vibe of a down-home, '70s era watering hole with an expertly crafted cocktail menu. A refreshing mix of high and low, you can get a cold Schlitz for a couple bucks or a house cocktail made by some of Savannah's best bartenders for under $10. Try The Glamorous Life, the pitch-perfect house daiquiri, or the Zippah, an invigorating crisp mix of gin, absinthe, and lemon with a touch of earthiness. A mix of townies, students, and neighborhood folks gather around the wood-paneled bar and booths and nosh on dinner from the food trucks frequently parked outside. ✉ *2429 Lincoln St., Thomas Square.*

THE ISLANDS AND THUNDERBOLT

BARS AND NIGHTCLUBS

Coach's Corner. This is the place to be if you're trying to catch the big game. Although it's a few miles east of downtown, Coach's Corner serves burgers and other traditional pub grub and is known for some of the best wings in all of Savannah. Check their Facebook page for the occasional live music offerings. ⊠ *3016 E. Victory Dr., Thunderbolt* ☎ *912/352–2933* ⊕ *www.coachs.net.*

PERFORMING ARTS

HISTORIC DISTRICT

FESTIVALS AND SPECIAL EVENTS

St. Patrick's Day Parade. The city's largest annual festival has evolved over the past two centuries to become one of the largest of its kind in the country. Each March, roughly 700,000 participants tip their hats (and their glasses) to the rolling hills of Ireland. River Street becomes a sea of green: clothes, beer, food, and even the water in city fountains is dyed the color of the clover. ■ TIP→ **Hotel rates during this period can be as much as three times the norm, so reserve well in advance.** ⊠ *Downtown* ⊕ *www.savannahsaintpatricksday.com.*

Savannah Book Festival. Held each February, the festival jump-starts the city's spring cultural season with dozens of high-profile authors, many with a connection to the region like Anne Rice, Patton Oswalt, and Nicholas Sparks. The literary event, which takes place in bookstores and other locations around Downtown Savannah, is marked by book signings, discussions, and plenty of activities for kids. ⊠ *Historic District* ☎ *912/598–4040* ⊕ *www.savannahbookfestival.org.*

Savannah Craft Brew Fest. Held every Labor Day weekend along the Savannah River, the brew fest is a buzz-worthy annual event for beer connoisseurs. Featuring small breweries from around the country, the weekend festival features educational seminars, gourmet meals, live music, and a grand tasting event. ⊠ *1 International Dr., Hutchinson Island* ⊕ *www.savannahcraftbrewfest.com.*

Savannah Jazz Festival. A local favorite since 1982, this free outdoor musical event is held annually in late September. Thousands of concertgoers pack Forsyth Park's expansive lawn with chairs, blankets, and picnic spreads for several nights of live jazz performances. Given the ideal weather this time of year, this festival puts Savannah's foremost greenspace to great use. After the evening headliner, head to local clubs to check out the nightly jam sessions, where unexpected collaborations are the norm. ⊠ *Forsyth Park, Gaston St., between Drayton and Whitaker Sts., Historic District* ⊕ *www.savannahjazzfestival.org.*

★ **Fodor's**Choice **Savannah Music Festival.** Georgia's largest and most acclaimed music festival brings together musicians from around the world for more than two weeks of unforgettable performances in late-March and early-April. The multigenre entertainment ranges from foot-stomping gospel to moody blues to mainstream rock to new takes on classical music. Performances take place in Savannah's premier theaters, as well as nontraditional venues like historic churches. ⊠ *Downtown* ⊕ *www.savannahmusicfestival.org.*

★ **Fodor's**Choice **SCAD Savannah Film Festival.** This star-studded affair, hosted by the Savannah College of Art and Design in late October and early November, offers multiple daily screenings of award-winning films in various venues on or near Broughton Street. Sir Patrick Stewart, Salma Hayek, and Hugh Jackman are among the celebrities who've attended in recent years. Q&A sessions with visiting celebrities and industry professionals are always popular. ⊠ *Downtown* ⊕ *filmfest.scad.edu.*

★ **Fodor's**Choice **Savannah Stopover Music Festival.** This intimate indie music festival held every March is a yearly "stopover" for bands headed to the massive South by Southwest event in Austin. The event features almost 100 acts in about a dozen different venues, providing indie music fans with an unmatched opportunity to experience their favorite up-and-coming acts. ⊠ *Historic District* ⊕ *www. savannahstopover.com.*

★ **Fodor's**Choice **SCAD Sidewalk Arts Festival.** Savannah College of Art and Design's Sidewalk Arts Festival, held the last Saturday of April, is a great opportunity to experience Forsyth Park in abundant glory. At no other time in the year is the park so packed with people of all ages, coming out in droves to see students past and present take to the

Did You Know?

Savannah's photogenic side has long served as a popular backdrop for movies. In the 1970s, some scenes from the legendary television miniseries *Roots* were shot at various spots around Savannah. In 1989 the Academy Award–winning film *Glory*, starring Denzel Washington and Morgan Freeman, was filmed near Fort Pulaski. One of Savannah's most famous film appearances came in 1994, when scenes for *Forrest Gump* were set on the north end of Chippewa Square. *Midnight in the Garden of Good and Evil* was filmed in the Historic District in 1997, and two years later *The General's Daughter* was shot at Wormsloe Plantation. *The Legend of Bagger Vance,* starring Will Smith, brought film crews to Savannah and Jekyll Island in 2000. Robert Redford's historical drama about Mary Surratt, *The Conspirator,* used Savannah for its backdrop in 2009.

Sparks flew between Miley Cyrus and Liam Hemsworth in 2010's beachside romance *The Last Song,* and Alan Rickman and Harry Potter co-star Rupert Grint came to town to shoot the story of legendary New York City nightclub CBGB in 2012. Broughton Street was transformed into Salty Shoals for box office smash *The SpongeBob Movie: Sponge Out of Water,* starring Antonio Banderas, in 2015. Funnymen Adam Sandler and David Spade filmed *The Do-Over* in 2016—Spade even surprised locals with an impromptu comedy set at local dive The Wormhole.

Tybee Island has welcomed heartthrob visitors like Channing Tatum for *Magic Mike XXL* and Zac Efron and Dwayne "The Rock" Johnson for 2017's *Baywatch.*

park's winding sidewalks with rainbow colors of chalk. By the day's end, the park is lined with out-of-this-world drawings as far as the eye can see, plus fun stains of chalk throughout the grass and on scraggling artists. ⊠ *Forsyth Park, Gaston St., between Drayton and Whitaker Sts., Historic District.*

VENUES

El-Rocko Lounge. This trendy, '70s-inspired nightclub, adorned in vintage decor, golden lighting, and authentic pachinko machines, serves a variety of audiences. At happy hour, you'll find young professionals enjoying a barrel-aged cocktail, conversation, and punching requests into the analog jukebox. After the sun sets, catch local and touring rock, hip-hop, and indie acts onstage. Late night, students flood the space to dance beneath the golden disco ball until last call. ⊠ *117 Whitaker St., Downtown* ✛ *At corner of Whitaker and State St.* ☎ *912/495–5808.*

The Historic Savannah Theatre. One of the country's oldest continuously operating theaters, the beautifully maintained Savannah Theatre presents family-friendly comedies and musical revues. The 600-seat theater is a throwback to the glory days of the stage. Don't miss the *Savannah Live* variety show. ⊠ *222 Bull St., at Chippewa Sq., Historic District* ☎ *912/233–7764* ⊕ *www.savannahtheatre.com.*

★ Fodor'sChoice **Lucas Theatre for the Arts.** Slated for demolition in 1921, the Lucas Theatre is now one of Savannah's most celebrated spaces. The beautifully renovated space hosts a variety of performances throughout the year, from ballet to bluegrass bands. It's a go-to venue for events hosted by the Savannah College of Art and Design, the Savannah Film Festival, and the Savannah Music Festival. ⊠ *32 Abercorn St., Historic District* ☎ *912/525–5050* ⊕ *www. lucastheatre.com.*

Savannah Civic Center. The Savannah Civic Center hosts numerous events and performances throughout the year, including big-ticket concerts, sporting events, and comedy. The Johnny Mercer Theatre, a separate venue inside the auditorium, hosts smaller events in a seated theater environment. ⊠ *301 W. Oglethorpe Ave., Orleans Sq., Historic District* ☎ *912/651–6550* ⊕ *www.savannahcivic.com.*

★ Fodor'sChoice **Trustees Theater.** When it opened in 1946, the Trustees Theater was one of the largest movie screens in the South. Now run by the Savannah College of Art and Design, it hosts a variety of events, including the Savannah Film Festival. It's also a popular venue for concerts and lectures. ⊠ *216 E. Broughton St., Historic District* ☎ *912/525–5050* ⊕ *www.trusteestheater.com.*

THE STARLAND DISTRICT, THOMAS SQUARE, AND MIDTOWN

FESTIVALS AND SPECIAL EVENTS

FAMILY **First Fridays in Starland.** This creative collaborative event takes place on the first Friday evening of each month throughout the Starland neighborhood. The event includes food trucks, music, and multiple art receptions and exhibits. Check out Instagram or their Facebook page for more information. ⊠ *Thomas Square.*

TYBEE ISLAND

FESTIVALS AND SPECIAL EVENTS

FAMILY **Tybee Island Pirate Fest.** Swashbucklers and wenches descend on Tybee Island in early October for the Pirate Fest. Don your best pirate-theme costumes for the Buccaneer Ball at the Crab Shack to kick off the weekend's festivities. Saturday is the popular Pirate Victory Parade, where Butler Avenue becomes a sea of ships filled with buccaneers tossing beads and booty. Venture over to the Thieves' Market, where vendors from across the country peddle their pirate wares and arts and crafts. Fun for the whole family, the festival includes magicians, puppet shows, and storytellers. Live entertainment rounds out the experience with concert headliners like Vince Neil and Quiet Riot. ⊠ *Strand Ave., between Tybrisia St. and 17th Pl., Tybee Island* ⊕ *tybeepiratefest.com* ⊒ *From $12 per day, $25 for weekend.*

SPORTS AND THE OUTDOORS

6

Updated
by Anna
Chandler

SAVANNAH RESIDENTS TAKE ADVANTAGE OF life on the coast. The neighboring areas and barrier islands of the Low-country are conducive to nearly all types of water sports. Swimming, stand-up paddle boarding, sailing, kiteboarding, fishing, kayaking, parasailing, and surfing are popular pastimes. The Savannah River flows alongside the city on its way to the Atlantic Ocean and is easily accessible by boat. A multitude of tidal creeks and marshlands intertwine the river and the barrier islands, most notably Tybee, where you can enjoy the sun-drenched beaches, friendly people, and a quirky vibe. The water here is generally warm enough for swimming from May through September.

For those who would prefer to stay on land, bicycling and jogging, golf and tennis dominate. During the hot and humid summer months, limit the duration of strenuous activity, remember to drink lots of water, and protect your skin from the sun.

HISTORIC DISTRICT

BIKING

Savannah is table-flat, to the enjoyment of many bicyclists. Like many towns and cities across the country, Savannah has introduced a bike-share program, allowing daily or weekly access to bikes at several solar-powered stations downtown. The city has also added a number of bike racks around the Historic District to make it easier for cyclists to find adequate parking without blocking foot traffic.

Sunday is the best day for riding downtown, but be aware that throughout much of downtown there are restrictions for bikers. Riding through the middle of squares and on the sidewalks of Broughton Street is illegal and carries a stiff fine if you're busted.

Bikers should always ride with traffic, not against it, and obey the lights. Riding after dark requires bicycles to display a white light visible from 300 feet on the front and a red reflector on the back. Helmets are legally required for those under the age of 16 (and a good idea for everyone). Be sure to lock up your bike securely if you're leaving it unattended, even for a few minutes.

CAT Bike. Keeping pace with booming metropolises like New York and Washington D.C., the City of Savannah and Chatham Area Transit introduced a public bike-share

BEST OUTDOOR ACTIVITIES

■ **Baseball.** A baseball game under a summer sky is an all-American pleasure. It's also a family-bonding opportunity, and the Savannah Bananas (a Coastal Plain League team) offer competitions and fun hijinks for the whole crew. Buy a hot dog and a frozen banana and join in the fun. There are fireworks on Saturday night, so you can double your fun for the cost of admission.

■ **Biking.** Forsyth and Daffin parks are favored destinations for locals. Tom Triplett Park, east of town on U.S. 80, offers three bike loops—3.5 miles, 5 miles, and 6.3 miles. You can explore quaint Tybee Island by bike for nearly half of what it costs to rent a bike downtown.

■ **Golf.** The weather here, particularly in the spring and fall, is custom ordered for a round or two of golf. Though the courses aren't as well regarded as those on Hilton Head, players looking for a challenge can count on gems like the Westin's Club at Savannah Harbor and the Wilmington Island Club, both of which are more moderately priced than the Hilton Head courses.

■ **Water Sports.** Water sports are the obvious choice for a city surrounded by rivers, creeks, marshes, and the Atlantic Ocean. Kayaking, sailing, stand-up paddle boarding, and kiteboarding are all popular, and there are plenty of options for guided tours, charter boats, and equipment rental (if you haven't brought your own).

6

program in 2014. Two solar-powered stations are located at Ellis Square and Rivers Exchange. Rates start at $5 for a 24-hour pass or $20 for a weekly pass. ⊠ *Historic District* ☎ *912/233–5767* ⊕ *catbike.bcycle.com.*

Perry Rubber Bike Shop. At the pulsing corner of Bull and Liberty Streets, Perry Rubber is the go-to shop for repairs and your best bet for rentals. It offers trendy hybrid or city bikes at $20 for a half day or $35 for the full day—helmet, lock, and basket included. ⊠ *240 Bull St., Downtown* ☎ *912/236–9929* ⊕ *www.perryrubberbikeshop.com.*

Sekka Bike. Stop by this popular storefront shop for hourly or daily bike rentals. Take an afternoon spin at $10 for three hours, or opt for a weekly rental for only $60. ⊠ *206 E. Broughton St., Historic District* ☎ *912/233–3888* ⊕ *sekkabike.com.*

BOATING AND FISHING

FAMILY **Dolphin Magic Tours.** Explore the natural beauty of Savannah's coastal waters on a narrated boat tour with Dolphin Magic Tours. From River Street, you cruise out to the marshlands and tidal creeks near Tybee Island. The search for dolphin encounters lasts two hours and costs $27; sightings are guaranteed. Departure times vary according to the tides and the weather. ⊠ *312 E. River St., Historic District* ☎ *912/897–4990* ⊕ *www.reelemn.com/dolphinmagic.*

GOLF

★ Fodor'sChoice **The Club at Savannah Harbor.** The area's only PGA course, this resort property on Hutchinson Island is a free ferry ride from Savannah's riverfront. The lush championship course winds through pristine wetlands and has unparalleled views of the river and downtown. It is also home to the annual Liberty Mutual Legends of Golf tournament, which attracts golfing's finest each spring. A bit pricier than most local clubs, prices vary according to the season, but the course is packed with beauty and amenities. ⊠ *Westin Savannah Harbor, 2 Resort Dr., Hutchinson Island* ☎ *912/201–2240* ⊕ *www.theclubatsavannahharbor.com* ⚑ *Dynamic pricing $85–$145* ⚐ *18 holes, 7300 yds, par 72* ⚑ *Reservations essential.*

ROLLER DERBY

Savannah Derby Devils. This women's flat-track roller derby team, the Derby Devils, is composed of an all-volunteer squad, coaches, medics, refs, and jeer-leaders. They play in "bouts" several times a year against worthy Southeastern opponents. The truly daring might try "suicide seating," on the edge of the rink, just inches away from bone-checking, jaw-dropping action. ⊠ *Savannah Civic Center, 301 W. Oglethorpe Ave., Historic District* ☎ *912/220–9744* ⊕ *www.savannahderby.com* ⚑ *$13.*

Georgia Football

This is the Deep South, so naturally locals can't get enough of Georgia football. They eat it for breakfast. Many locals take a couple of days off from their busy schedules to attend one of the first University of Georgia Bulldogs football games of the season.

If you want to make friends fast, express an interest in the Bulldogs—or "Dawgs," as they're better known in these parts. The famous mascot, nicknamed "Uga," hails from a line of white bulldogs that has been owned since the 1950s by Savannah resident Sonny Seiler. Once an attorney so prominent that he was featured in Hollywood's adaptation of *Midnight in the Garden of Good and Evil*, he is a local celebrity in his own right. And don't be surprised if your waiter raises the sleeve of his T-shirt to show you his symbolic University of Georgia tattoo—"One big G!"

If you want to attend a game, plan accordingly as the University of Georgia is in Athens, about four hours northwest of Savannah, and tickets are almost impossible to come by.

THE VICTORIAN DISTRICT AND EASTSIDE

BIKING

Bike Walk Savannah. Savannah's foremost bicycle advocate, this nonprofit membership organization helps to educate cyclists, motorists, and elected officials about cyclist and pedestrian safety and promotes improved bicycle facilities in Chatham County. They also host monthly rides and annual special events, such as the Moonlight Garden Ride. Many events are family-oriented and open to the public. Visit their website for information on upcoming activities. ✉ *3101 Lincoln St. , Suite A* ☎ *912/228–3096* ⊕ *www.bicyclecampaign.org.*

THE STARLAND DISTRICT, THOMAS SQUARE, AND MIDTOWN

BASEBALL

FAMILY **Savannah Bananas.** Since 2016, the Savannah Bananas have entertained locals and made national headlines for their unabashed sense of fun and silliness. A Bananas game is more than a baseball game: it's an entertainment event, with plenty of activities for the kids, dancing players, and lots of banana-themed snacks. If you've never seen a banana with abs, keep an eye out for mascot Split, who proudly cheers on the Coastal Plain League team. The Bananas' home, Grayson Stadium, is one of the country's oldest minor league stadiums; legends including Babe Ruth have run its bases. ⊠ *1401 E. Victory Dr., Daffin Park* ☏ *912/351–9150* ⊕ *www.savannahbananas.com.*

> ### SPORTS BARS
>
> Don't forget the sport of cheerleading! If you can't get tickets to the game, the next best thing is joining locals around a neighborhood bar to root for the home team. Spots like Congress Street Social Club and Coach's Corner make an art out of it.

THE MOON RIVER DISTRICT

BOATING AND FISHING

Moon River Kayak Tours. Setting out from either Wilmington or Skidaway islands, Moon River Kayak offers a different experience than many of the tours originating on Tybee Island. Paddling Turner's Creek, Skidaway Narrows, and Johnny Mercer's Moon River gives you a more inland perspective rich with sightings of such spectacular birds as ospreys and eagles. Be sure to bring your binoculars. ⊠ *Rodney J. Boat Ramp & Park, 45 Diamond Causeway, Skidaway Island* ☏ *912/897–3474* ⊕ *www.moonriverkayak.com.*

SOUTHSIDE, GATEWAY, AND GREATER SAVANNAH

GOLF

Bacon Park Golf Course. Completely renovated in 2014, Savannah's municipal golf club offers two courses: the 18-hole Donald Ross and the 9-hole Legends Course. Located on Savannah's Southside, Bacon Park is the best bang for your golfing buck in the area. ✉ *1 Shorty Cooper Dr.* ☎ *912/354–2625* ⊕ *baconparkgolf.com* 🖭 *9-hole Legends Course, $16; 18-hole Donald Ross, $22* 🏌 *Donald Ross course: 18 holes, 6418 yards, par 71.*

Crosswinds Golf Club. This 18-hole championship course features parkland-style play in an isolated setting 12 miles from downtown Savannah. Crosswinds has a reputation for being exceedingly well maintained; a 9-hole executive course is available, as is a driving range. ✉ *232 James Blackburn Dr.* ☎ *912/966–1909* ⊕ *www.crosswindsgolfclub.com* 🖭 *Championship Course, $53; Par-3 Course, $20* 🏌 *Championship Course: 18 holes, 6748 yards, par 72; Par-3 Course: 9 holes, 1126 yards, par 27* ♤ *Reservations essential.*

Henderson Golf Club. Located 15 miles from downtown, Henderson Golf Club might not be Savannah's biggest course, but its abundance of natural beauty makes it a draw for locals and visitors alike. This lush municipal course is surrounded by live oaks and wandering wetlands. Cart rental is included in the price. ✉ *1 Al Henderson Dr.* ☎ *912/920–4653* ⊕ *www.hendersongolfclub.com* 🖭 *$30, $27 after 1 pm* 🏌 *18 holes, 6700 yards, par 71* ♤ *Reservations essential.*

Southbridge Golf Club. Nestled within one of Savannah's most exclusive private housing communities, Southbridge is a popular Bermuda grass course. Discounted rates are available. ✉ *415 Southbridge Blvd.* ☎ *912/651–5455* ⊕ *www.southbridgegolfclub.com* 🖭 *$60 Fri.–Sun. and holidays, $50 Mon.–Thurs.* 🏌 *18 holes, 6922 yards, par 72* ♤ *Reservations essential.*

6

THE ISLANDS AND THUNDERBOLT

BOATING AND FISHING

Bull River Marina. This is your one-stop-shop for all your boating needs. Bull River offers rentals, tours, and charters in boats big and small. Starting at $29 per person for six or more passengers, expert guides will take you to hunt sharks' teeth; on a sightseeing tour of area forts and lighthouses; or on a 90-minute dolphin tour. For the more adventuresome, charters start at $350 for four people. If you prefer to captain your own boat, rentals start at $200 for four hours. ⊠ *8005 U.S. Hwy. 80, Wilmington Island* ☎ *912/897–7300* ⊕ *www.bullrivermarina.com.*

Compass Sailing. Boarding at Bull River Marina, Captain Steve's personal and private tours explore the ocean and salt marshes via a 38-foot sailing yacht. Passengers are encouraged to bring their own lunch or coolers; soft drinks are provided. ⊠ *Bull River Marina, 8005 U.S. Hwy. 80* ☎ *912/441–3265* ⊕ *www.compasssailing.com.*

Miss Judy Charters. Captain Judy Helmey, a longtime fishing guide and legendary local character, heads up Miss Judy Charters. The company offers packages ranging from 3-hour sightseeing tours to 14-hour deep-sea fishing expeditions. Inshore rates start at around $350 for three to four people for three hours; offshore rates start at $600 for up to six people for three hours. ⊠ *124 Palmetto Dr., Wilmington Island* ☎ *912/897–4921* ⊕ *www.missjudycharters.com.*

★ **Fodor's Choice Savannah Canoe and Kayak.** Leading you through inlets and tidal creeks, Savannah Canoe and Kayak has highly skilled guides that provide expert instruction for newbies and challenges for seasoned paddlers. You'll also learn about the history of these historic waterways. Half-day tours start at $65 for three hours. ⊠ *414 Bonaventure Rd.* ☎ *912/341–9502* ⊕ *www.savannahcanoeandkayak. com.*

FAMILY **Telecaster Charters.** Captain Kevin Rose leads fishing excursions on his 18-foot Pioneer flats boat for speckled trout, black drum, redfish, sheepshead, whiting, and even sharks. Fully licensed and insured, his four-hour trips start from one of several locations. The excursions start at $300 for two people and includes bait and licenses. Rose also offers island shuttles and nature tours. Children are welcome. ⊠ *Thunderbolt* ☎ *912/308–4622* ⊕ *www.telecastercharters.com.*

Wilderness Southeast. Discover Coastal Georgia wildlife in its natural habitat with a unique kayaking tour. Wilderness Southeast offers private and personalized kayak tours for spotting dolphins, birds, and alligators in maritime forests, salt marshes, swamps, beaches, and creeks, learning about history, and enjoying Savannah's outdoor offerings. ✉ *Savannah* ☎ *912/236–8115* ⊕ *www.naturesavannah.org*.

TYBEE ISLAND

BEACHES

North Beach. Tybee Island's North Beach is an all-in-one destination for beachgoers of every age. Located at the mouth of the Savannah River, the scene is generally low-key and is a great vantage point for viewing the cargo ships making their way to the Port of Savannah. A large, metered parking lot gives you convenient access to the beach, Fort Screven, and the adjacent Tybee Island Lighthouse and Museum, a 178-step lighthouse with great views of the surrounding area. The North Beach Grill, located in the parking lot, is perfect for an ice-cold beverage or bite to eat. To get here from Highway 80, turn left on Campbell Street and follow the signs to the Tybee Island Lighthouse. ■TIP→ **The local police are notorious for parking tickets, so make sure you feed the meter. Amenities:** food and drink; lifeguard; parking (fee); toilets. **Best for:** solitude; sunrise; swimming; walking. ✉ *Meddin Dr. at Gulick St., north of 1st St., Tybee Island*.

South End. If your idea of a good beach day involves empty stretches of sand, unobstructed views, plenty of privacy, and the sound of crashing waves, then you should test the waters at the south end. As its name suggests, the south end is located at the southern tip of the island where Tybee's Back River meets the Atlantic Ocean. ⚠ **Riptides and strong currents are prevalent here, so use extreme caution when swimming.** At low tide, the waters recede to expose a stunning system of sandbars that are great for shelling and spotting sea life. Check the tides to make sure you don't get stranded on the sandbars. This is one of Tybee's prettiest beaches, and is worshipped by locals for its seclusion. There are no restaurants in the immediate vicinity, so it's a good idea to bring a cooler packed with snacks and beverages. Parking is tough—just two very small metered lots. In high season, arrive on the early or the late side, when crowds are thinner.

6

Amenities: parking (fee). **Best for:** sunset; walking; windsurfing; sea kayaking. ⊠ *Butler Ave., at 19th St., Tybee Island.*

Tybee Island Pier and Pavilion. This is Tybee's "grand strand," the center of the summer beach action. Anchored by a 700-foot pier that is sometimes host to summer concerts, this stretch of shoreline is your best bet for people-watching and beach activities. Just off the sand at the bustling intersection of Tybrisa Street and Butler Avenue, a cluster of watering holes, souvenir shops, bike shacks, and oyster bars makes up Tybee's main business district. ■TIP→ **There's metered street parking as well as two good-size lots. Both fill up fast during the high season, so arrive early.** There are public restrooms at the Pier and at 15th and Tybrisa Streets. The pier is popular for fishing and is also the gathering place for fireworks displays. **Amenities:** food and drink; lifeguard; parking (fee); toilets. **Best for:** partiers; sunrise; surfing; swimming. ⊠ *Tybrisa St. at Butler Ave., Tybee Island* ☎ *912/652–6780.*

BIKING

Tim's Bike & Beach Gear. Filled with ocean-view trails, Tybee Island offers a bike-friendly environment and rentals at half the cost of downtown. Tim's Beach Gear rents bikes for adults and kids, as well as pull-behind carriers and jogging strollers. The shop offers free delivery and pickup on the island. Daily rates are $12 and include helmets and cup holders. And talk about one-stop shopping: umbrellas, beach chairs, towels, and games like bocce ball and horseshoes are also available. ⊠ *1101 U.S. Hwy. 80 E, Tybee Island* ☎ *912/786–8467* ⊕ *www.timsbeachgear.com.*

BOATING AND FISHING

★ Fodor'sChoice **Captain Mike's Dolphin Tours.** If boat-bound
FAMILY adventure is what you seek, look no further than Captain Mike. Widely popular with tourists and locals alike, Captain Mike's tours have been featured on the Discovery Channel, *Good Morning America,* and in the pages of *Southern Living.* Choose from a 90-minute dolphin tour from $15 per person, or an $18 sunset tour (available May to September). Captain Mike has a 32-foot cabin cruiser in his fleet and offers inshore and offshore fishing charters. This business is family-owned and operated, and kids are welcome. ⊠ *Lazaretto Creek Marina, 1 Old U.S. Hwy. 80, Tybee Island* ☎ *912/786–5848* ⊕ *tybeedolphins.com.*

North Island Surf & Kayak. Virtually unsinkable and great for navigating the shallowest of creeks, sit-on-top kayaks are available at North Island Surf & Kayak. All rentals include paddles, lifejackets, and seat backs. Prices are $45 per day for a single, $55 for a double. Paddle to the beautiful uninhabited island of Little Tybee or to Cockspur Lighthouse. Discounts are available for multiday rentals, so you can even camp on one of the islands. Stand-up paddle boards are $40 for the day. If you've always wanted to learn how to surf, $50 will get you a board rental and a two-hour lesson. ⊠ *1C Old Hwy. 80, Tybee Island* ☎ *912/786–4000* ⊕ *www.northislandkayak.com.*

Sea Kayak Georgia. Owned by professional paddlers and instructors Marsha Henson and Ronnie Kemp, Sea Kayak Georgia provides gear, tours, and courses for beginners and advanced kayakers alike, not to mention stand-up paddle board rentals and the unique experience of teacher-led stand-up paddle board yoga. Seasoned guides and naturalists lead half-day salt-marsh paddle tours beginning at $50. ⊠ *1102 U.S. Hwy. 80, Tybee Island* ☎ *912/786–8732* ⊕ *www.seakayakgeorgia.com.*

Sundial Charters. Discover fossils, cast a net, spot birds or dolphins, or try crabbing with Sundial's custom charter tours. Popular tours include a jaunt to the remote and lush Daufuskie Island, inshore fishing charters, Georgia Coastal History Boat Tour, and a trip to the natural heritage preserve of Little Tybee Island. ⊠ *Tybee Island* ☎ *912/786–9470* ⊕ *www.sundialcharters.com.*

Tybee Jet Ski & Watersports. For those who enjoy more fast-paced activities, little compares to the rush of jet skiing on the island waterways or riding the swells of the beach. Tybee Jet Ski & Watersports rents Jet Skis/waverunners starting at $99 per hour. In addition, this shop offers everything you need for sea kayaking excursions. Rates for a single kayak start at $35 for a half day. If you'd like a guided tour of the coastal marshes and tidal streams, Little Tybee Island, or the historic Cockspur Lighthouse, the cost is $38 for 90 minutes. ⊠ *1C Old Hwy. 80, Tybee Island* ☎ *912/786–5554* ⊕ *tybeejetski.com.*

6

WATER SPORTS

AOK Watersports. AOK Watersports is a one-stop shop for coastal adventurers. Whether you're taking a lesson in paddle boarding or kiteboarding, renting or purchasing gear, or finding balance through stand-up paddle board yoga, professional guidance awaits you. AOK also offers guided paddle board tours. ✉ *1510 Butler Ave., Tybee Island* ☎ *912/786–8080* ⊕ *www.aokwatersports.com.*

East Coast Paddleboarding. With its tidal creeks and small waves, Tybee Island is the perfect place to learn stand-up paddle boarding. Beginners can take a two-hour flat water introductory class for $100 or learn the art of paddle surfing at $125 for a 1½-hour course. Private and group classes are also available, as are paddle board rentals. Tours of Little Tybee and Horsepen Creek include a lesson and gear and give paddlers the opportunity to see coastal wildlife. ✉ *Tybee Island* ☎ *912/484–3200* ⊕ *eastcoastpaddleboarding.com.*

SHOPPING

Updated
by Anna
Chandler

ANYONE WITH EVEN THE SLIGHTEST inclination toward shopping would be hard pressed to leave Savannah empty-handed. The downtown streets are alive with an array of boutiques and shops running the gamut from kitschy to glamorous, locally owned to nationally renowned.

A 2014 infusion of capital into Broughton Street has seen the city's "main street" come full circle over the past 30 years, and what was once a string of abandoned storefronts has been transformed into a world-class shopping district. As you stroll along Broughton, note the original tenant names etched into historic facades and the sidewalk entries.

Antiques malls and junk emporiums with eye-catching facades and eclectic offerings beckon you to take home treasures from the city's rich past. Meanwhile, contemporary design shops feature the latest lighting and sleek designer furnishings. Some of the newest additions to the shopping landscape are specialty food stores that offer tastings throughout the day. And don't miss trendy boutiques that offer modern fashions with a Southern twist.

Since a great many of the city's attractions are centrally located, a day of shopping can go hand-in-hand with visits to nearby museums or long meals at one of the well-regarded restaurants. The tree-lined streets promise a vista at every turn, so be sure to bring along your camera and a comfortable pair of walking shoes. Should you tire along the way, horse-drawn carriages, trolley tours, or pedicabs abound to help you get off your feet without sacrificing a full itinerary. ·

SHOPPING DISTRICTS

Broughton Street. Savannah's "main street" has long served as an indicator of the city's changing economic and demographical trends. The first of Savannah's department stores, Adler's and Levy's, emerged on Broughton, followed by the post-WWII introduction of national chains Sears & Roebuck, JCPenney, and Kress. During the 1950s, ladies donning white gloves and heels did their shopping, while kids gathered at the soda counter or caught the matinee. Downtown's decline began in the late 1950s and continued through the '70s, when boarded-up storefronts were the norm rather than the exception. Today, Broughton is again thriving, not only

BEST BETS FOR SHOPPING

■ **Art Galleries.** The Savannah College of Art and Design has indelibly imprinted the city with a love of fine arts. Numerous galleries are associated with the school, and many more feature works by some of the many successful alums.

■ **Clothing and Accessories.** Broughton Street is the place for designer clothing, chic shoes, and one-of-a-kind jewelry and accessories to outfit the most discerning shoppers. J. Parker Ltd. is where Savannah's Southern gentlemen pick up their seersucker suits.

■ **Edible Gifts.** The Savannah Bee Company's flagship store is a haven of honey-based delights. Pair that with a gift box from The Tea Room and homemade treats from Byrd Cookie Company for a take-home taste of Savannah.

■ **Home Decor and Antiques.** The charming Paris Market & Brocante occupies two floors with a feel reminiscent of a turn-of-the-20th-century French bazaar. But don't neglect the city's many antiques shops, including Picker Joe's and Alex Raskin Antiques.

with local boutiques and world-class shops, but with theaters, restaurants, and coffeehouses. ⊠ *Broughton St., between Congress and State Sts., Historic District* ⊕ *www.broughtonstreetcollection.com.*

Downtown Design District. Known for its array of fine antiques shops, galleries, lighting showrooms, and interior design boutiques, the Downtown Design District is worth a visit. Stop in some of Savannah's trendier fashion stores, many of them housed in charming historic storefronts. Nearby are the famed Mercer-Williams House and the landmark Mrs. Wilkes' Dining Room, known for some of the area's best family-style Southern food. The picturesque surrounding neighborhoods are also amenable for a nice afternoon stroll. ⊠ *Whitaker St., between Charlton and Gaston Sts., Historic District.*

Madison Square. You'll discover an array of unique local shops nestled around historic Madison Square. Grab lunch on the rooftop of the Public Kitchen and Bar before stopping in longtime favorites like Saints & Shamrocks and E. Shaver, Bookseller. ShopSCAD offers some of the finest gifts, clothing, and home decor items designed and produced by students of the highly regarded Savannah College of Art and Design. Take afternoon tea at the college's Gryphon Tea Room, located inside a remodeled old-time pharmacy. For something a little stronger, head to Artillery, a speakeasy-inspired bar housed in a restored cavalry artillery; the bartenders make some of the city's best handcrafted cocktails. ⊠ *Bull St., bordered by Liberty and Charlton Sts., Historic District.*

Riverfront/Factors Walk. Though it's often crowded and a little rowdy after dark, no visit to Savannah would be complete without a stroll through Riverfront/Factors Walk. These nine blocks of renovated waterfront warehouses were once the city's cotton exchange. Today, you'll discover more than 75 boutiques, galleries, restaurants, and pubs, as well as a spectacular view of the Savannah River. Glimpse impressive cargo ships as they head to port while you shop for souvenirs, specialty treats, and local art. Tired of shopping? Catch a dolphin tour or dinner boat and see the waterfront from a different perspective. ■TIP→ **River Street's cobblestones and Factors Walk's steep stairwells can be rough, so be sure to wear comfortable footwear.** ⊠ *River St., Historic District.*

SHOPPING REVIEWS

HISTORIC DISTRICT

ANTIQUES

★ Fodor'sChoice **Alex Raskin Antiques.** This shop is inside the four-story Noble Hardee Mansion, a gilded Italianate home. You can wander through almost all 12,000 square feet of the former grand residence and see how the landed gentry once lived. The building is a bit musty, with peeling wallpaper and patches of leaky ceiling, but the antiques within are in great condition and represent a colorful scrapbook of Savannah's past. They specialize in furniture, rugs, and paintings, but take note of more rare artifacts like tramp art frames and antique doll furniture. Take in the view of Forsyth Park from one of the upper-level porches. ■TIP→ **The building lacks air-conditioning, so avoid the heat of midday or bring along a fan.** ⊠ *441 Bull St., Historic District* ☎ *912/232–8205* ⊕ *www.alexraskinantiques.com* ⊘ *Closed Sun.*

ART GALLERIES

The Butcher Art Gallery. Half gallery, half tattoo studio, the Butcher is a true original. Its rotating exhibitions feature younger, more contemporary artists. The staff is hip, friendly, and knowledgeable, and the space is a modern twist on a vintage storefront. ⊠ *19 E. Bay St., Historic District* ☎ *912/234–6505* ⊕ *www.whatisthebutcher.com.*

Gallery Espresso. Gallery Espresso has a new show every couple of weeks focusing on work by local artists. Pastries, cheesecakes, muffins, scones, and luscious desserts are house-made and complement the heavy dose of caffeine and art. ⊠ *234 Bull St., Historic District* ☎ *912/233–5348* ⊕ *www.galleryespresso.com.*

★ **Fodor'sChoice Kobo Gallery.** Between the bustling hubs of Broughton Street and City Market sits the city's foremost cooperative art gallery. Near Ellis Square, the tasteful space is teeming with fine art across countless mediums. Noteworthy is industrial style jewelry by Danielle Hughes Rose, the colorful landscapes of Dana Richardson, and Dicky Stone's intricate wordworking. ⊠ *33 Barnard St., Historic District* ☎ *912/201–0304* ⊕ *kohogallery.com.*

Ray Ellis Gallery/Compass Prints. Ray Ellis Gallery/Compass Prints sells original artwork, prints, and books by acclaimed landscape artist Ray Ellis. ⊠ *205 W. Congress St., Historic District* ☎ *912/234–3537* ⊕ *www.rayellis.com.*

★ **Fodor'sChoice Roots Up Gallery.** Opened in 2014 by longtime Savannah residents Leslie Lovell and Francis Allen, Roots Up is a testament to the charm and mystique of southern folk art. Located in the heart of the Downtown Design District, Roots Up is home to such artists as Howard Finster, Willie Tarver, Jimmy Lee Sudduth, Antonio Esteves, and Mr. Imagination. The collection includes everything from handmade dolls to vintage pieces. ⊠ *412–C Whitaker St., Historic District* ☎ *912/677–2845* ⊕ *www.rootsupgallery. com* ☉ *Closed Mon. and Tues.*

7

Tiffani Taylor Gallery. Renowned local artist Tiffani Taylor's textured paintings are romantic yet bold, influenced by nature and her extensive travels. Her work has been exhibited in the Salvador Dalí Museum in St. Petersburg, Florida, and her clients include Oprah Winfrey and Diane von Furstenberg. In addition to her paintings, Taylor's original pottery and stationery make great gifts. ⊠ *11 Whitaker St., Historic District* ☎ *912/507–7860* ⊕ *www.tiffani-taylor-art.com.*

BOOKS

The Book Lady. Located on the garden level of a Liberty Street row house, the Book Lady stocks around 50,000 new, used, and vintage books spanning 40 genres. The friendly staff is always available for a lively literary discussion, and the shop hosts the occasional book signing by noted authors. ✉ *6 E. Liberty St., Historic District* ☎ *912/233–3628* ⊕ *www. thebookladybookstore.com* ⊙ *Closes Sun. at 4.*

★ **Fodor'sChoice E. Shaver, Bookseller.** Among the city's most beloved bookshops, E. Shaver is the source for 17th- and 18th-century maps and new books on local history, recipes, artists, and authors. This shop occupies multiple rooms of a historic building, which alone is something to see. The whole family can explore the children's book sections. The booksellers are welcoming and knowledgeable about their wares. ✉ *326 Bull St., Historic District* ☎ *912/234–7257* ⊕ *eshaverbooks.com.*

V&J Duncan. An intricate iron sign and gate point the way to V&J Duncan, an off-the-beaten path Savannah relic located on the garden level of a historic home on Monterey Square. The shop specializes in antique maps and prints and carries a vast collection of engravings, photographs, and lithographs. There are also rare books on Southern culture. Their hours aren't strictly observed, so call ahead to make sure they're open. ■TIP→ **With so much to see, plan to spend some time here.** ✉ *12 E. Taylor St., Historic District* ☎ *912/232–0338* ⊕ *vjduncan.com* ⊙ *Closed Sun.*

CLOTHING

Copper Penny. Venture to this Broughton Street mainstay for women's clothing and footwear that is, as they say, "curated with the Southern eye." You'll find seasonal looks by Michael Stars, BB Dakota, and Citizens of Humanity, as well as shoes and accessories by Rebecca Minkoff, Vince Camuto, and Sam Edelman. ✉ *22 W. Broughton St., Historic District* ☎ *912/629–6800* ⊕ *www.shopcopperpenny. com.*

J. Parker Ltd. This is where savvy gentlemen go to suit up. Look for outerwear, sportswear, and dresswear by top men's designers like Filson, Southern Tide, High Cotton, and Mountain Khakis. If you need a seersucker suit on short notice, this is your best bet. ✉ *20 W. Broughton St., Historic District* ☎ *912/234–0004* ⊕ *www.jparkerltd.com.*

James Hogan. Tucked in a storefront in the Historic District, this shop has brought a touch of glamour to the city. Featured here is apparel designed by James Hogan himself, as well as upscale women's fashions from well-regarded American and European designers. ✉ *412B Whitaker St., Historic District* ☎ *912/234–0374* ⊕ *www.jameshogan. com* ☾ *Closed Sun.*

Red Clover. This is the place to be if you want fashionable and affordable apparel, shoes, and handbags. It features sharp looks from up-and-coming designers, all at under $100. It's also a great place to search for unique jewelry. ✉ *244 Bull St., Historic District* ☎ *912/236–4053* ⊕ *shopredclover.com.*

FOOD AND WINE

Le Chai Galerie du Vin. This is a long-cherished establishment for Savannah's wine aficionados. With a devoted following, proprietor Christian Depken has a trained palate for old-world wines—trust him to recommend the perfect accompaniment to any dish. Plus, its temperature- and humidity-controlled environment is the only one of its kind in Georgia. ✉ *15 E. Park St., Historic District* ☎ *912/713–2229* ⊕ *www.lechai.com.*

Paula Deen Store. The "First Lady of Southern Cooking" sells her wares at this shop on Congress Street. You can find some very Southern spices and sauces, such as a smokin' barbecue sauce, and salad dressings—like peach pecan and blueberry walnut—that are so sweet they could double as dessert toppings. Two full floors of Paula's own label of cooking goodies and gadgets are cleverly displayed against bare brick walls. The shop is adjacent to Deen's famous Southern-style restaurant, the Lady and Sons. ✉ *108 W. Congress St., Historic District* ☎ *912/232–1579* ⊕ *www. ladyandsons.com/retail-store/.*

Pie Society. This British-style bakery sells everything from traditional meat pies to savory quiches to crusty bread, all of it baked fresh daily. The owners hail from Staffordshire and make remarkable and authentic meat pies in such varieties as steak and ale, chicken and thyme, and steak and kidney. ✉ *19 Jefferson St., City Market* ☎ *912/856–4785* ⊕ *www.thebritishpiecompany.com.*

7

River Street Sweets. Savannah's self-described "oldest and original" candy store, River Street Sweets opened in 1973. The aroma of creamy homemade fudge will draw you in, and once you're inside you won't be able to resist the piping hot pralines, made all day long. The store is also known for milk chocolate bear claws. The old-fashioned taffy machine pulls 50 different flavors. You'll always receive excellent customer service here. ✉ *13 E. River St., Historic District* ☎ *912/234–4608* ⊕ *www.riverstreetsweets.com.*

The Salt Table. More than 200 flavors of salts are on offer here, as well as specialty sugars, peppers, and teas. Noteworthy are the popular black truffle, smoked bacon, and ghost pepper sea salts. Gourmands should not miss the Himalayan pink salt plates. These solid salt bricks or slabs come in various sizes and can be used as cutting boards for preparing meats, vegetables, seafood, or even cheeses. They can also be placed directly on the stovetop, adding flavor to every dish. ✉ *51 Barnard St., Downtown* ☎ *912/447–0200* ⊕ *www.salttable.com.*

★ **Fodor'sChoice Savannah Bee Company.** Ted Dennard's Savannah FAMILY Bee Company has been featured in such national magazines as *O, Vogue, InStyle,* and *Newsweek,* and with good reason—the whimsical shop features locally cultivated honey and bath products that are simply wonderful. You can sample and buy multiple varieties of honey and even raw honeycombs, and there's an entire bar dedicated to mead, a delicate honey wine; enjoy a tasting for a sweet experience. Children enjoy the life-size beehive. ✉ *104 W. Broughton St., Historic District* ☎ *912/233–7873* ⊕ *www. savannahbee.com.*

Savannah Candy Kitchen. One of the largest candy stores in the South, Savannah Candy Kitchen has made its home on historic River Street for more than 30 years. Owner and head confectioner Stan Strickland grew up in Woodbine, Georgia, watching his mother bake pecan log rolls, pralines, and peanut brittle. You'll find every scrumptious delight imaginable here, but don't miss the world-famous praline layer cake. There's a second location in City Market. ✉ *225 E. River St., Historic District* ☎ *912/233–8411* ⊕ *www. savannahcandy.com.*

GIFTS AND SOUVENIRS

★ **Fodor's**Choice **La Paperie.** Gorgeous stationery, journals, and writing implements are on offer at this shop in the Downtown Design District. It also carries an impressive array of designer wrapping paper and handpressed botanical prints. Don't forget the final touches: embossers, stamps, and wax seals are all available. ✉ *409 Whitaker St., Historic District* ☎ *912/443–9349* ⊕ *www.lapaperiesavannah.com.*

Saints & Shamrocks. In a neo-Gothic storefront rich with architectural detail, Saints & Shamrocks features hand-smocked children's clothing, Irish imports, and religious gifts. The gift selection embraces Irish and Southern heritage in the form of jewelry, bath products, and seasonal items. ✉ *307 Bull St., Historic District* ☎ *912/233–8858* ⊕ *www. saintsandshamrocks.com.*

★ **Fodor's**Choice **ShopSCAD.** Inside historic Poetter Hall, the Savannah College of Art and Design's shop is filled with handcrafted items guaranteed to be one of a kind. Handmade and hand-dyed silk accessories are cutting-edge, as are original fashion pieces and experimental purses by design students. Just remember that these originals do not come cheap. ✉ *340 Bull St., Historic District* ☎ *912/525–5180* ⊕ *www.shopscad.com.*

HOME DECOR

Hygge Savannah. Inspired by the Danish lifestyle of "hygge," which prioritizes coziness, comfort, and thoughtful enjoyment of life's simplicities, Hygge Savannah offers products for home, body and mind. Find unique souvenirs and gifts like Love Wild Design blooming tea, which unfurls like a flower in your cup, or peruse a selection of handmade ceramics, linen attire, and hand-carved wooden toys. ✉ *600 E. Broughton St., Downtown* ☎ *912/231–3512* ⊕ *www. shophyggesavannah.com* ⊙ *Closed Sun. and Mon.*

One Fish Two Fish. Whimsically named for the classic Dr. Seuss book, *One Fish Two Fish* is a high-end home decor shop located in the Downtown Design District. Look for contemporary furnishings, fine linens, and bedroom and bathroom accessories. Every corner of the store has something charming to offer, including elegant handbags and jewelry and colorful modern lighting fixtures. For fine wearables, cross over Whitaker Street to visit the Annex, its sister store. ✉ *401 Whitaker St., Historic District* ☎ *912/447–4600* ⊕ *onefishstore.com.*

7

★ **Fodor'sChoice The Paris Market & Brocante.** A Francophile's dream, this two-story emporium hung with glittering chandeliers is a classy reproduction of a Paris flea market, selling elegant furnishings, vintage art, garden planters, and home decor items. Although the staff is happy to ship your purchases, there are numerous treasures that can be easily carried away, like soaps, candles, vintage jewelry, and dried lavender. A café serves baguette sandwiches, fresh coffee, and beautiful baked goods. ✉ *36 W. Broughton St., Historic District* ☎ *912/232–1500* ⊕ *www.theparismarket.com.*

★ **Fodor'sChoice 24e.** Owner Ruel Joyner has a keen eye for design. His eclectically sophisticated downtown shop is stocked floor to ceiling with luxurious housewares like velvet sofas, stunning chandeliers, and conversation-starting accessories from an array of revered design houses. 24e has also made a name for itself with custom-built furniture. Simply perusing the two stories of spectacular specimens is an inspiring way to spend some time—even if the store's big-ticket items are a little out of your price range. ✉ *24 E. Broughton St., Historic District* ☎ *912/233–2274* ⊕ *www.24estyle.com.*

JEWELRY AND ACCESSORIES

ZIA. Savannah's most-lauded jewelry boutique features pieces designed by artists around the world and assembled by owner Zia Sachedina. The opulent and eye-catching wearable art—including magnificent necklaces, rings, and bracelets made from such unexpected materials as titanium, amber, quartz, and even Hawaiian lava—is individually made. The jewelry represents a broad array of styles, materials, and price points. ✉ *325 W. Broughton St., Historic District* ☎ *912/233–3237* ⊕ *www.ziacouture.com* ⊙ *Closed Sun.*

SHOES, HANDBAGS, AND LEATHER GOODS

Globe Shoe Co. Hands down Savannah's best shoe store, Globe has served both well-heeled women and well-soled men since 1892. There's an expansive storefront display, so it's easy to window shop for the perfect pair. It features footwear and accessories by Stuart Weitzman, Donald Pliner, Cole Haan, Sam Edelman, VanElli, Thierry Rabotin, Gentle Souls, and Jeffrey Campbell, to name a few. ✉ *17 E. Broughton St., Historic District* ☎ *912/232–8161.*

★ **Fodor's**Choice **Satchel.** This artisanal-leather studio and shop is owned by Elizabeth Seeger Jolly, a New Orleans native and graduate of the SCAD. The store specializes in custom leather clutches, handbags, travel bags, and accessories and offers a wide selection of leathers to choose from, including python and alligator. At lower price points are the sharp and handy beverage cozies, cuff bracelets, and wallets. ⊠ *4 E. Liberty St., Historic District* ☎ *912/233–1008* ⊕ *shopsatchel.com* ⊘ *Closed Sun. at 3.*

SPAS

Savannah Day Spa. In addition to traditional spa services, Savannah Day Spa offers a complete line of skin-care products, accessories for home, and a line of vegan body products. This former mansion is a delightful place to take your treatments, be it one of the creative massages or a therapeutic facial for your particular skin type. It's also one of the more romantic settings for couples massages. ⊠ *18 E. Oglethorpe St., Downtown* ☎ *912/234–9100* ⊕ *www. savannahdayspa.com.*

★ **Fodor's**Choice **Spa Bleu.** Consistently ranked as one of Savannah's top ways to pamper yourself, Spa Bleu offers a more contemporary feel. In keeping with trends of the "New South," Spa Bleu offers true Southern comfort in a modern space. The signature Organic Thermal Body Treatments are not to be missed, and neither are spa nights where you can stay late and indulge in hors d'oeuvres and Champagne. ⊠ *101 Bull St., Historic District* ☎ *912/236–1490* ⊕ *www. spableu-sav.com.*

Westin Heavenly Spa. Across the Savannah River from downtown, the Westin Heavenly Spa feels a world away with it's standard menu of services and then some. The "quiet room," with its solarium-like setting, is a highlight. It's a little on the pricey side, but it's worth it for the relaxing, luxurious environment. It's also a great destination for bridal parties. ■TIP→ **If you're coming from downtown, consider traveling by water taxi.** ⊠ *Westin Savannah Harbor Golf Resort & Spa, 1 Resort Dr., Hutchinson Island* ☎ *912/201–2250* ⊕ *www.westinsavannah.com.*

7

VICTORIAN DISTRICT AND EASTSIDE

ART GALLERIES

Grand Bohemian Gallery. Neatly tucked inside the Mansion on Forsyth Park, one of the city's most luxurious hotels, this gallery showcases the Kessler Collection, acquired by the gallery's owner and hotelier, native Georgian Richard Kessler. You'll find more than 400 works by acclaimed artists, especially contemporary paintings, blown glass, whimsical sculptures, and some incredibly innovative jewelry. ☒ *The Mansion on Forsyth Park, 700 Drayton St., Historic District* ☎ *912/721–5007* ⊕ *www.grandbohemiangallery.com.*

CLOTHING

Brown Dog Market at Cohen's Retreat. Built in 1934 as Cohen's Old Men Retreat, Cohen's main building is resplendent with historic charm as well as noteworthy high-end modern upgrades. These days, locals flock to Cohen's for its restaurant's Southern-inspired eats, but down the hall there's local art, crafts, home decor items, and designer furniture in the Brown Dog Market. ☒ *5715 Skidaway Rd., Eastside* ☎ *912/355–3336* ⊕ *www.cohensretreat.com.*

SPAS

Poseidon Spa. The very chic Poseidon Spa in the Mansion on Forsyth Park offers a number of rejuvenating treatments, including manicures, pedicures, massages, and skin and body treatments. Included in the rates is access to the white-marble courtyard and pool, a 24-hour fitness center, and a relaxation area. One wet and three dry treatment rooms, separate women's and men's locker rooms, and a steam shower make up the facilities. ☒ *The Mansion on Forsyth Park, 700 Drayton St., Historic District* ☎ *912/721–5004* ⊕ *www.kesslercollection.com/mansion/.*

THE STARLAND DISTRICT, THOMAS SQUARE, AND MIDTOWN

ANTIQUES

★ Fodor'sChoice **Picker Joe's Antique Mall & Vintage Market.** A haven for lovers of architectural salvage, vintage treasures, mid-century furniture, and antique decor, Picker Joe's offers 10,000 square feet of discovery. A consistent receiver of local awards, the shop's many booths offer a true variety of quality finds for pickers of all walks of life. ☒ *217 E. 41st St., Thomas Square* ☎ *912/239–4657* ⊕ *www. pickerjoes.com.*

CLOTHING

The Rat on Bull. In the heart of the Starland District, The Rat on Bull offers apparel, accessories, and apothecary items for men and women. Located inside a former barbershop, there's a thoughtfully curated selection of hip, ethical brands like Res Ispa, a shoe company known for upcycling kilim rugs into elegant loafers. The shop also spotlights local designers and their unique creations, from fine leather backpacks to 3D-printed jewelry. ✉ *1612 Bull St.* ☎ *912/999–6328* ⊕ *www.theratonbull.com* ☾ *Closed Sun.*

SPAS

★ Fodor'sChoice **Glow Medical Spa & Beauty Boutique.** Consistently ranked by locals as the best in Savannah, this sparkling day spa is known for its extensive menu of services. Specializing in the latest treatments for face and skin, this full-service facility offers exceptional massages and a wide selection of high-end cosmetics that are hand-selected by owner Courtney Buntin Victor. ■TIP→ **The original location is about 8 miles from downtown, but there's a new location on Chippewa Square at 3 E. Perry Street.** ✉ *415 Eisenhower Dr. , Suite 1, Midtown* ☎ *912/303–9611* ⊕ *www.glowsavannah.com.*

MOON RIVER DISTRICT

ANTIQUES

Sandfly Market Place. Shoppers will find an ever-changing, unique selection of antiques and mid-century, rustic, and Victorian finds like lamps, chairs, toys, jewelry, and more. ✉ *8511 Ferguson Ave.* ☎ *912/777–4081* ⊕ *www.sandflymarket.com* ☾ *Closed Sun. and Mon.*

SOUTHSIDE, GATEWAY, AND GREATER SAVANNAH

FOOD

Byrd Cookie Company & Gourmet Marketplace. Founded in 1924, this shop sells picture tins of Savannah and gourmet foodstuffs such as condiments and dressings. This shop—along with their other locations in City Market, on River Street, and in Pooler—is the best place to buy benne wafers ("the seed of good luck") and trademark Savannah cookies, notably key lime, and house-made crackers. Free samples of all are available. ✉ *6700 Waters Ave., Southside* ☎ *912/355–1716* ⊕ *www.byrdcookiecompany.com.*

MARKETS

Keller's Flea Market. More than 400 vendors descend upon Keller's every weekend bringing with them kitschy souvenirs, antiques, collectibles, and everything in between. Keep an eye out for the 15-foot-tall cow statue—you can't miss it. ✉ *5901 Ogeechee Rd.* ☎ *912/927–4848* ⊕ *ilovefleas.com* ⊗ *Closed weekdays.*

HILTON HEAD
AND THE
LOWCOUNTRY

TOP REASONS TO GO

Beachcombing: Hilton Head Island has 12 miles of beaches. You can swim, soak up the sun, or walk along the sand.

Beaufort: This small antebellum town offers large doses of heritage and culture; nearly everything you might want to see is within its downtown historic district.

Challenging Golf: Hilton Head's many challenging courses have an international reputation.

Serving Up Tennis: Home to hundreds of tennis courts, Hilton Head is home to legend Stan Smith and one of the nation's top tennis destinations.

Staying Put: This semitropical island has been a resort destination for decades, and it has all the desired amenities for visitors: a vast array of lodgings, an endless supply of restaurants, and excellent shopping.

Updated by Stratton Lawrence

HILTON HEAD ISLAND IS A unique and incredibly beautiful resort town that anchors the southern tip of South Carolina's coastline. What makes this semitropical island so unique? At the top of the list is the fact that visitors won't see large, splashy billboards or neon signs. What they will see is an island where the environment takes center stage—a place where development is strictly regulated.

There are 12 miles of sparkling white-sand beaches, amazing world-class restaurants, top-rated golf courses—Harbour Town Golf Links annually hosts the Heritage Golf Tournament, a PGA Tour event—and a thriving tennis community. Wildlife abounds, including loggerhead sea turtles, alligators, snowy egrets, wood storks, great blue heron, and, in the waters, dolphins, manatees, and various species of fish. There are lots of activities offered on the island, including parasailing, charter fishing, and kayaking.

The island is home to several private gated communities, including Sea Pines, Hilton Head Plantation, Shipyard, Wexford, Long Cove, Port Royal, Indigo Run, Palmetto Hall, and Palmetto Dunes. Within these you'll find upscale housing (some of it doubling as vacation rentals), golf courses, shopping, and restaurants. Sea Pines is one of the most famous of these communities, as it is known for the candy-cane-striped Harbour Town Lighthouse. There are also many areas on the island that are not behind security gates.

ORIENTATION AND PLANNING

GETTING ORIENTED

Hilton Head is just north of South Carolina's border with Georgia. The 42-square-mile island is shaped like a foot, hence the reason locals often describe places as being at the "toe" or "heel" of Hilton Head. This part of South Carolina is best explored by car, as its points of interest are spread across a flat coastal plain that is a mix of wooded areas, marshes, and sea islands. The more remote areas are accessible only by boat or ferry.

Hilton Head's neighbor, Bluffton, is an artsy town rich with history. In the last several years the tiny community has grown to cover about 50 square miles. South of Hilton Head is the city of Savannah, which is about a 45-minute drive from the island. North of Hilton Head is Beaufort, a cultural treasure and a graceful antebellum town. Beaufort is also about 45 minutes from Hilton Head.

Hilton Head Island. One of the Southeast coast's most popular tourist destinations, Hilton Head is known for its golf courses and tennis courts. It's a magnet for time-share owners and retirees. Bluffton is Hilton Head's quirky neighbor to the west. The old-town area is laden with history and charm.

Beaufort. This charming town just inland from Hilton Head is a destination in its own right, with a lively dining scene and cute bed-and-breakfasts.

Daufuskie Island. A scenic ferry ride from Hilton Head, Daufuskie is now much more developed than it was during the days when Pat Conroy wrote *The Water Is Wide,* but it's still a beautiful island to explore, even on a day trip. You can stay for a few days at a variety of fine rental properties, tool down shady dirt roads in a golf cart, and delight in the glorious, nearly deserted beaches.

PLANNING

WHEN TO GO

The high season follows typical beach-town cycles, with June through August and holidays year-round being the busiest and most costly. Mid-April, during the annual RBC Heritage Golf Tournament, is when rates tend to be highest. Thanks to the Lowcountry's mostly moderate year-round temperatures, tourists are ever-present. Spring is the best time to visit, when the weather is ideal for tennis and golf. Autumn is almost as active for the same reason.

To get a good deal, it's imperative that you plan ahead. The choicest locations can be booked six months to a year in advance, but booking agencies can help you make room reservations and get good deals during the winter season, when the crowds fall off.

WILL IT RAIN?

In summer, the weather forecast may say there's a 30% chance of rain for Hilton Head. It can be a gorgeous day and suddenly a storm will pop up late in the afternoon. That's because the hot air rises and mixes with cooler air, causing the atmosphere to become unstable, thereby creating thunderstorms. Don't worry, though: these storms pass quickly.

Villa-rental companies often offer snowbird rates for monthly stays during the winter season. Parking is always free at the major hotels, but valet parking can cost from $17 to $25; the smaller properties have free parking, too, but no valet service.

PLANNING YOUR TIME

No matter where you stay, spend your first day relaxing on the beach or hitting the links. After that, you'll have time to visit some of the area's attractions, including the Coastal Discovery Museum and the Sea Pines Resort. You can also visit the Tanger outlet malls on U.S. 278 in Bluffton. Old-town Bluffton is a quaint area with many locally owned shops and art galleries. If you have a few more days, visit Beaufort on a day trip or even spend the night there. This historic antebellum town is rich with history. Savannah is also a short drive away.

GETTING HERE AND AROUND

AIR TRAVEL

Most travelers use the Savannah/Hilton Head International Airport, less than an hour from Hilton Head, which is served by Allegiant, American Airlines, Delta, Frontier, JetBlue, and United. Hilton Head Island Airport is served by American Airlines, Delta, and United.

Air Contacts Hilton Head Island Airport.⊠ *120 Beach City Rd., North End* ☎ *843/255–2950* ⊕ *www.hiltonheadairport.com.* **Savannah/Hilton Head International Airport.**⊠ *400 Airways Ave., Northwest* ☎ *912/964–0514* ⊕ *www.savannahairport.com.*

BOAT AND FERRY TRAVEL

Hilton Head is accessible via boat, with docking available at Harbour Town Yacht Basin, Skull Creek Marina, and Shelter Cove Harbor.

Boat Docking Information **Harbour Town Yacht Basin.** ✉ *Sea Pines, 149 Lighthouse Rd., South End* ☎ *843/363–8335* ⊕ *www. seapines.com.* **Shelter Cove Harbour & Marina.** ✉ *Shelter Cove, 1 Shelter Cove La., Mid-Island* ☎ *866/661–3822* ⊕ *www.sheltercove-hiltonhead.com.* **Skull Creek Marina.** ✉ *1 Waterway La., North End* ☎ *843/681–8436* ⊕ *www.theskullcreekmarina.com.*

BUS TRAVEL

Palmetto Breeze has buses that leave Bluffton in the morning for Hilton Head, Beaufort, and some of the islands. The fare is $2, and exact change is required.

Bus Contacts **Palmetto Breeze Transit.** ☎ *843/757–5782* ⊕ *www. palmettobreezetransit.com.*

CAR TRAVEL

Driving is the best way to get onto Hilton Head Island. Off Interstate 95, take Exit 8 onto U.S. 278 East, which leads you through Bluffton (where it's known as Fording Island Road) and then to Hilton Head. Once on Hilton Head, U.S. 278 forks: on the right is William Hilton Parkway, and on the left is the Cross Island Parkway (a toll road that costs $1.25 each way). If you take the Cross Island (as the locals call it) to the south side where Sea Pines and many other resorts are located, the trip will take about 10 to 15 minutes. If you take William Hilton Parkway the trip will take about 30 minutes. Be aware that at check-in and checkout times on Friday, Saturday, and Sunday, traffic on U.S. 278 can slow to a crawl. ■ TIP→ **Be careful of putting the pedal to the metal, particularly on the Cross Island Parkway. It's patrolled regularly.**

Once on Hilton Head Island, signs are small and blend in with the trees and landscaping, and nighttime lighting is kept to a minimum. The lack of streetlights makes it difficult to find your way at night, so be sure to get good directions.

TAXI TRAVEL

There are several taxi services available on Hilton Head, including Uber, Lyft, Yellow Cab HHI, and Diamond Transportation, which has SUVs and passenger vans available for pickup at Savannah/Hilton Head International Airport and Hilton Head Airport. Prices range from $20 to $120, depending on where you're headed.

Taxi Contacts **Diamond Transportation.** *843/247–2156* *hiltonheadrides.com.* **Yellow Cab HHI.** *843/686–6666* *www.yellowcabhhi.net.*

TRAIN TRAVEL

Amtrak gets you as close as Savannah or Yemassee, South Carolina. It's a little more than 45 minutes from either station to the island.

Train Contacts **Savannah Amtrak Station.** *2611 Seaboard Coastline Dr., Savannah* *800/872–7245* *www.amtrak.com/stations/sav.* **Yemassee Amtrak Station.** *Salkehatchie Rd. and Railroad Ave., Yemassee* *800/872–7245* *www.amtrak.com/stations/yem.*

RESTAURANTS

The number of fine-dining restaurants on Hilton Head is extraordinary, given the size of the island. Because of the proximity to the ocean and the small farms on the mainland, most locally owned restaurants are still heavily influenced by the catch of the day and seasonal harvests. Most upscale restaurants open at 11 and don't close until 9 or 10, but some take a break between 2 and 4. Many advertise early-bird menus, and sometimes getting a table before 6 can be a challenge. During the height of the summer season, reservations are a good idea, though in the off-season you may need them only on weekends. There are several locally owned breakfast joints and plenty of great delis where you can pick up lunch or the fixings for a picnic. Smoking is prohibited in restaurants and bars in Bluffton, Beaufort, and on Hilton Head. Beaufort's restaurant scene has certainly evolved, with more trendy restaurants serving contemporary cuisine moving into the downtown area.

HOTELS

Hilton Head is known as one of the best vacation spots on the East Coast, and its hotels are a testimony to its reputation. The island is awash in regular hotels and resorts, not to mention beachfront or golf-course-view villas, cottages, and luxury private homes. You can expect the most modern conveniences and world-class service at the priciest places. Clean, updated rooms and friendly staff are everywhere, even at lower-cost hotels—this is the South, after all. Staying in cooler months, for extended periods of time, or commuting from nearby Bluffton can save money.

WHAT IT COSTS				
	$	**$$**	**$$$**	**$$$$**
Restaurants	under $15	$15–$19	$20–$24	over $24
Hotels	under $150	$150–$200	$201–$250	over $250

Restaurant prices are for a main course at dinner, excluding sales tax. Hotel prices are for two people in a standard double room in high season, excluding service charges and tax.

TOURS

Hilton Head's Adventure Cruises hosts dolphin-watching cruises, sport crabbing, and more. Several companies, including H20 Sports, Live Oac, Outside Hilton Head, and Low Country Nature Tours run dolphin-watching, shark-fishing, kayak, sunset, and delightful environmental trips.

Gullah Heritage Trail Tours gives a wealth of history about slavery and the Union takeover of the island during the Civil War; tours leave from the Coastal Discovery Museum at Honey Horn Plantation.

There's a wide variety of tours available at Harbour Town Yacht Basin, including sunset cruises, fireworks, and dolphin tours.

Tour Contacts Captain Mark's Dolphin Cruise.⊠ *Shelter Cove Marina, 9 Harbourside La., Mid-Island* ☎ *843/785–4558* ⊕ *www. cruisehiltonhead.com.* **Gullah Heritage Trail Tours.**⊠ *Coastal Discovery Museum, 70 Honey Horn Dr., North End* ☎ *843/681–7066* ⊕ *www.gullaheritage.com.* **Hilton Head Island Sailing.**⊠ *Shelter Cove Marina, 1 Shelter Cove La., Mid-Island* ☎ *843/686–2582* ⊕ *www. hiltonheadislandsailing.com.* **Live Oac.**⊠ *Hilton Head Harbor, 43A Jenkins Rd., North End* ☎ *843/384–1414* ⊕ *www.liveoac.com.* **Low Country Nature Tours.**⊠ *Shelter Cove Marina, 1 Shelter Cove La., Mid-Island* ☎ *843/683–0187* ⊕ *www.lowcountrynaturetours.com.*

VISITOR INFORMATION

As you're driving into town, you can pick up brochures and maps at the Visitor and Convention Bureau.

Visitor Information Hilton Head Island-Bluffton Chamber of Commerce and Visitor and Convention Bureau.⊠ *1 Chamber of Commerce Dr., Mid-Island* ☎ *843/785–3673* ⊕ *www.hiltonhead-chamber.org.*

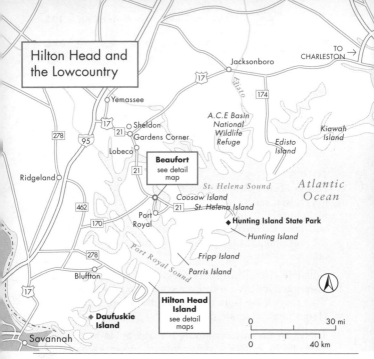

TO CHARLESTON →

Jacksonboro

17

174

Yemassee

17

21

Sheldon

Gardens Corner

278

95

Lobeco

A.C.E Basin National Wildlife Refuge

Kiawah Island

Edisto Island

Ridgeland

Beaufort see detail map

21

St. Helena Sound

Atlantic Ocean

Coosaw Island

St. Helena Island

21

462

Port Royal

170

◆ **Hunting Island State Park**

Hunting Island

278

Port Royal Sound

Fripp Island

Bluffton

Parris Island

17

Hilton Head Island see detail maps

◆ **Daufuskie Island**

Savannah

0		30 mi
0		40 km

HILTON HEAD ISLAND

Hilton Head Island is known far and wide as a vacation destination that prides itself on its top-notch golf courses and tennis programs, world-class resorts, and beautiful beaches. But the island is also part of the storied American South, steeped in a rich but troubled history. It has seen Native Americans and explorers, battles from the Revolutionary War to the Civil War, plantations and slaves, and development and environmentally focused growth.

More than 10,000 years ago, the island was inhabited by Paleo-Indians. From 8000 to 2000 BC, Woodland Indians lived on the island. A shell ring made from their discarded oyster shells and animal bones from that period can be found in the Sea Pines Nature Preserve.

The recorded history of the island goes back to the early 1500s, when Spanish explorers sailing coastal waters came upon the island and found Native American settlements. Over the next 200 years, the island was claimed at various times by the Spanish, the French, and the British. In 1663, Captain William Hilton claimed the island for the British crown (and named it for himself), and the island became home to indigo, rice, and cotton plantations.

During the Revolutionary War, the British harassed islanders and burned plantations. During the War of 1812, British troops again burned plantations, but the island recovered from both wars. During the Civil War, Union troops took Hilton Head in 1861 and freed the more than 1,000 slaves on the island. Mitchelville, one of the first settlements for freed blacks, was created. There was no bridge to the island, so its freed slaves, called "Gullah," subsisted on agriculture and the seafood-laden waters.

Over the years, much of the plantation land was sold at auction. Then, in 1949, General Joseph Fraser purchased 17,000 acres, much of which would eventually become various communities, including Hilton Head Plantation, Palmetto Dunes, and Spanish Wells. The general bought another 1,200 acres, which his son, Charles, used to develop Sea Pines. The first bridge to the island was built in 1956, and modern-day Hilton Head was born.

What makes Hilton Head so special now? Charles Fraser and his business associates focused on development while preserving the environment. And that is what tourists will see today: an island that values its history and its natural beauty.

GETTING HERE AND AROUND

8

Hilton Head Island is 19 miles east of Interstate 95. Take Exit 8 off Interstate 95 and then U.S. 278 east, directly to the bridges. If you're heading to the southern end of the island, your best bet to save time and avoid traffic is the Cross Island Parkway toll road. The cost is $1.25 each way.

EXPLORING

Your impression of Hilton Head depends on which of the island's developments you make your temporary home. The oldest and best known of Hilton Head's developments, Sea Pines occupies 4,500 thickly wooded acres. It's not wilderness, however; among the trees are three golf courses, tennis clubs, riding stables, and shopping plazas. A free trolley shuttles visitors around the resort. Other well-known communities are Palmetto Dunes and Port Royal Plantation.

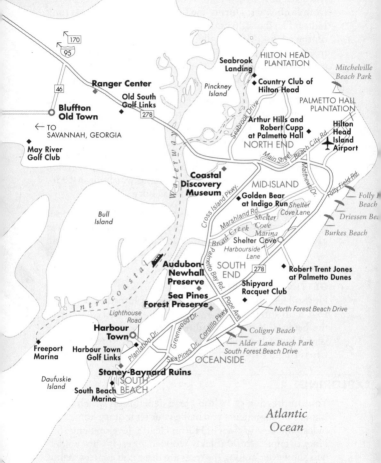

Hilton Head Island

Port Royal Sound

170
95
46

Ranger Center

Bluffton Old Town

← TO SAVANNAH, GEORGIA

May River Golf Club

Old South Golf Links

278

Pinckney Island

Seabrook Landing

HILTON HEAD PLANTATION

Country Club of Hilton Head

Mitchelville Beach Park

PALMETTO HALL PLANTATION

Arthur Hills and Robert Cupp at Palmetto Hall

Hilton Head Island Airport

NORTH END

Main Street

Beach City Rd.

Matthews Dr.

Folly Field Rd.

Folly Beach

Coastal Discovery Museum

MID-ISLAND

Golden Bear at Indigo Run

Shelter Cove Lane

Driessen Beach

Cross Island Pkwy.

Marshland Rd.

Shelter Cove Marina

Shelter Cove Lane

Burkes Beach

Bull Island

Broad Creek

Harbourside Lane

Shelter Cove

Palmetto Bay Rd.

SOUTH END

Robert Trent Jones at Palmetto Dunes

278

Shipyard Racquet Club

Audubon-Newhall Preserve

Sea Pines Forest Preserve

Pope Ave.

North Forest Beach Drive

Intracoastal

Lighthouse Road

Harbour Town

Greenwood Dr.

Cordillo Pkwy.

Coligny Beach

Alder Lane Beach Park

South Forest Beach Drive

Freeport Marina

Harbour Town Golf Links

Plantation Dr.

Sea Pines Dr.

OCEANSIDE

Daufuskie Island

Stoney-Baynard Ruins

SOUTH BEACH

South Beach Marina

Atlantic Ocean

0   1/2 mi

0   1/2 km

KEY

Beach

Ferry

TOP ATTRACTIONS

★ **Fodors**Choice **Coastal Discovery Museum.** This interactive
FAMILY museum features a butterfly enclosure, hands-on programs
for children, and guided walks of the 68-acre property that
includes marshes, live oaks, and the state's largest Southern
red cedar tree, which dates back to 1595. Exhibits cover
the history of the Lowcountry, including the early development of Hilton Head as an island resort after the Civil
War. Although the museum is just off the Cross Island
Parkway, the peaceful grounds make it feel miles away. ⊠ *70
Honey Horn Dr., off Hwy. 278, North End* ☎ *843/689–
6767* ⊕ *www.coastaldiscovery.org* ⊠ *$5 donation; lectures
and tours additional.*

★ **Fodors**Choice **Old Town Bluffton.** Charming Old Town Bluffton
has historic homes and churches on oak-lined streets drip-
ping with Spanish moss, intermingled with new businesses
like the Salt Marsh Brewing Company. The Promenade
Street area is newer and features trendy bars and restaurants. At the end of Wharf Street in this artsy community
is the Bluffton Oyster Company (*63 Wharf Street*), a place
to buy fresh raw local shrimp, fish, and oysters. Grab some
picnic fixings from the Downtown Deli (*1223 May River
Road*) and head to the Calhoun Street Public Dock for a
meal with a view. Another incredibly beautiful spot for a
picnic is the grounds of the Church of the Cross. ⊠ *May
River Rd. and Calhoun St., Bluffton* ⊕ *www.oldtownbluff-
ton.com.*

★ **Fodors**Choice **Sea Pines Forest Preserve.** Walking and biking
FAMILY trails take you past a stocked fishing pond, a waterfowl
pond, and a 3,400-year-old Native American shell ring at
this 605-acre public wilderness tract. Pick up the extensive
activity guide at the Sea Pines Welcome Center to take
advantage of goings-on—moonlight hayrides, storytelling
around campfires, and alligator- and bird-watching boat
tours. The preserve is part of the grounds at Sea Pines
Resort. Overlooking a small lake, the outdoor chapel has
five wooden pews and a wooden lectern engraved with
the Prayer of St. Francis. ⊠ *Sea Pines Resort, 32 Greenwood Dr., South End* ☎ *843/671–1343* ⊕ *www.seapines.
com* ⊠ *$8 per car.*

8

WORTH NOTING

FAMILY **Audubon Newhall Preserve.** There are walking trails, a self-guided tour, and seasonal walks on this small, 50-acre preserve. Native plant life is tagged and identified in this pristine forest. ⌧ *Palmetto Bay Rd., off Cross Island Pkwy., South End* ⊕ *www.hiltonheadaudubon.org* ⧉ *Free.*

★ **Fodor'sChoice Harbour Town.** The closest thing the Sea Pines
FAMILY development has to a downtown is Harbour Town, a charming area centered on a circular marina that's filled with interesting shops and restaurants. Rising above it all is the landmark candy-cane-stripe Hilton Head Lighthouse, which you can climb to enjoy a view of Calibogue Sound. ⌧ *Lighthouse Rd., South End* ☎ *866/561–8802* ⊕ *www. seapines.com.*

FAMILY **Stoney-Baynard Ruins.** This historic site—the remnants of a plantation home and slave quarters built in the 1700s by Captain John "Saucy Jack" Stoney—hides within the Sea Pines neighborhood. A cotton planter named William Edings Baynard bought the place in 1840. On the National Register of Historic Sites, only parts of the oyster shell tabby walls are still standing. The ruins are not easy to find, so ask for directions at the Sea Pines Welcome Center at the Greenwood Drive gate. ⌧ *Plantation Dr., near Baynard Cove Rd., South End* ⧉ *Free.*

BEACHES

Hilton Head as 12 miles of beaches perfect for strolling, playing, swimming, or surfing. A delightful stroll on the beach can end with an unpleasant surprise if you don't put your towels, shoes, and other earthly possessions way up on the sand. Tides here can fluctuate as much as 7 feet. Check the tide chart at your hotel.

Beach Rules: Animals are not permitted on Hilton Head beaches between 10 and 5 from Memorial Day through Labor Day, and must otherwise always be on leash. Other rules include no alcohol, glass, littering, indecent exposure, unauthorized vehicles, fires and fireworks, shark fishing, removal of any live beach fauna, sleeping between midnight and 6 am, and kites not under manual control.

FAMILY **Alder Lane Beach Park.** A great place for solitude during the winter—and popular with families during the summer season—this beach has hard-packed sand at low tide, making it great for walking. It's accessible from the Marriott Grande

May River Sandbar

Known as the "Redneck Riviera," the May River Sandbar is pure party. Basically, the sandbar is just that: a small island of sand on the May River in Bluffton, which is the town that vacationers must go through on U.S. 278 to get to Hilton Head. The sandbar is accessible only by boat and only at low tide. Locals will plan their weekends around the time of low tide to head out to the sandbar. Boaters drop anchor and the party begins. Horseshoe and cornhole games are set up, picnic baskets unpacked, and cold drinks poured. To get there, go north by boat on Calibogue Sound and turn left west at the May River. The sandbar is at Red Marker 6.

Ocean Resort. **Amenities:** lifeguards; parking; showers; toilets. **Best for:** swimming; walking. ⊠ *Alder La., off South Forest Beach Rd., South End.*

Burkes Beach. This beach is usually not crowded, mostly because it is a bit hard to find and there are no lifeguards on duty. At sunrise, birds and deer bring the adjacent marsh to life. ■TIP→ **Time a visit around low tide—the marsh flooding during high tide can cut off access.** **Amenities:** parking; showers. **Best for:** solitude; sunrise; swimming; windsurfing. ⊠ *60 Burkes Beach Rd. , at William Hilton Pkwy., Mid-Island.*

★ Fodor'sChoice **Coligny Beach.** The island's most popular beach is
FAMILY a lot of fun, but during high season it can get very crowded. Accessible from the Beach House resort (with its beachside Tiki Hut) and several other hotels, it has choreographed fountains that delight little children, bench swings, and beach umbrellas and chaise longues for rent. If you have to go online, there's also Wi-Fi access. **Amenities:** food and drink; lifeguards; parking (no fee); showers; toilets. **Best for:** partiers; swimming; windsurfing. ⊠ *1 Coligny Circle, at Pope Ave. and South Forest Beach Dr., South End.*

FAMILY **Driessen Beach.** A good destination for families, Driessen Beach has a playground and an attractive boardwalk and sandy path through the dunes. It's often peppered with people flying kites, making it colorful and fun. **Amenities:** lifeguards; parking; showers; toilets. **Best for:** sunrise; surfing; swimming; walking. ⊠ *43 Bradley Beach Rd., at William Hilton Pkwy., Mid-Island.*

8

Where to Eat on Hilton Head Island

Port Royal Sound

← 170
← 95

46

278

Bluffton

← TO
SAVANNAH, GEORGIA

Seabrook Landing

Pinckney Island

Seabrook Drive

HILTON HEAD PLANTATION

PALMETTO HALL PLANTATION

Hilton Head Island Airport

Beach City Rd.

NORTH END

Main Street

Matthews Dr.

PORT ROYAL PLANTATION

MID-ISLAND

Cross Island Pkwy.

Marshland Rd.

Broad Creek

Shelter Cove Lane

Shelter Cove Marina

Harbourside Lane

Shelter Cove

Folly Field Rd.

PALMETTO DUNES RESORT

Bull Island

SOUTH END

278

Sea Pines Forest Preserve

North Forest Beach Drive

Intracoastal Waterway

Lighthouse Road

Harbour Town

Greenwood Dr.

Cordillo Pkwy.

South Forest Beach Drive

Freeport Marina

Daufuskie Island

Plantation Dr.

Sea Pines Dr.

OCEANSIDE

SOUTH BEACH

Atlantic Ocean

N

| 0 | 1/2 mi |
| 0 | 1/2 km |

Black Marlin Bayside Grill, **9**
Captain Woody's, **13**
Charlie's L'Etoile Verte, **14**
Coast, **20**
Frankie Bones, **4**
Hilton Head Social Bakery, **6**
Hinoki, **15**
Hudson's Seafood House, **1**
Kenny B's, **19**
Lucky Rooster, **8**
Michael Anthony's Cucina Italiana, **16**

Mi Tierra, **12**
Old Fort Pub, **3**
One Hot Mama's, **17**
Red Fish, **11**
Santa Fe Cafe, **7**
The Sea Shack, **18**
Signe's Heaven Bound Bakery & Café, **10**
Skull Creek Boathouse, **2**
Truffles Cafe, **21**
WiseGuys, **5**

SAND DOLLARS

Hilton Head Island's beaches hold many treasures, including starfish, sea sponges, and sand dollars. Note that it is strictly forbidden to pick up any live creatures on the beach, especially live sand dollars. How can you tell if they are alive? Live sand dollars are brown and fuzzy and will turn your fingers yellow and brown. You can take sand dollars home only if they're white. Soak them in a mixture of bleach and water to remove the scent once you get home.

FAMILY **Folly Field Beach Park.** Next to Driessen Beach, Folly Field is a treat for families. It can get crowded in high season, but even so it's a wonderful spot for a day of sunbathing and swimming. The islands best waves for surfing break are here. **Amenities:** lifeguards; parking; showers; toilets. **Best for:** sunrise; surfing; swimming; walking. ⊠ *55 Starfish Dr., off Folly Field Rd., North End.*

Mitchelville Beach Park. Not ideal for swimming because of the many sharp shells on the sand and in the water, Mitchelville Beach Park is a terrific spot for a walk or shell and shark tooth hunting. It is not on the Atlantic Ocean, but rather on Port Royal Sound. **Amenities:** parking; showers; toilets. **Best for:** sunrise; solitude; walking. ⊠ *124 Mitchelville Rd., Hilton Head Plantation, North End.*

8

WHERE TO EAT

$$$ ✕**Black Marlin Bayside Grill.** *Seafood.* This lively seafood eatery draws a steady stream of customers most days, but weekend brunches are the highlights for eggs Benedict and live entertainment. There's an early dining menu from 4 to 5:30, and the kitchen cranks out entrées—fish and lobster tacos are a favorite—until 10 every night. **Known for:** a hopping happy hour; an outdoor Hurricane Bar; weekend oyster roasts during winter. $ *Average main: $23* ⊠ *86 Helmsman Way, South End* ☎ *843/785–4950* ⊕ *www. blackmarlinhhi.com.*

$$$ ✕**Captain Woody's.** *Seafood.* If you're looking for a fun,
FAMILY casual, kid-friendly seafood restaurant, this vibrant joint
offers creamy crab bisque, oysters on the half shell, and a
sampler platter that includes crab legs, shrimp, and oysters.
The restaurant has a second location in Bluffton. **Known
for:** grouper sandwiches, including the buffalo grouper,
grouper melt, and grouper Reuben; a lively atmosphere;
football-watching crowds on fall weekends. Ⓢ *Average
main: $22* ✉ *6 Target Rd., South End* ☎ *843/785–2400*
⊕ *www.captainwoodys.com.*

$$$$ ✕**Charlie's L'Etoile Verte.** *French.* This family-owned culinary
landmark shows off its personality with eclectic, country
French decor and homey ambience. The menu is hand-
written daily on a blackboard and features French classics
like escargot and leeks and rack of American lamb with
rosemary au jus. **Known for:** extensive wine list (more than
500) from California, Bordeaux, and the Rhone Valley; 14
varying seafood entrées offered nightly; fine dining in a
relaxed atmosphere. Ⓢ *Average main: $27* ✉ *8 New Orleans
Rd., Mid-Island* ☎ *843/785–9277* ⊕ *www.charliesgreenstar.
com* ☾ *Closed Sun. No lunch Sat.*

★ **Fodor's**Choice ✕**Coast.** *Seafood.* An oceanfront restaurant
$$$ can often count on its real estate to bring in diners, but
this casual yet upscale seafood spot at the Sea Pines Beach
Club doesn't cut corners in the kitchen. There is plenty of
Southern-inspired fare for landlubbers, but the real gems
are the raw bar platter and the day's featured fish entrée.
Known for: lively patio (and indoor) dining with horizon
views across the ocean; a Cajun-influenced lobster roll;
the adjacent Ocean Lounge cocktail bar. Ⓢ *Average main:
$24* ✉ *87 North Sea Pines Dr., South End* ☎ *843/842–1888*
⊕ *www.seapines.com.*

$$$$ ✕**Frankie Bones.** *Italian.* The early '60s theme here appeals
to an older crowd that likes the traditional Italian dishes
on the early dining menu, but during happy hour, the bar
and the surrounding cocktail tables are populated with
younger patrons who order flatbread pizzas and small
plates. Some dishes have innovative twists, including the
16-ounce rib eye with a sweetened coffee rub. **Known for:**
cool twists on traditional dishes; drinks for dessert, like a
key lime colada martini and house-made limoncello; the
24-ounce "Godfather Cut" prime rib. Ⓢ *Average main:
$26* ✉ *1301 Main St., North End* ☎ *843/682–4455* ⊕ *www.
frankieboneshhi.com.*

Shrimp Boats Forever

Watching shrimp trawlers coming into their home port at sunset, with mighty nets raised and an entourage of hungry seagulls, is a cherished Lowcountry tradition. The shrimping industry has been an integral staple of the South Carolina economy for nearly a century. (Remember Bubba Gump?) It was booming in the 1980s. But alas, cheap, farm-raised shrimp from foreign markets and now the cost of diesel fuel are deci-mating the shrimpers' numbers. The season for fresh-caught shrimp is May to December. Lowcountry residents support the freelance fishermen by buying only certified, local wild shrimp in restaurants and in area fish markets and super-markets. Visitors can follow suit by patronizing local restaurants and markets that display the logo that reads "Certified Wild American Shrimp." Or you can simply ask before you eat.

★ **Fodor'sChoice** ✕ **Hilton Head Social Bakery.** *Bakery.* It's impos-
$ sible to stop in just for a baguette or sourdough loaf at this unassuming French-owned bakery and bistro—you'll inevitably be tempted by the lush *pain au chocolat* and cinnamon buns. The owner/chef, a Normandy native, was the executive chef at New York's Tavern On the Green and Windows on the World before relocating to Hilton Head. **Known for:** savory tarts and croque-monsieur for lunch; thoughtfully sourced ingredients; decadent eclairs washed down with good coffee. ⑤ *Average main: $6* ⊠ *Shelter Cove Harbour & Marina, 17 Harborside La., Mid-Island* ☎ *843/715-3349* ⊕ *www.hiltonheadsocialbakery.com* ⊘ *Closed Mon. and Tues. seasonally.*

$$$ ✕ **Hinoki.** *Japanese.* Slip into a peaceful oasis through a tun-nel of bamboo at Hinoki, which has some of the best sushi on the island. Try the Hilton Head roll, which is whitefish tempura and avocado, the Hinoki roll with asparagus, spicy fish roe, tuna and avocado, or the to-die-for tuna sashimi salad with spicy mayo, cucumbers, onions, salmon roe, and crabmeat. **Known for:** superfresh sushi with more than 50 menu items; extensive sake menu; udon noodle dishes and bento boxes. ⑤ *Average main: $23* ⊠ *Orleans Plaza, 37 New Orleans Rd., South End* ☎ *843/785-9800* ⊕ *hinokihhi.com* ⊘ *Closed Sun., no lunch Mon. or Sat.*

8

★ FodorśChoice ✕ **Hudson's Sea-**
$$$ **food House.** *Seafood.* Built
FAMILY over the water on Port
Royal Sound, this classic
seafood joint buys its fish
and shrimp directly from the
boats that dock there, and
the staff raises their own
oysters and soft-shell crabs
with an in-house maricul-
ture program. Dining here
feels like stepping back
50 years into an authentic
waterfront dive, including
the locally sourced, same-
day-fresh seafood that's
now often hard to find.

> **MODERN TAKEOUT**
>
> When you just don't feel like going out for a bite, a local delivery service is here to help. Hiltonheaddelivers.com delivers restaurant food to homes, condos, and hotels from 5 to 9:45 pm seven days a week for a 15% or $5.50 delivery charge. A variety of restaurants take part, including One Hot Mama's, WiseGuys, and Skull Creek Boathouse.

Known for: sunsets at the open air waterfront bar; happy
hour mai tais and seafood specials; oysters grown by the
restaurant-owned Shell Ring Oyster Company. ⑤ *Average
main: $22* ⊠ *1 Hudson Rd., North End* ☎ *843/681–2772*
⊕ *www.hudsonsonthedocks.com.*

$ ✕ **Kenny B's.** *Cajun.* Surrounded by Mardi Gras memo-
FAMILY rabilia, Kenny himself cooks up jambalaya, gumbo, and
muffaletta sandwiches. His wife runs the dining room,
serving hungry working folks golden-fried oyster po'boys
topped with real remoulade sauce. **Known for:** colorful
mural and decor; the Sunday brunch buffet's eggs Bene-
dict stations; beignets like they're made in New Orleans.
⑤ *Average main: $14* ⊠ *Bi-Lo Circle, 70 Pope Ave., South
End* ☎ *843/785–3315* ⊘ *Closed Mon.*

★ FodorśChoice ✕ **Lucky Rooster.** *Southern.* From its unassuming
$$$ perch at the corner of a strip mall, the ever-changing daily
menus at this chef-owned farm-to-table establishment sit
quietly on par with the very best dining in neighboring
Charleston. Whether it's braised short rib, Korean-style
fried chicken, or roasted octopus, the Rooster's kitchen
serves plates brimming with pride and inspiration. **Known
for:** the island's best cocktail program, including speakeasy
mixes on tap; every ingredient sourced with care; Sunday
night burger deals. ⑤ *Average main: $22* ⊠ *841 William
Hilton Pkwy, Mid-Island* ☎ *843/681–3474* ⊕ *www.lucky-
roosterhhi.com* ⊘ *No lunch.*

★ FodorśChoice ✕ **Michael Anthony's Cucina Italiana.** *Italian.*
$$$$ Owned by a talented, charismatic Philadelphia family, this
restaurant has a convivial spirit, and its innovative pairings

and plate presentations are au courant. Expect fresh, top-quality ingredients, simple yet elegant sauces, and waiters who know and care about the food and wine they serve. **Known for:** cooking demonstrations/classes; on-site market with fresh pasta; wine tastings. ⑤ *Average main: $30* ⊠ *Orleans Plaza, 37 New Orleans Rd., Suite L, South End* ☎ *843/785–6272* ⊕ *www.michael-anthonys. com* ⊘ *Closed Sun. and Mon. No lunch.*

> **COOKING CLASS**
>
> Learn to prepare Italian cuisine in a hands-on cooking class at Michael Anthony's. Classes include samples of the dishes and wine. Demonstration classes, wine tastings, and programs for visiting corporate groups are also available. There is a high demand for these classes, so reserve your place as far in advance as possible.

$$ ✕ **Mi Tierra.** *Mexican.* There's nothing fancy here, just great Mexican food and decor that has a Southwestern feel, with tile floors, colorful sombreros, and paintings of chili peppers hanging on the walls. Don't forget to order the guacamole and bean dip with your margarita and *enchiladas suizas*, tortillas filled with chicken and topped with green tomatillo sauce, sour cream, and avocado. **Known for:** authentic comfort food; signature dish arroz con camarones—butterfly shrimp sautéed with garlic butter and vegetables; daily specials and affordable kids' menu. ⑤ *Average main: $15* ⊠ *130 Arrow Rd., South End* ☎ *843/342–3409.*

$$$$ ✕ **Old Fort Pub.** *Modern American.* Overlooking the sweeping marshlands of Skull Creek, this romantic restaurant has almost panoramic views. The building is old enough to have some personality, and the professional staffers diligently do their duty, but more importantly, the kitchen serves flavorful food, highlighted by dishes like roasted calamari with sun-dried tomatoes and olives, bouillabaisse, and filet mignon with chanterelles. The wine list is extensive, and there's outdoor seating on a third-floor porch for toasting the sunset. Sunday brunch is celebratory and includes a mimosa. **Known for:** amazing, decadent entrées beautifully presented; a lovely Sunday brunch; gorgeous views; romantic atmosphere. ⑤ *Average main: $33* ⊠ *Hilton Head Plantation, 65 Skull Creek Dr., North End* ☎ *843/681–2386* ⊕ *www.oldfortpub.com* ⊘ *No lunch Mon.–Sat.*

$$ ✕ **One Hot Mama's.** *Barbecue.* This heavenly barbecue joint
FAMILY is a Hilton Head institution because of its upbeat atmosphere, graffiti-strewn walls, and melt-in-the-mouth pulled

8

pork and fall-off-the-bone ribs. In addition to food that will wake up your taste buds, there are also 15 beers on tap, about a dozen flat-screen TVs, and an outdoor patio with a big brick fireplace for the cooler months. **Known for:** lots of fun in the "Barmuda Triangle" (other bars are just steps away); award-winning wings with sauces like strawberry-jalapeño; a delectable rib sampler that includes chocolate barbecue and "Hot Asian". ⑤ *Average main: $19* ⊠ *7A Greenwood Dr., South End* ☎ *843/682–6262* ⊕ *onehotmamas.com.*

$$$$ ✕**Red Fish.** *American.* This seafood eatery's "naked" catch of the day—seafood grilled with olive oil, lime, and garlic—is a heart-healthy specialty that many diners say is the best thing on the menu. The restaurant's wine cellar is filled with some 1,000 bottles, and there's also a retail wineshop so you can take a bottle home. Although the commercial-strip location isn't inspired, the lively crowd, the soft candlelight, and the subdued artwork more than make up for it. There's a sister location in Bluffton. **Known for:** an award-winning burger; fabulous service; produce grown on the restaurant's own farm. ⑤ *Average main: $30* ⊠ *8 Archer Rd., South End* ☎ *843/686–3388* ⊕ *www.redfishofhiltonhead.com* ⊗ *No lunch Sun.*

$$$$ ✕**Santa Fe Cafe.** *Southwestern.* The sights, sounds, and aromas of New Mexico greet you here: Native American rugs, Mexican ballads, steer skulls and horns, and the pungent smells of chilies and mesquite on the grill. The restaurant is perhaps best experienced on a rainy, chilly night when the adobe fireplaces are cranked up. Plan on listening to *guitarra* music in the rooftop cantina Wednesday to Saturday night. **Known for:** rooftop cantina with a cozy fireplace and live music; signature grouper served with chipotle Parmesan au gratin; one of the island's best margaritas. ⑤ *Average main: $28* ⊠ *807 William Hilton Pkwy., Mid-Island* ☎ *843/785–3838* ⊕ *santafehhi.com* ⊗ *No lunch weekends.*

★ Fodor'sChoice ✕**The Sea Shack.** *Seafood.* Heaping plates of
$ fried seafood and hearty po'boys are worth the long line at this local staple counter-serve. The humble dining room and open kitchen suit the mouthwatering platters perfectly. Local tip: During the busy summer months, call in your order for pickup and skip the line. **Known for:** eclectic seafood options like gator, frog legs, and conch fritters; blueberry key lime pie; over a dozen varieties of fish on the daily menu. ⑤ *Average main: $14* ⊠ *6 Executive Park Rd., South End* ☎ *843/785–2464* ⊗ *Closed Sun.*

$ ✕ **Signe's Heaven Bound Bakery & Café.** *American.* Every morning, locals roll in for the deep-dish French toast, crispy polenta, and whole wheat waffles. Since 1972, European-born Signe has been feeding islanders her delicious soups and quiches, curried chicken salad, and loaded hot and cold sandwiches. **Known for:** melt-in-your-mouth cakes and the rave-worthy breads; the "beach bag" (a lunch packed with goodies to take to the beach); cozy, friendly atmosphere. ⑤ *Average main: $8* ⊠ *93 Arrow Rd., South End* ☎ *843/785–9118* ⊕ *www.signesbakery.com* ⊗ *Closed Sun.*

$$ ✕ **Skull Creek Boathouse.** *Seafood.* Soak up the salty atmo-
FAMILY sphere in this complex of dining areas where almost every table has a view of the water. Outside is a third dining area and a bar called the Marker 13 Buoy Bar, where Adirondack chairs invite you to sit back, listen to live music, and catch the sunset. **Known for:** an adjacent outdoor "Sunset Landing" beer garden; tasty sandwiches and po'boys with a Southern twist; sushi, ceviche, and carpaccio from the "Dive Bar". ⑤ *Average main: $17* ⊠ *397 Squire Pope Rd., North End* ☎ *843/681–3663* ⊕ *www.skullcreekboathouse.com.*

$$$$ ✕ **Truffles Cafe.** *Modern American.* When a restaurant keeps its customers happy for decades, there's a reason: you won't find any of the namesake truffles on the menu, but there's grilled salmon with a mango-barbecue glaze and barbecued baby back ribs. There's a Bluffton branch that has a lovely outdoor seating area. **Known for:** wide-ranging, crowd-pleasing menu with plenty of seafood; very popular with locals; an on-site market with thoughtful gifts. ⑤ *Average main: $26* ⊠ *Sea Pines Center, 71 Lighthouse Rd., South End* ☎ *843/671–6136* ⊕ *www.trufflescafe.com.*

$$$$ ✕ **WiseGuys.** *Steakhouse.* The red-and-black decor is modern and sophisticated at this steak house—it's a little art deco, a little contemporary. The food is a spin on the classics, starting with seared tuna sliders and an incredible beef tenderloin carpaccio topped with baby arugula and horseradish cream. **Known for:** a delightful crème brûlée flight and deep-fried bread pudding; attentive waitstaff that's knowledgeable about the extensive wine list; charred rib-eye steak entrée. ⑤ *Average main: $32* ⊠ *1513 Main St., North End* ☎ *843/842–8866* ⊕ *wiseguyshhi.com* ⊗ *No lunch.*

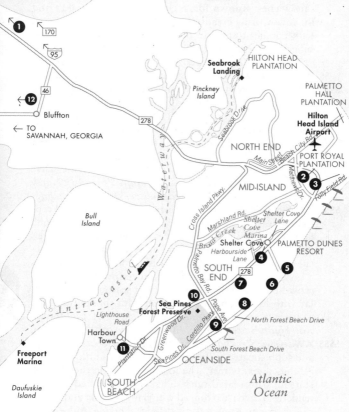

Where to Stay on Hilton Head Island

KEY
Beach
Ferry

Port Royal Sound

170
95
46
Bluffton
← TO SAVANNAH, GEORGIA

Seabrook Landing

HILTON HEAD PLANTATION

Pinckney Island

PALMETTO HALL PLANTATION

Hilton Head Island Airport

278

Seabrook Drive

Main Street

Beach City Rd.

Matthews Dr.

NORTH END

PORT ROYAL PLANTATION

Fatty Fright Rd.

MID-ISLAND

Cross Island Pkwy.

Marshland Rd.

Broad Creek

Shelter Cove Lane

Shelter Cove Marina

Shelter Cove

Harbourside Lane

Palmetto Bay Rd.

PALMETTO DUNES RESORT

Bull Island

Intracoastal Waterway

SOUTH END

278

Sea Pines Forest Preserve

Lighthouse Road

Harbour Town

Freeport Marina

Greenwood Dr.

Cordillo Pkwy.

Pope Ave.

North Forest Beach Drive

South Forest Beach Drive

OCEANSIDE

Sea Pines Dr.

Plantation Dr.

SOUTH BEACH

Daufuskie Island

Atlantic Ocean

0   1/2 mi
0   1/2 km

Beach House
Hilton Head Island, **9**

Candlewood Suites, **1**

Disney's Hilton Head Island
Resort, **4**

Hampton Inn on
Hilton Head Island, **2**

Hilton Head Marriott
Resort & Spa, **5**

The Inn at Harbour Town, **11**

Montage Palmetto Bluff, **12**

Omni Hilton Head
Oceanfront Resort, **6**

Park Lane Hotel & Suites, **7**

Sea Pines Resort, **10**

Sonesta Resort
Hilton Head Island, **8**

Westin Hilton Head Island
Resort & Spa, **3**

WHERE TO STAY

$$$ ⊞ **Beach House Hilton Head Island.** *Resort.* On one of the
FAMILY island's most popular stretches of sand, this Holiday Inn-
branded resort is within walking distance of Coligny Plaza's
shops and restaurants. **Pros:** the central location cannot
be beat for families; renovations have made this a very
desirable destination; professional staff. **Cons:** in summer
the number of kids raises the noise volume; small front
desk can get backed up; not a spot for a quiet getaway.
⑤ *Rooms from: $229* ⊠ *1 S. Forest Beach Dr., South End*
☎ *843/785–5126* ⊕ *www.beachhousehhi.com* ⇆ *202 rooms*
⏰ *No meals.*

$$$$ ⊞ **Disney's Hilton Head Island Resort.** *Resort.* The cheery colors
FAMILY and whimsical designs at Disney's popular resort create a
look that's part Southern beach resort, part Adirondack
hideaway. **Pros:** family-friendly vibe; young and friendly
staffers; a huge heated pool with a waterslide. **Cons:** books
up far in advance; expensive rates; it's a drive to the beach.
⑤ *Rooms from: $414* ⊠ *22 Harbourside La., Mid-Island*
☎ *843/341–4100* ⊕ *hiltonhead.disney.go.com* ⇆ *123 units*
⏰ *No meals.*

$$$ ⊞ **Hampton Inn on Hilton Head Island.** *Hotel.* Although it's not
FAMILY on the beach, this attractive hotel is a good choice for bud-
get travelers and the lovely pool area and fitness room are
much-appreciated amenities. **Pros:** good customer service;
moderate prices; more amenities than you might expect.
Cons: not on a beach; parking lot views; lacks the charm of
the island's resort hotels. ⑤ *Rooms from: $219* ⊠ *1 Dillon
Rd., Mid-Island* ☎ *843/681–7900* ⊕ *www.hamptoninn.com*
⇆ *121 rooms* ⏰ *Free Breakfast.*

★ **Fodor's**Choice ⊞ **Hilton Head Marriott Resort & Spa.** *Hotel.* Private
$$$$ balconies with views of the palm-shaded grounds are the
FAMILY best reason to stay at this resort facing the Atlantic Ocean.
Pros: steps from the beach; lots of amenities; one of the
best-run operations on the island. **Cons:** rooms could be
larger; in summer, kids are everywhere; one of the older
beachfront resorts on the island. ⑤ *Rooms from: $359* ⊠ *1
Hotel Circle, Mid-Island* ☎ *843/686–8400* ⊕ *www.marriott.
com/hotels/travel/hhhgr-hilton-head-marriott-resort-and-
spa* ⇆ *513 rooms* ⏰ *No meals.*

★ **Fodor's**Choice ⊞ **The Inn at Harbour Town.** *Hotel.* The most buzz-
$$$$ worthy of Hilton Head's properties, this European-style
boutique hotel pampers you with British service and a dose
of Southern charm—butlers are on hand any time of the
day or night, and the kitchen delivers around the clock.

Pros: the service spoils you from arrival to checkout; idyllic location; complimentary parking. **Cons:** it's a drive to the beach; two-day minimum on most weekends; less appealing for families. ⑤ *Rooms from: $309* ✉ *Sea Pines Resort, 7 Lighthouse La., South End* ☎ *843/785–3333* ⊕ *www. seapines.com* ↝ *60 rooms* ⚏ *No meals.*

★ **Fodor's**Choice ⚏ **Montage Palmetto Bluff.** *B&B/Inn.* About 15
$$$$ minutes from Hilton Head, the Lowcountry's most luxuri-
FAMILY ous resort sits on 20,000 acres that have been transformed into a perfect replica of a small island town, complete with its own clapboard church; as a chauffeured golf cart takes you to your cottage or room, you'll pass the club-house, which resembles a mighty antebellum great house. **Pros:** 18-hole May River Golf Club on-site; tennis/bocce/croquet complex has an impressive retail shop; the river adds both ambience and boat excursions. **Cons:** the mock Southern town is not the real thing; isolated from the amenities of Hilton Head; escaping in luxury is priced accordingly. ⑤ *Rooms from: $580* ✉ *1 Village Park Sq., Bluffton* ☎ *843/706–6500, 855/264–8705* ⊕ *www.mon-tagehotels.com/palmettobluff* ↝ *50 cottages, 75 inn rooms* ⚏ *No meals.*

$$$$ ⚏ **Omni Hilton Head Oceanfront Resort.** *Resort.* At this beach-
FAMILY front hotel with a Caribbean sensibility, the spacious accom-modations range from studios to two-bedroom suites. **Pros:** competes more with condos than hotels because of the size of its accommodations; lots of outdoor dining options; well suited for both families and couples; packages are often good deals, and many include breakfast, bottles of wine, or outdoor cabana massages. **Cons:** wedding parties can be noisy; the two hot tubs are often full; noise travels through room walls. ⑤ *Rooms from: $349* ✉ *23 Ocean La., Palmetto Dunes, Mid-Island* ☎ *843/842–8000* ⊕ *www. omnihiltonhead.com* ↝ *323 rooms* ⚏ *No meals.*

$$ ⚏ **Park Lane Hotel & Suites.** *Hotel.* This all-suites property has
FAMILY a friendly feel, which is probably why many guests settle in for weeks. **Pros:** one of the island's most reasonably priced lodgings; parking and Wi-Fi are free; playground for the kids. **Cons:** doesn't have an upscale feel; more kids means more noise, especially around the pool area; going to the beach or to dinner requires a drive. ⑤ *Rooms from: $176* ✉ *12 Park La., South End* ☎ *843/686–5700* ⊕ *www. hiltonheadparklanehotel.com* ↝ *156 suites* ⚏ *No meals.*

$$$$ ⚏ **Sonesta Resort Hilton Head Island.** *Resort.* Set in a luxu-
FAMILY riant garden that always seems to be in full bloom, the Sonesta Resort is the centerpiece of Shipyard Plantation,

How to Talk to Locals

Hilton Head is known as a place where people come to start a new life, or to happily live out their golden years. It is politically incorrect to immediately ask someone you just met, "Where did you come from?" or "What brought you here?" or "What did you do in your former life?" Residents are asked these questions all the time, and it gets old, especially if they moved here decades ago. Their reluctance to tell all does not mean that they necessarily have skeletons in their closets. Now, conversely, they are allowed to ask *you* where you are from—not to mention, "How long you are staying?"— or they may be considered unwelcoming. But do let them tell you about themselves in time, or over a cocktail. You may learn that your golfing partner was the CEO of a big national corporation, or the guy next to you at the bar is a best-selling author, or the friendly fellow in line at the store is a billionaire entrepreneur who might even be a household name.

which means you'll have access to all its various amenities, including golf and tennis. **Pros:** close to all the restaurants and nightlife in Coligny Plaza; spacious rooms; free parking. **Cons:** crowded during summer; service is sometimes impersonal; doesn't have the views of competing resorts. ⑤ *Rooms from: $299* ✉ *Shipyard Plantation, 130 Shipyard Dr., South End* ☎ *843/842–2400* ⊕ *www.sonesta.com/hiltonheadisland* ⌁ *340 rooms* ⭑◉⭑ *No meals.*

$$$$ ⛢ **Westin Hilton Head Island Resort & Spa.** *Resort.* A circular
FAMILY drive winds around a sculpture of long-legged marsh birds as you approach this beachfront resort, whose lush landscape lies on the island's quietest stretch of sand. **Pros:** great for destination weddings; the beach here is absolutely gorgeous; pampering spa; guests have access to the Port Royal Golf & Racquet Club. **Cons:** lots of groups in the off-season; crowds during summer can backup the check-in process; onsite Carolina Room restaurant gets mixed reviews. ⑤ *Rooms from: $314* ✉ *2 Grass Lawn Ave., Port Royal Plantation, North End* ☎ *800/933–3102, 843/681–4000* ⊕ *www.marriott.com/hotels/hotel-information/restaurant/ hhhwi-the-westin-hilton-head-island-resort-and-spa/* ⌁ *416 rooms* ⭑◉⭑ *No meals.*

8

BLUFFTON

$ Ⓕ **Candlewood Suites.** *Hotel.* At this suites-only hotel, the
FAMILY   guest rooms are comfortable and tastefully decorated in
muted browns and beiges. **Pros:** location makes it convenient to Hilton Head, Beaufort, and Savannah; every room
has a full kitchen; free guest laundry. **Cons:** it's a half-hour
drive to the beach; set back from road, it can be difficult to
find; lacks the charm of on-island resorts. Ⓢ *Rooms from:
$129* ✉ *5 Young Clyde Court, Bluffton* ☎ *843/705–9600*
⊕ *www.ihg.com/candlewood/hotels/us/en/bluffton/btocw/
hoteldetail* ⇥ *124 suites* �� *No meals.*

PRIVATE VILLA RENTALS

Hilton Head has some 6,000 villas, condos, and private
homes for rent, almost double the number of the island's
hotel rooms. Villas and condos seem to work particularly
well for families with children, especially if they want to
avoid the extra costs of staying in a resort. Often these
vacation homes cost less per diem than hotels of the same
quality. Guests on a budget can further economize by cooking some of their own meals.

Villas and condos are primarily rented by the week, Saturday to Saturday. It pays to make sure you understand
exactly what you're getting before making a deposit or
signing a contract. For example, a property owner in the
Hilton Head Beach & Tennis Club advertised that his villa
sleeps six. That villa had one small bedroom, a foldout
couch, and a hall closet with two very narrow bunk beds.
That's a far cry from the three-bedroom villa you might
have expected. ■TIP➔ **Before calling a vacation rental company,
make a list of the amenities you want.** Ask for pictures of each
room and ask when the photos were taken. If you're looking for a beachfront property, ask exactly how far it is to
the beach. Make sure to ask for a list of all fees, including
those for parking, cleaning, pets, security deposits, and
utility costs. Finally, get a written contract and a copy of
the refund policy.

RENTAL AGENTS

Hilton Head Rentals. Representing more than 150 vacation
rentals ranging in size from one to seven bedrooms, this
agency has villas, condos, and homes with oceanfront
views. It offers various packages that include golf and
other activities. Rentals are generally for three to seven
days. ✉ *578 William Hilton Pkwy.* ☎ *843/785–8687* ⊕ *www.
hiltonheadvacation.com.*

FAMILY **Resort Rentals of Hilton Head Island.** This company represents some 500 homes and villas, including many located inside the gated communities of Sea Pines, Palmetto Dunes, and Shipyard Plantation. Others are in North and South Forest Beach and the Folly Field area. Stays are generally Saturday to Saturday during the peak summer season; three- or four-night stays may be possible off-season. Most of the properties are privately owned, so decor and amenities can vary. ⊠ *32 Palmetto Bay Rd., Suite 1B, Mid-Island* ☎ *800/845–7017* ⊕ *www.hhivacations.com.*

★ Fodor'sChoice **Sea Pines Resort.** The vast majority of the over-
FAMILY night guests at Sea Pines Resort rent one of the 500 suites, villas, and beach houses. The community is home to three golf courses, a tennis facility, a beach club, the Inn at Harbour Town and the Harbour Town village. One- and two-bedroom villas have a minimum stay of four nights. For stays of four or more nights, you must arrive on Saturday, Sunday, Monday, or Tuesday. Three- and four-bedrooms villas have a minimum stay of seven nights, and you've got to check in on Saturday. All houses have Internet access, and most have Wi-Fi. Housekeeping is usually an additional charge. ⊠ *32 Greenwood Dr., South End* ☎ *843/785–3333, 866/561–8802* ⊕ *www.seapines.com/vacation-rentals.*

FAMILY **Wyndham Vacation Rentals.** Wyndham boasts that it has the most exclusive vacation-rental accommodations (500-plus) on Hilton Head, from oceanfront to golf views, all in premier locations. A quality rating helps prospective guests know the type of decor their accommodation will have. ☎ *866/739–1554* ⊕ *www.wyndhamvacationrentals.com/hilton-head-island.*

NIGHTLIFE AND PERFORMING ARTS

NIGHTLIFE

Bars, like everything else on Hilton Head, are often in gated communities or shopping centers. Some are hangouts frequented by locals, and others get a good mix of both locals and visitors. There are a fair number of clubs, many of them restaurants that crank up the music after diners depart.

Big Bamboo. Decked out like a World War II–era officers' club, this South Pacific–theme bar and restaurant features live music most nights of the week. ⊠ *Coligny Plaza, 1 N. Forest Beach Dr., South End* ☎ *843/686–3443* ⊕ *www.bigbamboocafe.com.*

Comedy Magic Cabaret. Several nights a week this lounge brings top-flight comedic talent to Hilton Head. There's a light menu of appetizers and sandwiches, and a full bar. Tickets are $28 to $32 per person. ■TIP→ **Book ahead during summer, because the shows sell out fairly quickly.** ⊠ *South Island Square, 843 William Hilton Pkwy., South End* ☎ *843/681–7757* ⊕ *www.comedymagiccabaret.com.*

★ Fodor'sChoice **The Jazz Corner.** The elegant supper-club atmosphere at this popular spot makes it a wonderful setting in which to enjoy an evening of jazz, swing, or blues. There's a special martini menu, an extensive wine list, and a late-night menu. ■TIP→ **The club fills up quickly, so make reservations.** ⊠ *The Village at Wexford, 1000 William Hilton Pkwy., Suite C-1, South End* ☎ *843/842–8620* ⊕ *www. thejazzcorner.com.*

Reilley's Plaza. Dubbed the "Barmuda Triangle" by locals, the bars at this plaza include One Hot Mama's, Reilley's, the Lodge burger bar, and Jump & Phil's Bar & Grill. It's the closest thing Hilton Head Island has to a raging club scene. ⊠ *Hilton Head Plaza, Greenwood Dr., right before gate to Sea Pines, South End.*

★ Fodor'sChoice **The Salty Dog Cafe.** If there's one thing you
FAMILY shouldn't miss on Hilton Head Island, it's the iconic Salty Dog Cafe. It's the ideal place to escape, sit back, and enjoy the warm nights and ocean breezes in a tropical setting at the outdoor bar. There's live music (think Jimmy Buffett) seven nights a week during high season. Bring the family along for kid-friendly entertainment, including music, magic, and face painting at 7 pm throughout the summer. ⊠ *South Beach Marina, 224 S. Sea Pines Dr., South End* ☎ *843/671–2233* ⊕ *www.saltydog.com.*

PERFORMING ARTS

★ Fodor'sChoice **Arts Center of Coastal Carolina.** Locals love the theater productions at this arts hub that often has notable, worthwhile exhibits at its Walter Greer Gallery. Programs for children are also popular. ⊠ *14 Shelter Cove La., Mid-Island* ☎ *843/686–3945* ⊕ *www.artshhi.com.*

FAMILY **Hilton Head Island Gullah Celebration.** This showcase of Gullah life through arts, music, and theater is held at a variety of sites throughout the Lowcountry in February. ☎ *843/255–7304* ⊕ *www.gullahcelebration.com.*

CLOSE UP

Island Gators

The most famous photo of Hilton Head's brilliant developer, Charles Fraser, ran in the *Saturday Evening Post* in the late 1950s. It shows him dressed as a dandy, outfitted with a cane and straw hat, with an alligator on a leash.

These prehistoric creatures are indeed indigenous to this subtropical island. What you will learn if you visit the Coastal Discovery Museum, where the old photograph is blown up for an interpretive board on the island's early history, is that someone else had the gator by the tail (not shown) so that it would not harm Fraser or the photographer.

Nowadays, in Sea Pines Center, there is a life-size, metal sculpture of an alligator that all the tourists, and especially their kids, climb on to have their pictures taken. But if you should happen to see a live gator while exploring the island or playing a round of golf, please don't feed or approach it. A woman was fatally attacked by an alligator in Sea Pines Resort in August 2018, a horrifying reminder of the deadly power these reptilian neighbors possess.

★ **Fodor's**Choice **Hilton Head Symphony Orchestra.** A selection of summer concerts—including the popular Symphony Under The Stars—are among the year-round performances by the symphony. Most events are at the First Presbyterian Church. ⊠ *First Presbyterian Church, 540 William Hilton Pkwy., Mid-Island* ☎ *843/842–2055* ⊕ *www.hhso.org.*

FAMILY **Main Street Youth Theatre.** A variety of classic and modern theatrical performances showcasing young local talent are presented by this local troupe. ⊠ *25 New Orleans Rd., Mid-Island* ☎ *843/689–6246* ⊕ *www.msyt.org.*

SPORTS AND THE OUTDOORS

Hilton Head Island is a mecca for the sports enthusiast and for those who just want a relaxing walk or bike ride on the beach. There are 24 public golf courses, more than 50 miles of public bike paths, and more than 300 tennis courts. There's also tons of water sports, including kayaking and canoeing, parasailing, fishing, and sailing.

8

BIKING

More than 50 miles of public paths crisscross Hilton Head Island, and pedaling is popular along the firmly packed beach. The island keeps adding more to the boardwalk network as visitors are using it and because it's such a safe alternative for kids. Bikes with wide tires are a must if you want to ride on the beach. They can save you a spill should you hit loose sand on the trails. Keep in mind when crossing streets that, in South Carolina, vehicles have the right-of-way. ■TIP→ For a map of trails, visit www.hiltonhead-islandsc.gov.

Bicycles from beach cruisers to mountain bikes to tandem bikes can be rented either at bike stores or at most hotels and resorts. Many can be delivered to your hotel, along with helmets, baskets, locks, child carriers, and whatever else you might need.

FAMILY **Hilton Head Bicycle Company.** This local outfit rents bicycles, helmets, bike trailers, and adult tricycles. ⊠ *112 Arrow Rd., South End* ☎ *843/686–6888, 800/995–4319* ⊕ *www.hiltonheadbicycle.com.*

FAMILY **Pedals Bicycles.** Rent beach bikes for adults and children, kiddy karts, jogging strollers, and mountain bikes at this local operation in business since 1981. ⊠ *71A Pope Ave., South End* ☎ *888/699–1039* ⊕ *www.pedalsbicycles.com.*

FAMILY **South Beach Bike Rentals.** Rent bikes, helmets, tandems, and adult tricycles at this spot in Sea Pines. ⊠ *230 S. Sea Pines Dr., Sea Pines, South End* ☎ *843/671–2453* ⊕ *www.south-beach-cycles.com.*

CANOEING AND KAYAKING

This is one of the most delightful ways to commune with nature on this commercial but physically beautiful island. Paddle through the creeks and estuaries and try to keep up with the dolphins.

★ Fodor's Choice **Outside Hilton Head.** Boats, canoes, kayaks, and
FAMILY paddleboards are available for rent from this local outfitter that also offers nature tours, surf camps, and dolphin-watching excursions. ⊠ *Shelter Cove Marina, 1 Shelter Cove La., Mid-Island* ☎ *843/686–6996, 800/686–6996* ⊕ *www.outsidehiltonhead.com.*

FISHING

Although anglers can fish in these waters year-round, in April things start to crank up and in May most boats are heavily booked. May is the season for cobia, especially in Port Royal Sound. In the Gulf Stream you can hook king mackerel, tuna, wahoo, and mahimahi. ■TIP→ **A fishing license is necessary if you are fishing from a beach, dock, or pier. They are $11 for 14 days.** Licenses aren't necessary on charter fishing boats because they already have their licenses.

FAMILY **Bayrunner Fishing Charters.** With more than four decades of experience fishing these waters, Captain Miles Altman takes anglers out for trips lasting three to eight hours. Evening shark trips are offered May to August. ⊠ *Shelter Cove Marina, 1 Shelter Cove La., Mid-Island* ☎ *843/290–6955* ⊕ *www.bayrunnerfishinghiltonhead.com.*

FAMILY **Bulldog Fishing Charters.** Captain Christiaan offers his guests 4-, 6-, 8-, and 10-hour fishing tours on his 32-foot boat. ⊠ *1 Hudson Rd., departs from docks at Hudson's Seafood House on the Docks, North End* ☎ *843/422–0887* ⊕ *bull-dogfishingcharters.com.*

FAMILY **Capt. Hook Party Boat.** If you're on a budget, have the family in tow, or just want to get on the water, deep-sea fishing tours are available on this large party boat, which sells concessions as well. The friendly crew teaches children how to bait hooks and reel in fish. ⊠ *Shelter Cove Marina, 1 Shelter Cove La., Mid-Island* ☎ *843/785–1700* ⊕ *www. captainhookhiltonhead.com.*

FAMILY **Fishin' Coach.** Captain Dan Utley offers a variety of inshore fishing tours on his 22-foot boat to catch redfish and other species year-round. ⊠ *2 William Hilton Pkwy., North End* ☎ *843/368–2126* ⊕ *www.fishincoach.com.*

FAMILY **Hilton Head Island Charter Fishing.** Cap. Jeff Kline offers off-shore fishing trips and four-hour family trips on a trio of 30-plus foot boats, the *Gullah Gal, True Grits,* and *Honey B.* ⊠ *Shelter Cove Marina, 1 Shelter Cove La., Mid-Island* ☎ *843/842–7002* ⊕ *www.hiltonheadislandcharterfishing. com.*

FAMILY **Integrity Charters.** The 38-foot charter boat *Integrity* offers offshore and near-shore fishing. ⊠ *Harbour Town Yacht Basin, Mariners Way, Sea Pines, South End* ☎ *843/422– 1221* ⊕ *www.integritycharterfishing.com.*

8

TEE OFF ON A BUDGET

Golfing on Hilton Head can be very expensive after you tally up the green fee, cart fee, rental clubs, gratuities, and so on. But there are ways to save money. There are several courses in Bluffton that are very popular with the locals, and some are cheaper to play than the courses on Hilton Head Island. Another way to save money is to play late in the day. If you're flexible, call around midday and courses with availability may let you on in the afternoon at a discount.

FAMILY **Palmetto Lagoon Charters.** Captain Trent Malphrus takes groups for half- or full-day excursions to the region's placid saltwater lagoons. Redfish, bluefish, flounder, and black drum are some of the most common trophy fish. ⊠ *Shelter Cove Marina, 1 Shelter Cove La., Mid-Island* ☎ *866/301–4634* ⊕ *www.palmettolagooncharters.com.*

FAMILY **The Stray Cat.** The Stray Cat will help you decide whether you want to fish "inshore" or go offshore into the deep blue—Cap. Jim Clark offers both on his 27-foot catamaran. ⊠ *2 Hudson Rd., North End* ☎ *843/683–5427* ⊕ *www.straycatcharter.com.*

GOLF

Apart from the beach, Hilton Head's main attraction is its golf. The island has two dozen championship courses (public, semiprivate, and private), and the outlying area has 16 more. Each offers its own packages, some of which are great deals. Almost all charge the highest green fees in the morning and lower fees as the day goes on. Lower rates can also be found in the hot summer and mid-winter months. It's essential to book tee times in advance, especially in the busy spring and fall months; resort guests and club members get first choices. Most courses can be described as casual-classy, so you will have to adhere to certain rules of the greens. ■TIP→ **The dress code on island golf courses does not permit blue jeans, gym shorts, or jogging shorts. Men's shirts must have collars.**

★ FodorśChoice **The RBC Heritage PGA Tour Golf Tournament.** The most internationally famed golf event in Hilton Head is the annual RBC Heritage, held mid-April. There are a wide range of ticket packages available. Tickets are also available at the gate. ⊠ *Sea Pines Resort, 2 Lighthouse La., South End* ⊕ *www.rbcheritage.com.*

GOLF SCHOOLS

Golf Learning Center at Sea Pines Resort. The well-regarded golf academy offers hourly private lessons by PGA-trained professionals and one- to three-day clinics to help you perfect your game. ⊠ *Sea Pines, 100 N. Sea Pines Dr., South End* ☎ *843/785–4540* ⊕ *www.golfacademy.net.*

Palmetto Dunes Golf Academy. There's something for golfers of all ages at this academy: instructional videos, daily clinics, and multiday schools. Lessons are offered for ages three and up, and there are special programs for women. Free demonstrations are held with Doug Weaver, former PGA Tour pro and director of instruction for the academy. Take advantage of the free swing evaluation and club-fitting. ⊠ *Palmetto Dunes Oceanfront Resort, 7 Trent Jones La., Mid-Island* ☎ *888/909–9566* ⊕ *www.palmettodunes.com.*

GOLF COURSES

★ FodorśChoice **Atlantic Dunes by Davis Love III.** One of three courses within Sea Pines Resort, Atlantic Dunes is an excellent and more affordable alternative to playing Harbour Town. Built along the route of Hilton Head's first golf course, the Ocean Course, the Davis Love III redesign features native grasses and plants that maintain the seaside feel—the 17th green even dips out into the dunes with views across the ocean. ⊠ *100 N Sea Pines Dr., South End* ☎ *843/842–1477* ⊕ *www.seapines.com/golf* ⅄ *18 holes, 7065 yards, par 72.*

Arthur Hills and Robert Cupp Courses at Palmetto Hall Plantation. There are two prestigious courses at Palmetto Hall: Arthur Hills and Robert Cupp. Arthur Hills is a player favorite, with its trademark undulating fairways punctuated with lagoons and lined with moss-draped oaks and towering pines. Robert Cupp is a very challenging course, but is great for the higher handicappers as well. ⊠ *Palmetto Hall, 108 Fort Howell Dr., North End* ☎ *843/466–6100* ⊕ *www. palmettohallcc.com* ⌸ *$99* ⅄ *Arthur Hills: 18 holes, 6257 yards, par 72. Robert Cupp: 18 holes, 6025 yards, par 72* ⌂ *Reservations essential.*

Country Club of Hilton Head. Although it's part of a country club, the semi-private course is open for public play. A well-kept secret, it's rarely too crowded. This 18-hole Rees Jones–designed course is a more casual environment than many of the other golf courses on Hilton Head. ⊠ *Hilton Head Plantation, 70 Skull Creek Dr., North End* ☎ *843/681–2582* ⊕ *www.clubcorp.com/Clubs/Country-Club-of-Hilton-Head* ⌑ *$105* ⚑ *18 holes, 6543 yards, par 72.*

Golden Bear Golf Club at Indigo Run. Located in the upscale Indigo Run community, Golden Bear Golf Club was designed by golf legend Jack Nicklaus, and received new champion Bermuda grass and an updated driving range in 2017. The course's natural woodlands setting offers easygoing rounds. It requires more thought than muscle, yet you will have to earn every par you make. Though fairways are generous, you may end up with a lagoon looming smack ahead of the green on the approach shot. ⊠ *Indigo Run, 100 Indigo Run Dr., North End* ☎ *843/689–2200* ⊕ *www.clubcorp.com/Clubs/Golden-Bear-Golf-Club-at-Indigo-Run* ⌑ *$99* ⚑ *18 holes, 6643 yards, par 72.*

★ **Fodor's**Choice **Harbour Town Golf Links.** Considered by many golfers to be one of those must-play-before-you-die courses, Harbour Town Golf Links is extremely well known because it has hosted the RBC Heritage Golf Tournament every spring for the last four decades. Designed by Pete Dye, the layout is reminiscent of Scottish courses of old. Forecaddies are a requirement, which adds to the special nature of a round here. The 18th hole lies along the marsh and river, driving toward the iconic lighthouse. The Golf Academy at the Sea Pines Resort is ranked among the top 10 in the country. ⊠ *Sea Pines Resort, 11 Lighthouse La., South End* ☎ *843/842–8484, 800/732–7463* ⊕ *www.seapines.com/golf* ⌑ *$350* ⚑ *18 holes, 7099 yards, par 71* ⚐ *Reservations essential.*

★ **Fodor's**Choice **Robert Trent Jones at Palmetto Dunes.** One of the island's most popular layouts, this course's beauty and character are accentuated by the 10th hole, a par 5 that offers a panoramic view of the ocean (one of only two on the entire island). It's among the most beautiful courses in the Southeast, with glittering lagoons punctuating 11 of the 18 holes. It received updated green layouts in 2016. ⊠ *Palmetto Dunes, 7 Robert Trent Jones La., North End*

☏ 843/785–1138 ⊕ www.palmettodunes.com ⌂ $105 ⚑ 18 holes, 6570 yards, par 72 ⚓ Reservations essential.

BLUFFTON GOLF COURSES

There are several beautiful golf courses in Bluffton, which is just on the other side of the bridges to Hilton Head Island. These courses are very popular with locals and can often be cheaper to play than the courses on Hilton Head Island.

Crescent Pointe. An Arnold Palmer Signature Course, Crescent Pointe is fairly tough, with somewhat narrow fairways and rolling terrain. There are numerous sand traps, ponds, and lagoons that make for demanding yet fun holes. Some of the par 3s are particularly challenging. The scenery is magnificent, with large live oaks, pine-tree stands, and rolling fairways. Additionally, several holes have spectacular marsh views. ✉ Crescent Pointe, 1 Crescent Pointe, Bluffton ☏ 843/706–2600 ⊕ crowngolfmanagement.com ⌂ $69 ⚑ 18 holes, 6447 yards, par 71.

Eagle's Pointe. This Davis Love III–designed course is one of the area's most playable, thanks to its women-friendly tees, spacious fairways, and large greens. There are quite a few bunkers and lagoons throughout the course, which winds through a natural woodlands setting that attracts an abundance of wildlife. ✉ Eagle's Pointe, 1 Eagle's Pointe Dr., Bluffton ☏ 843/757–5900 ⊕ crowngolfmanagement. com ⌂ $59 ⚑ 18 holes, 6399 yards, par 72.

Island West Golf Club. Fuzzy Zoeller and golf course designer Clyde Johnston designed this stunningly beautiful course set amongst majestic live oaks, plenty of wildlife, and expansive marsh views on several holes. There are several holes where the undulating fairways are rather generous, while others can be demanding, making it a fun and challenging course for golfers of all handicaps. ✉ Island West, 40 Island West Dr., Bluffton ☏ 843/815–6660 ⊕ www.islandwestgolf.net ⌂ $45 ⚑ 18 holes, 6208 yards, par 72.

The May River Golf Club. This 18-hole Jack Nicklaus course at the Montage Palmetto Bluff resort has several holes along the banks of the scenic May River and will challenge all skill levels. The greens are Champion Bermuda grass and the fairways are covered by Paspalum, the latest eco-friendly turf. Caddy service is always required. No carts are allowed earlier than 9 am to encourage walking. ✉ Palmetto Bluff, 476 Mount Pelia Rd., Bluffton ☏ 855/377–3198 ⊕ www.

8

montagehotels.com/palmettobluff/experiences/golf/ $315 ⛳ *18 holes, 7171 yards, par 72* ⛳ *Reservations essential.*

Old South Golf Links. There are many scenic holes overlooking marshes and the intracoastal waterway at this Clyde Johnson–designed course. It's a public course, but that hasn't stopped it from winning awards. It's reasonably priced, and reservations are recommended. ✉ *50 Buckingham Plantation Dr., Bluffton* ☎ *843/785–5353* ⊕ *www.oldsouthgolf. com* 🖅 *$70* ⛳ *18 holes, 6772 yards, par 72.*

PARASAILING

For those looking for a bird's-eye view of Hilton Head, it doesn't get better than parasailing. Newcomers will get a lesson in safety before taking off. Parasailers are then strapped into a harness, and as the boat speeds up, the parasailer is lifted hundreds of feet into the sky.

★ **Fodor's Choice H20 Sports.** Check out views up to 25 miles in
FAMILY all directions with this popular company located in Sea Pines. They also offer sailing, kayak and SUP tours, Jet Ski rentals, and a ferry to Daufuskie Island. ✉ *149 Lighthouse Rd., Sea Pines, South End* ☎ *843/671–4386, 877/290–4386* ⊕ *www.h2osports.com.*

FAMILY **Sky Pirate Parasail.** You can glide 500 feet in the air over the Low country on a trip out of Broad Creek Marina. The outfitter also offers boat rentals, tubing trips, and paddleboard rentals. ✉ *Broad Creek Marina, 18 Simmons Rd., Mid-Island* ☎ *843/842–2566* ⊕ *www.skypirateparasail.com.*

TENNIS

There are more than 300 courts on Hilton Head. After golf, tennis comes in at a close second as the island's premier sport. Hilton Head has a large international organization of coaches, and is one of the nation's best tennis destinations. ■TIP→ **Spring and fall are the peak seasons for cooler play, with numerous tennis packages available at the resorts and through the schools.**

★ **Fodor's Choice Palmetto Dunes Tennis & Pickleball Center.** Ranked
FAMILY among the best in the world, this facility at the Palmetto Dunes Oceanfront Resort has 21 clay tennis courts (four of which are lighted for night play) and 16 pickleball courts. There are lessons geared to players of every skill level given by enthusiastic staffers. Daily round-robin tournaments add to the festive atmosphere. ✉ *Palmetto Dunes Oceanfront Resort, 6 Trent Jones La., Mid-Island* ☎ *888/909–9566* ⊕ *www.palmettodunes.com.*

Fun for Kids

Hilton Head Island is a really fun place for little ones. Check out these kid-friendly sites.

Fodor'sChoice Adventure Cove. With two 18-hole golf courses (Paradise Falls and Lost Lagoon) and a large arcade, this minigolf haven pleases all ages. ⌧ *18 Folly Field Rd., Mid-Island* ☎ *843/842–9990* ⊕ *www.adventurecove.com.*

Fodor'sChoice Pirates of Hilton Head. Families board the Black Dagger pirate ship and head to sea in search of treasure and adventure, with kids in full pirate gear and face paint. The ship sets sail from Harbour Town. ⌧ *Mariners Way, Sea Pines Resort, South End* ☎ *843/363–7000* ⊕ *www.piratesofhiltonhead.com.*

Island Playground. Near the bridges to Hilton Head, this indoor play area has giant inflatable slides, a fairy-tale castle, toddler exploration area, and snack counter. ⌧ *1538 Fording Island Rd., Bluffton* ☎ *843/837–8383* ⊕ *www.Island-playground.com.*

Fodor'sChoice The Sandbox. This interactive, hands-on children's museum includes a cockpit where kids can put on a pilot's uniform and pretend to fly the friendly skies. In the Builders of Tomorrow exhibit, children dress up like construction workers and move materials to the building site, raise walls, and maneuver equipment. There's also a Learner's Loft where kids play with a puppet theater, puzzles, games, and toys. ⌧ *18A Pope Ave., South End* ☎ *843/842–7645* ⊕ *www.thesandbox.org.*

Station 300. Two dozen state-of-the-art bowling lanes, an arcade, and a restaurant keep this modern entertainment complex in Bluffton buzzing. ⌧ *25 Innovation Dr., Bluffton* ☎ *843/815–2695* ⊕ *station300.com.*

8

FAMILY **Port Royal Racquet Club.** Magnolia trees dot the grounds of the Port Royal Racquet Club, which has eight clay courts and two pickleball courts. The professional staff, stadium seating, and frequent tournaments help it consistently rank among the best in the world. ⌧ *Port Royal Plantation, 15 Wimbledon Court, Mid-Island* ☎ *843/686–8803* ⊕ *www.hiltonheadgolf.net/port-royal/.*

FAMILY **Sea Pines Racquet Club.** This highly rated club has 21 clay courts, as well as a pro shop and instructional programs, including weekend clinics with Wimbledon champ, Stan Smith. Guests of Sea Pines receive two hours of complimentary court time each day. ⌧ *5 Lighthouse La., Sea Pines*

Resort, South End ☎ *843/363–4495* ⊕ *www.seapines.com/ tennis.*

Van der Meer Tennis Center. Recognized for its tennis instruction for players of all ages and skill levels, this highly rated club in Shipyard Plantation has 17 hard courts, 4 of which are covered and lighted for night play. The Van der Meer Tennis Center also offers courts at the Shipyard Racquet Club, which has 20 courts. ✉ *19 DeAllyon Ave., Shipyard Plantation, South End* ☎ *800/845–6138* ⊕ *www.vandermeertennis.com.*

ZIPLINE TOURS

★ **Fodor's Choice ZipLine Hilton Head.** Take a thrilling tour on a
FAMILY zipline over ponds and marshes and past towering oaks and pines. This company offers eight ziplines, two suspended sky bridges, and a dual-cable racing zipline. Guests are harnessed and helmeted, and must be at least 10 years old and weigh between 80 and 250 pounds. ✉ *33 Broad Creek Marina Way, Mid-Island* ☎ *843/682–6000* ⊕ *ziplinehiltonhead.com.*

SHOPPING

Hilton Head is a great destination for shopping, starting with the Tanger outlet malls. Although they're officially in Bluffton, visitors drive by the outlets on U.S. 278 en route to Hilton Head Island. Notable high-end stores include Saks OFF 5th, Kate Spade, Michael Kors, and Vineyard Vines.

ART GALLERIES

★ **Fodor's Choice Ben Ham Images.** The extraordinary black-and-white large format photography of Ben Ham includes many iconic Lowcountry landscapes. ✉ *90 Capital Dr., Suite 104, Mid-Island* ☎ *843/842–4163* ⊕ *www.benhamimages.com.*

★ **Fodor's Choice Red Piano Gallery.** Sculptures, Lowcountry landscapes, and eccentric works by contemporary artists can be found at this upscale gallery in Bluffton. ✉ *40 Calhoun St. , Suite 201, Bluffton* ☎ *843/842–4433* ⊕ *redpianoartgallery.com.*

SOBA Gallery. There is always something interesting at the Society of Bluffton Artists' small gallery that showcases the work of local painters, sculptors, and photographers. ✉ *8 Church St., Bluffton* ☎ *843/757–6586* ⊕ *www.sobagallery.com.*

Walter Greer Gallery. Part of the Arts Center of Coastal Carolina, this modern gallery showcases local artists. ⊠ *Arts Center of Coastal Carolina, 14 Shelter Cove La., Mid-Island* ☎ *843/681–5060* ⊕ *www.artshhi.com/greer-gallery.*

GIFTS

FAMILY **Harbourtown Lighthouse Gift Shop.** The Hilton Head Lighthouse is the island's iconic symbol, and this shop celebrates the red-and-white-stripe landmark with tasteful South Carolina-theme gifts. ⊠ *149 Lighthouse Rd., Sea Pines, South End* ☎ *866/305–9814* ⊕ *www.harbourtown-lighthouse.com/shop.*

★ Fodor'sChoice **Markel's.** The helpful and friendly staff at Markel's is known for wrapping gifts with giant bows. You'll find unique Lowcountry gifts, including hand-painted wineglasses and beer mugs, lawn ornaments, baby gifts, greeting cards, and more. ⊠ *1008 Fording Island Rd., Bluffton* ☎ *843/815–9500* ⊕ *www.markelsgifts.com* ☉ *Closed Sun.*

Pretty Papers & Gifts. This is the go-to local spot for wedding invitations, fine stationery, and gifts. ⊠ *The Village at Wexford, 1000 William Hilton Pkwy., Suite E7, Mid-Island* ☎ *843/341–5116* ⊕ *www.prettypapershhi.com* ☉ *Closed Sun.*

FAMILY **Salty Dog T-Shirt Factory.** You can't leave Hilton Head without a Salty Dog T-shirt, so hit this factory store for the best deals. The iconic T-shirts are hard to resist, and there are lots of choices for kids and adults in various colors and styles. ⊠ *67 Arrow Rd., South End* ☎ *843/842–6331* ⊕ *www.saltydog.com.*

FAMILY **The Storybook Shoppe.** This charming, whimsical children's bookstore has a darling area for little ones to read as well as educational toys for infants to teens. ⊠ *41A Calhoun St., Bluffton* ☎ *843/757–2600* ⊕ *www.thestorybookshoppe.com* ☉ *Closed Sun.*

JEWELRY

The Bird's Nest. Local handmade jewelry, accessories, and island-theme charms are available at this popular, long-standing boutique. ⊠ *Coligny Plaza, 1 N. Forest Beach Dr. , #21, South End* ☎ *843/785–3737* ⊕ *www.thebirdsnesthiltonhead.com.*

Forsythe Jewelers. This is the island's leading jewelry store, offering pieces by famous designers. ⊠ *71 Lighthouse Rd., Sea Pines, South End* ☎ *843/671–7070* ⊕ *www.forsythejewelers.biz* ⊘ *Closed Sun.*

MALLS AND SHOPPING CENTERS

FAMILY **Coligny Plaza.** Things are always humming at this shopping center, which is within walking distance of the most popular beach on Hilton Head. Coligny Plaza has more than 60 shops and restaurants, including unique clothing boutiques, souvenir shops, and the expansive Piggly Wiggly grocery store. There are also bike rentals and free family entertainment throughout summer. ⊠ *Coligny Circle, 1 N. Forest Beach Dr., South End* ☎ *843/842–6050.*

★ **Fodor's Choice Harbour Town.** Distinguished by a candy-stripe
FAMILY lighthouse, Harbour Town wraps around a marina and has plenty of shops selling colorful T-shirts, casual resort wear, and beach-theme souvenirs, plus street musicians during summer. ⊠ *Sea Pines, 32 Greenwood Dr., South End* ☎ *866/561–8802* ⊕ *www.seapines.com/recreation/harbour-town.*

★ **Fodor's Choice Old Town Bluffton.** Charming Old Town Bluffton
FAMILY features local artist galleries, antiques, and restaurants. ⊠ *Downtown Bluffton, May River Rd. and Calhoun St., Bluffton* ☎ *843/706–4500* ⊕ *www.oldtownbluffton.com.*

FAMILY **Shelter Cove Towne Centre.** This sprawling, bikeable complex is anchored by chains like Belk and Talbots, but is also home to charming local spots like Spartina 449 and the Palmetto Running Company. There's also a Kroger grocery store, several restaurants and bars, and a barre studio. They host movie nights on Thursday at 9 pm during summer. ⊠ *40 Shelter Cove La., Mid-Island* ☎ *843/686–3090* ⊕ *www.mallatsheltercove.com.*

FAMILY **Shops at Sea Pines Center.** Clothing for men and women, the best local crafts, and fine antiques are the draw at this outdoor shopping center. You can even get a massage at the on-site day spa. ⊠ *71 Lighthouse Rd., South End* ☎ *843/363–6800* ⊕ *www.theshopsatseapinescenter.com.*

FAMILY **South Beach Marina Village.** Built to resemble a New England fishing village, South Beach is home to the Salty Dog Cafe and is the place for beach-friendly fashions. ⊠ *232 S. Sea Pines Dr., South End.*

Kid Stuff

Free outdoor children's concerts are held at Harbour Town in Sea Pines and Shelter Cove Harbor throughout the summer months. Guitarist Gregg Russell has been playing for children under Harbour Town's mighty Liberty Oak tree for decades. He begins strumming nightly at 8 in the summer, except on Saturday. It's also tradition for kids to get their pictures taken at the statue of Neptune at Harbour Town. At Shelter Cove, longtime island favorite Shannon Tanner performs a fun, family show at 6:30 pm and 8 pm weekdays from Memorial Day through Labor Day.

FAMILY **Tanger Outlets.** There are two halves to this popular shopping center: Tanger Outlet I has more than 40 upscale stores, as well as popular eateries like Olive Garden, Panera Bread, and Longhorn Steakhouse. Tanger Outlet II has Banana Republic, the Gap, and Nike, along with 60 others stores. There are also several children's stores, including Janie and Jack and Carter's. ✉ *1414 Fording Island Rd., Bluffton* ☎ *843/837–5410, 866/665–8679* ⊕ *www.tangeroutlet. com/hiltonhead.*

FAMILY **The Village at Wexford.** Upscale shops, including Lilly Pulitzer and Le Cookery, as well as several fine-dining restaurants can be found in this shopping area. There are also some unique gift shops and luxe clothing stores. ✉ *1000 William Hilton Pkwy.* ⊕ *www.villageatwexford.com.*

SPAS

Spa visits have become a recognized activity on the island, and for some people they are as popular as golf and tennis. In fact, spas have become one of the top leisure-time destinations, particularly for golf "widows." And this popularity extends to the men as well; previously spa-shy guys have come around, enticed by couples massage, deep-tissue sports massage, and even the pleasures of the manicure and pedicure.

There are East Indian–influenced therapies, hot-stone massage, Hungarian organic facials—the treatments span the globe. Do your research, go online, and call or stop by the various spas and ask the locals their favorites. The quality of therapists island-wide is noteworthy for their training, certifications, and expertise.

FACES DaySpa. This local institution has been pampering loyal clients for more than three decades, thanks to body therapists, stylists, and cosmetologists who really know their stuff. Choose from the line of fine cosmetics, enjoy a manicure and pedicure, or have a professional do your evening makeup for that special occasion. ☒ *The Village at Wexford, 1000 William Hilton Pkwy., D1, South End* ☎ *843/785–3075* ⊕ *www.facesdayspa.com.*

★ **Fodor's Choice Heavenly Spa by Westin.** This is the quintessential spa experience on Hilton Head. Prior to a treatment, clients are told to put their worries in a basket woven from local sweetgrass; de-stressing is a major component of the therapies here. The relaxation room with its teas and healthy snacks and the adjacent retail area with products like sweetgrass scents live up to the spa's name. In-room spa services are available, as are romance packages. ☒ *Westin Resort Hilton Head Island, 2 Grasslawn Ave., Port Royal Plantation, North End* ☎ *843/681–1019* ⊕ *www.westin-hiltonheadisland.com.*

Spa Montage Palmetto Bluff. Dubbed the "celebrity spa" by locals, this two-story facility is the ultimate pamper palace. The names of the treatments are almost as creative as the treatments themselves. There's the Coastal Waters body wrap, the Vitality of the Glaciers facial, and sensual soaks and couples massage. The spa also offers a variety of other services, including pedicures and manicures, facials and other skin treatments, and a hair salon. ☒ *Palmetto Bluff, 477 Mount Pelia Rd., Bluffton* ☎ *855/264–8705* ⊕ *www. montagehotels.com/palmettobluff/spa.*

Spa Soleil. A wide variety of massages and other treatments are offered at this haven inside the Marriott Resort. The tantalizing teas and snacks make your time here a soothing, therapeutic experience. ☒ *Hilton Head Marriott Resort & Spa, 1 Hotel Circle, Palmetto Dunes, Mid-Island* ☎ *843/686–8420* ⊕ *www.marriott.com/spas/hhhgr-hilton-head-marriott-resort-and-spa/spa-soleil/5012315/home-page.mi.*

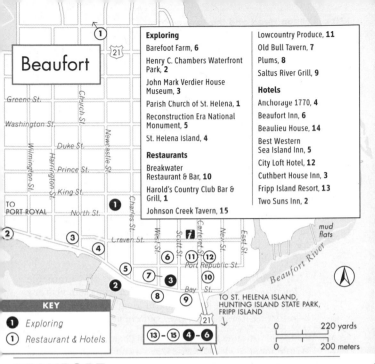

Exploring

Barefoot Farm, **6**

Henry C. Chambers Waterfront Park, **2**

John Mark Verdier House Museum, **3**

Parish Church of St. Helena, **1**

Reconstruction Era National Monument, **5**

St. Helena Island, **4**

Restaurants

Breakwater Restaurant & Bar, **10**

Harold's Country Club Bar & Grill, **1**

Johnson Creek Tavern, **15**

Lowcountry Produce, **11**

Old Bull Tavern, **7**

Plums, **8**

Saltus River Grill, **9**

Hotels

Anchorage 1770, **4**

Beaufort Inn, **6**

Beaulieu House, **14**

Best Western Sea Island Inn, **5**

City Loft Hotel, **12**

Cuthbert House Inn, **3**

Fripp Island Resort, **13**

Two Suns Inn, **2**

KEY

- **●** Exploring
- **①** Restaurant & Hotels

BEAUFORT

*38 miles north of Hilton Head via U.S. 278 and Rte. 170;
70 miles southwest of Charleston via U.S. 17 and U.S. 21.*

8

Charming homes and churches grace this old town on Port Royal Island. Come here on a day trip from Hilton Head, Savannah, or Charleston, or to spend a quiet weekend at a B&B while you shop and stroll through the historic district. Beaufort continues to gain recognition as an art town and supports a large number of galleries for its diminutive size. Visitors are drawn equally to the town's artsy scene and to the area's water-sports possibilities. The annual Beaufort Water Festival, which takes place over 10 days in July, is the premier event. For a calendar of Beaufort's annual events, check out ⊕ *www.beaufortsc.org*.

More and more transplants have decided to spend the rest of their lives here, drawn to Beaufort's small-town charms, and the area is burgeoning. A truly Southern town, its picturesque backdrops have lured filmmakers here to shoot *The Big Chill*, *The Prince of Tides*, and *The Great Santini*, the last two being Hollywood adaptations of best-selling books by author Pat Conroy. Conroy has waxed poetic about the Lowcountry and calls the Beaufort area home.

To support Beaufort's growing status as a tourist destination, it has doubled the number of hotels in recent years. Military events like the frequent graduations (traditionally Wednesday and Thursday) at the marine base on Parris Island tie up rooms.

GETTING HERE AND AROUND

Beaufort is 25 miles east of Interstate 95, on U.S. 21. The only way to get here is by private car or Greyhound bus.

ESSENTIALS

Well-maintained public restrooms are available at the Beaufort Visitors Center. You can't miss this former arsenal; a crenellated, fortlike structure, it is now beautifully restored and painted ocher.

The Beaufort County Black Chamber of Commerce (⊕ *www.bcbcc.org*) puts out an African American visitor's guide, which takes in the surrounding Lowcountry. The Beaufort Visitors Center gives out copies.

Visitor Information Beaufort Regional Chamber of Commerce. ⊠ *701 Craven St.* ☎ *843/525–8525* ⊕ *www.beaufortchamber.org.* **Beaufort Visitors Center.** ⊠ *713 Craven St.* ☎ *843/525–8500* ⊕ *www. beaufortsc.org.*

EXPLORING

Barefoot Farm. Pull over for boiled peanuts, a jar of gumbo and strawberry jam, or perfect watermelons at this roadside stand. ⊠ *939 Sea Island Pkwy., St. Helena Island* ☎ *843/838–7421.*

★ **Fodor's Choice Henry C. Chambers Waterfront Park.** Off Bay Street, FAMILY this park is a great place to survey the scene. Trendy restaurants and bars overlook these seven beautifully landscaped acres along the Beaufort River. In the evening, locals stroll along the river walk and enjoy the hanging bench swings. ⊠ *1006 Bay St.* ☎ *843/525–7070* ⊕ *www.cityofbeaufort.org.*

John Mark Verdier House Museum. Built in the Federal style, this 1804 house has been restored and furnished as it would have been prior to a visit by Marquis de Lafayette in 1825. It was the headquarters for Union forces during the Civil War. The house museum also features Civil War photographs, a diorama of Bay Street in 1863, and an exhibit on the first African American U.S. congressman, Robert Smalls.

Writer Pat Conroy on Beaufort

Many fans of the late best-selling author Pat Conroy consider Beaufort *his* town because of his autobiographical novel *The Great Santini,* which was set here. He, too, considered it home base: "We moved to Beaufort when I was 15. We had moved 23 times. (My father was in the Marines.) I told my mother, 'I need a home.' Her wise reply was: 'Well, maybe it will be Beaufort.' And so it has been. I have stuck to this poor town like an old barnacle. I moved away, but I came running back in 1993."

A number of Hollywood films have been shot here, not just Conroy's. "The beautiful white house on the Point was called the 'Big Santini House' until the next movie was shot and now it is known as 'The Big Chill House.' If a third movie was made there, it would have a new name.

"One of the great glories of Beaufort is found on St. Helena Island," said Conway. "You get on Martin Luther King Jr. Boulevard and take a right at the Red Piano Too Art Gallery to the Penn Center. Before making the right turn, on the left, in what was the Bishop family's general store, is Gullah Grub, one of the few restaurants that serve legitimate Gullah food."

He continues: "At the end of St. Helena, toward the beach, take Seaside Road. You will be in the midst of the Gullah culture. You end up driving down a dirt road and then an extraordinary avenue of oaks that leads to the Coffin Point Plantation, which was the house where Sally Field raised Forrest Gump as a boy."

✉ *801 Bay St., Downtown Historic District* ☎ *843/379–6335* ⊕ *historicbeaufort.org* 💲 *$10* ⊗ *Closed Sun.*

Parish Church of St. Helena. This 1724 church (founded in 1712) was turned into a hospital during the Civil War, and gravestones were brought inside to serve as operating tables. While on church grounds, stroll the peaceful cemetery and read the fascinating inscriptions. ✉ *505 Church St.* ☎ *843/522–1712* ⊕ *www.sthelenas1712.org.*

★ Fodor'sChoice **Reconstruction Era National Monument.** Established in 1862, the Penn Center was the first school for African Americans in the American South. It's now the centerpiece of the Reconstruction Era National Monument, which demonstrates the life and struggles of African Americans in the decades after the Civil War. The York W. Bailey Museum here has displays on the Gullah culture and heritage on the

Sea Islands, and the beautiful, live oak-shaded grounds host seasonal events, including a bi-weekly Saturday farmer's market, and the Center remains an active advocate for human rights through its programs and exhibits. ⊠ *16 Penn Center Circle West, St. Helena Island* ☎ *843/838–2432* ⊕ *www.penncenter.com* ⊠ *Museum $7* ⊙ *Museum closed Sun. and Mon.*

St. Helena Island. About 9 miles southeast of Beaufort, St. Helena Island is a stronghold of the Gullah culture. Several African American–owned businesses in its tight-knit community of Frogmore make this a worthy day trip or stop en route to Fripp and Hunting Islands. ⊠ *Rte. 21, St. Helena Island* ⊕ *www.beaufortsc.org/area/st.-helena-island.*

BEACHES

★ **Fodor'sChoice Hunting Island State Park.** This secluded park 18
FAMILY miles southeast of Beaufort has 5,000 acres of rare maritime forest and 4 miles of public beaches—some dramatically eroding. The light sand beach decorated with driftwood and the subtropical vegetation is breathtaking. You can kayak in the tranquil lagoon; stroll the 1,300-foot-long fishing pier (among the longest on the East Coast); and go fishing or crabbing. For sweeping views, climb the 167 steps of the 1859 **Hunting Island Lighthouse.** Bikers and hikers can enjoy 8 miles of trails. The nature center has exhibits, an aquarium, and lots of turtles; there is a resident alligator in the pond. **Amenities:** parking (fee); toilets. **Best for:** solitude; sunrise; swimming; walking. ⊠ *2555 Sea Island Pkwy., St. Helena Island* ☎ *843/838–2011* ⊕ *www.southcarolinaparks.com* ⊠ *$5.*

WHERE TO EAT

$$$$ ✕ **Breakwater Restaurant & Bar.** *Eclectic.* This classy downtown restaurant offers small tasting plates such as tuna crudo and fried shrimp, as well as main dishes like lamb meat loaf and filet mignon with a truffle demi-glace. The presentation is as contemporary as the decor. There's also an impressive and affordable wine list. **Known for:** contemporary approach to Lowcountry cuisine; elegant atmosphere; local loyalty. ⑤ *Average main: $26* ⊠ *203 Carteret St., Downtown Historic District* ☎ *843/379–0052* ⊕ *www.breakwatersc.com* ⊙ *Closed Sun.*

CLOSE UP

The World of Gullah

In the Lowcountry, Gullah refers to several things: a language, a people, and a culture. Gullah (the word itself is believed to be derived from *Angola*), an English-based dialect rooted in African languages, is the unique language, more than 300 years old, of the African Americans of the Sea Islands of South Carolina and Georgia. Most locally born African Americans of the area can understand, if not speak, Gullah.

Descended from thousands of slaves who were imported by planters in the Carolinas during the 18th century, the Gullah people have maintained not only their dialect but also their heritage. Much of Gullah culture traces back to the African rice-coast culture and survives today in the art forms and skills, including sweetgrass basket making, of Sea Islanders. During the colonial period, when rice was king, Africans from the West African rice kingdoms drew high premiums as slaves. Those with basket-making skills were extremely valuable because baskets were needed for agricultural and household use. Made by hand, sweetgrass baskets are intricate coils of marsh grass with a sweet, haylike aroma.

Nowhere is Gullah culture more evident than in the foods of the region. Rice appears at nearly every meal—Africans taught planters how to grow rice and how to cook and serve it as well. Lowcountry dishes use okra, peanuts, *benne* (a word of African origin for sesame seeds), field peas, and hot peppers. Gullah food reflects the bounty of the islands: shrimp, crabs, oysters, fish, and such vegetables as greens, tomatoes, and corn. Many dishes are prepared in one pot, a method similar to the stewpot cooking of West Africa.

On St. Helena Island, near Beaufort, Penn Center is the unofficial Gullah headquarters, preserving the culture and developing opportunities for Gullahs. In 1852 the first school for freed slaves was established at Penn Center, which is now preserved as the Reconstruction Era National Monument. You can delve into the culture further at the site's York W. Bailey Museum.

On St. Helena, many Gullahs still shrimp with hand-tied nets, harvest oysters, and grow their own vegetables. Nearby on Daufuskie Island, as well as on Edisto, Wadmalaw, and Johns islands near Charleston, you can find Gullah communities.

8

$ ✕ **Harold's Country Club Bar & Grill.** *American.* Not the "country club" you might expect, Harold's is a remodeled gas station in the little town of Yemassee, just east of Interstate 95. There's a buffet every Thursday, wings and things like seafood baskets and hamburgers on Friday, and steak or chicken with a variety of sides on Saturday. Seating is in one of the large, kitschy dining rooms and there's live entertainment Friday and Saturday night. **Known for:** cheerful ladies slapping meat on your plate cafeteria-style; great music; kitschy dining rooms; a worthy stop on your way in or out of town. Ⓢ *Average main: $13* ✉ *97 U.S. 17A, Yemassee* ✛ *30 minutes north of Beaufort* ☎ *843/589–4360* ⊕ *www. haroldscountryclub.com* ⊘ *Closed Sun.–Wed.*

$$ ✕ **Johnson Creek Tavern.** *American.* There are times when you just want a cold one accompanied by some raw oysters. If that's the case, head out to St. Helena Island to this relaxed hangout to sit outside and enjoy the marsh views. Or opt for a seat in the sporty bar, where every surface is covered with dollar bills. You may even feel compelled to add one of your own—ask for the staple gun and try to find an empty spot for your George Washington. **Known for:** decorated dollar bills stapled to the wall; fresh seafood; cheap happy hour specials. Ⓢ *Average main: $19* ✉ *2141 Sea Island Pkwy., St. Helena Island* ☎ *843/838–4166* ⊕ *www. johnsoncreektavern.com.*

★ **Fodor's**Choice ✕ **Lowcountry Produce.** *Southern.* If you don't $ impulsively order the tomato pie atop the glass display case—and you won't go wrong if you do—try the fried oysters, a lobster po'boy, or what may be the best shrimp and grits in town. There's table service and counter-order options, and plenty of jams, relishes, and pickled okra in their on-site market to stock your pantry at home. **Known for:** excellent selection of culinary gifts and souvenirs; colorful, airy decor that welcomes you in; hearty, satisfying breakfast entrées. Ⓢ *Average main: $14* ✉ *302 Carteret St., Downtown Historic District* ☎ *843/322–1900* ⊕ *www. lowcountryproduce.com.*

★ **Fodor's**Choice ✕ **Old Bull Tavern.** *European.* This neighborhood $$ gathering spot has a daily-changing menu heavy on pasta, FAMILY wood-fired pizza, and hearty entrées. The cocktail menu is equally appealing, as are the wines and local beers on tap. **Known for:** gourmet thin-crust pizza that's served until late; ricotta gnocchi that melts like heavenly pillows; tempting, creative cocktails. Ⓢ *Average main: $17* ✉ *205 West St., Downtown Historic District* ☎ *843/379–2855* ⊕ *oldbulltavern.com* ⊘ *Closed Sun. and Mon.*

Sea Monkeys

There is a colony of monkeys living on Morgan Island, a little isle near Fripp Island. If you are in a boat cruising or on a fishing charter and think you might be seeing monkeys running on the beach, you are not hallucinating from sun exposure. The state of South Carolina leases one of these tiny islands to raise monkeys for medical research. This deserted island and the subtropical climate and vegetation have proved ideal for their breeding. You can't land on the island or feed the monkeys, so bring binoculars or a long-lens camera.

$$$ ✕**Plums.** *American.* This comfortable local stalwart still uses old family recipes for its soups, crab-cake sandwiches, and curried chicken salad. Dinner is more sophisticated with creative pairings and artistic presentations, particularly with the pasta and seafood dishes. **Known for:** raw bar; inventive burgers and sandwiches for lunch; live music and hopping nightlife on weekends. ⑤ *Average main: $22* ✉ *904 Bay St., Downtown Historic District* ☎ *843/525–1946* ⊕ *www.plumsrestaurant.com.*

$$$$ ✕**Saltus River Grill.** *Seafood.* This hip eatery wins over diners with its sailing motifs, breezy patio, and modern Southern menu. Take in the sunset and a plate of seared sea scallops from the outdoor seating area overlooking the riverfront park. **Known for:** signature crab bisque; raw bar with a tempting array of oysters and sushi; thoughtful wine list. ⑤ *Average main: $32* ✉ *802 Bay St., Downtown Historic District* ☎ *843/379–3474* ⊕ *www.saltusrivergrill.com* ⊗ *No lunch.*

8

WHERE TO STAY

Even though accommodations in Beaufort have increased in number, prime lodgings can fill up fast, so call ahead.

★ **Fodor's**Choice ⛆ **Anchorage 1770.** *B&B/Inn.* Sophisticated and
$$$$ full of charm, this stately home has soaring ceilings, four-poster rice beds, and views across the river, but skips all of the dusty antiques and knickknacks often common in family-run B&Bs. **Pros:** wide porches on both stories with gorgeous views across the water; breakfasts prepared with

gourmet ingredients and tailored to the guest; authentic Southern hospitality. **Cons:** not all rooms have views; cottage is attractive and private but set apart from the hotel; restaurant service can be slow when it's busy. ⑤ *Rooms from: $275 ✉ 1103 Bay St., Downtown Historic District ☎ 877/951–1770 ⊕ anchorage1770.com ⇨ 16 rooms* ⑩ *Free Breakfast.*

★ **Fodor's**Choice ⛅ **Beaufort Inn.** *B&B/Inn.* This 1890s Victorian
$$$ inn charms with its handsome gables and wraparound verandas. **Pros:** in the heart of the historic district; beautifully landscaped space; breakfast is complimentary at three nearby restaurants. **Cons:** atmosphere in the main building may feel too dated for those seeking a more contemporary hotel; no water views; can fill up with wedding parties during spring. ⑤ *Rooms from: $209 ✉ 809 Port Republic St., Downtown Historic District ☎ 843/379–4667 ⊕ www. beaufortinn.com ⇨ 48 rooms* ⑩ *Free Breakfast.*

$$$ ⛅ **Beaulieu House.** *B&B/Inn.* From the French for "beautiful place," this waterfront bed-and-breakfast on nearby Cat Island is a quiet, relaxing inn with airy rooms decorated in Caribbean colors. **Pros:** great views; scrumptious gourmet hot breakfast; short drive to Beaufort historic district. **Cons:** thin walls; hot water can be a problem; a bit off the beaten path. ⑤ *Rooms from: $205 ✉ 3 Sheffield Ct. ☎ 843/770– 0303 ⊕ beaulieuhouse.com ⇨ 5 rooms* ⑩ *Free Breakfast.*

$$ ⛅ **Best Western Sea Island Inn.** *Hotel.* This well-maintained
FAMILY motel in the heart of the Historic District puts you within walking distance of many shops and restaurants. **Pros:** only swimming pool in downtown Beaufort; directly across from marina and an easy walk to art galleries and restaurants; breakfast included. **Cons:** air-conditioning is loud in some rooms; breakfast room can be noisy; lacks of the charm of nearby B&B alternatives. ⑤ *Rooms from: $179 ✉ 1015 Bay St. ☎ 843/522–2090 ⊕ www.sea-island-inn.com ⇨ 43 rooms* ⑩ *Free Breakfast.*

$$ ⛅ **City Loft Hotel.** *Hotel.* This 1960s-era motel was cleverly transformed by its hip, young owners to reflect their high-tech, minimalist style. **Pros:** stylish decor; use of the adjacent gym; very accommodating staff. **Cons:** the sliding Asian screen that separates the bathroom doesn't offer full privacy; no lobby or public spaces; not as charming as a B&B. ⑤ *Rooms from: $189 ✉ 301 Carteret St., Downtown Historic District ☎ 843/379–5638 ⊕ www.citylofthotel.com ⇨ 22 rooms* ⑩ *No meals.*

Writer Pat Conroy on Fripp Island

CLOSE UP

When asked what Fripp Island meant to him, the late Pat Conroy, arguably the Lowcountry's most famous author, answered: "The year was 1964. I was living in Beaufort. And when the bridge to Fripp Island was built, I was a senior in high school. My English teacher *and* my chemistry teacher moonlighted as the island's first security guards. It was a pristine island; there were no houses on it yet, and it was as beautiful as any desert island.

"In 1978, my mother moved over there, and all our summers were spent on the island. It was to be her last home. That sealed the island in our family's history. In 1989, I bought a house there, both because it is a private island and thus good for a writer, but also so that our family—my brothers and sisters—could always have a home on Fripp to come to."

$$$ ☎**Cuthbert House Inn.** *B&B/Inn.* Named after the original Scottish owners, who made their money in cotton and indigo, this 1790 home is filled with 18th- and 19th-century heirlooms and retains the original Federal fireplaces and crown and rope molding. **Pros:** owners are accommodating; complimentary wine and hors d'oeuvres service; great walk-about location. **Cons:** some furnishings are a bit busy; some artificial flower arrangements; stairs creak. ⑤*Rooms from: $225* ⊠*1203 Bay St., Downtown Historic District* ☎*843/521–1315* ⊕*www.cuthberthouseinn.com* ⌦*10 rooms* ⦿*Free Breakfast.*

$$ ☎**Two Suns Inn.** *B&B/Inn.* With its unobstructed bay views and wraparound veranda complete with porch swing, this historic home—built in 1917 by an immigrant Lithuanian merchant—offers a distinctive Beaufort experience. **Pros:** most appealing is the Charleston room, with its own screened-porch and water views; it's truly peaceful; breakfast prepared by the French owners. **Cons:** decor is dated; although on Bay Street it's a bike ride or short drive downtown; third-floor skylight room is cheapest but least desirable. ⑤*Rooms from: $169* ⊠*1705 Bay St., Downtown Historic District* ☎*843/522–1122, 800/532–4244* ⊕*www.twosunsinn.com* ⌦*6 rooms* ⦿*Free Breakfast.*

8

FRIPP ISLAND

$$$$ ⛅ **Fripp Island Resort.** *Resort.* On the island made famous in
FAMILY *Prince of Tides,* with 3½ miles of broad, white beach and
unspoiled scenery, this resort has long been known as a safe
haven where kids are allowed to roam free, go crabbing at
low tide, bike the trails, and swim. **Pros:** fun for all ages;
the beachfront Sandbar has great frozen drinks and live
music; two golf courses: Ocean Creek and Ocean Point.
Cons: far from Beaufort; some dated decor; could use
another restaurant with contemporary cuisine. ⑤ *Rooms
from: $374* ⊠ *1 Tarpon Blvd., Fripp Island* ✦ *19 miles south
of Beaufort* ☎ *843/838–1558* ⊕ *www.frippislandresort.com*
⇄ *210 units* ⊚ *No meals.*

NIGHTLIFE AND PERFORMING ARTS

Luther's. A late-night waterfront hangout, Luther's is casual
and fun, with a young crowd watching the big-screen TVs
or dancing to rock music live bands on weekends. Luther's
also has an appealing late-night menu. The decor features
exposed brick, pine paneling, and old-fashioned posters
on the walls. ⊠ *910 Bay St., Downtown Historic District*
☎ *843/521–1888.*

SPORTS AND THE OUTDOORS

BIKING

Beaufort looks different from two wheels. In town, traffic
is moderate, and you can cruise along the waterfront and
through the historic district. Some local inns lend or rent
bikes to guests. However, if you ride on the sidewalks or
after dark without a headlight and a rear red reflector, you
run the risk of a city fine of nearly $150. If you stopped
for happy hour and come out as the light is fading, walk
your bike back "home."

FAMILY **Lowcountry Bicycles.** If you want a decent set of wheels—or
need yours fixed—this affordable shop is the hub of all
things bike-related in Beaufort. ⊠ *102 Sea Island Pkwy.*
☎ *843/524–9585.*

BOATING

Beaufort is where the Ashepoo, Combahee, and Edisto
rivers form the A.C.E. Basin, a vast wilderness of marshes
and tidal estuaries loaded with history. For sea kayaking,
tourists meet at the designated launching areas for fully
guided, two-hour tours.

FAMILY **Barefoot Bubba's.** This eclectic surf shop on the way to Hunting Island rents bikes and kayaks and will deliver them to the park or anywhere in the area. ✉ *2135 Sea Island Pkwy., St. Helena Island* ☎ *843/838–9222* ⊕ *barefootbubbasurfshop.com.*

★ Fodor'sChoice **Beaufort Kayak Tours.** Tours are run by profes-
FAMILY sional naturalists and certified historical guides, and are designed to go with the tides, not against them, so paddling isn't strenuous. The large cockpits in the kayaks make for easy accessibility, and offer an up-close observation of the Lowcountry wilds. Tours depart from various landings in the area. ☎ *843/525–0810* ⊕ *www.beaufortkayaktours. com* ⊑ *$50.*

FAMILY **Beaufort Lands End Tours.** Take a guided kayak tour around the historic Beaufort waterfront or in the isolated waterways around Hunting Island. This outfitter also rents kayaks and bicycles for self-guided trips. ✉ *1152 Sea Island Pkwy, St. Helena Island* ☎ *615/243–4684* ⊕ *beaufortlandsendtours.com.*

GOLF

Most golf courses are about a 10- to 20-minute scenic drive from Beaufort.

Dataw Island. This upscale island community is home to Tom Fazio's Cotton Dike golf course, with spectacular marsh views, and Arthur Hill's Morgan River golf course, with ponds, marshes, and wide-open fairways. The lovely 14th hole of the latter overlooks the river. To play you must be accompanied by a member or belong to another private club. ✉ *100 Dataw Club Rd., Dataw Island* ✚ *6 miles east of Beaufort* ☎ *843/838–3838* ⊕ *www.dataw.com* ⊑ *From $69* ⚑ *Cotton Dike: 18 holes, 6787 yards, par 72. Morgan River: 18 holes, 6657 yards, par 72.*

Fripp Island Golf & Beach Resort. This resort has a pair of championship courses. Ocean Creek was designed by Davis Love III and has sweeping views of saltwater marshes, while Ocean Point runs alongside the ocean for 10 holes. This is a wildlife refuge, so you'll see plenty of animals, particularly the graceful marsh deer. ✉ *2119 Sea Island Pkwy., Fripp Island* ☎ *843/838–1558* ⊕ *www.frippislandresort.com/golf* ⊑ *$99* ⚑ *Ocean Creek: 18 holes, 6613 yards, par 71. Ocean Point: 18 holes, 6556 yards, par 72.*

8

SHOPPING

ART GALLERIES

★ Fodor'sChoice **Red Piano Too Gallery.** More than 150 Lowcountry artists are represented at this spacious gallery out in the St. Helena Island countryside. It's one of the area's best art spaces and carries folk and Gullah art, sculpture and fine art, and books. ✉ *870 Sea Island Pkwy., St. Helena Island* ☎ *843/838–2241* ⊕ *redpianotoo.com.*

Rhett Gallery. This family gallery sells Lowcountry art by four generations of the Rhetts, including remarkable wood carvings. There are also antique maps, books, Civil War memorabilia, and Audubon prints. ✉ *901 Bay St., Downtown Historic District* ☎ *843/524–3339* ⊕ *rhettgallery.com.*

Thibault Gallery. This attractive, well-lit gallery, owned by painter Mary Thibault, is right on Bay Street and features a mix of fine art and accessible, affordable pieces by local artists and craftspeople. There are also gifts, prints and stationary. ✉ *815 Bay St., Downtown Historic District* ☎ *843/379–4278* ⊕ *www.thibaultgallery.com* ⊙ *Closed Sun.*

DAUFUSKIE ISLAND

13 miles (approximately 45 minutes) from Hilton Head via ferry.

From Hilton Head you can take a 45-minute ferry ride to nearby Daufuskie Island, the setting for Pat Conroy's novel *The Water Is Wide,* which was made into the movie *Conrack.* The boat ride may very well be one of the highlights of your vacation. The Lowcountry beauty unfolds before you, as pristine and unspoiled as you can imagine. The island is in the Atlantic, nestled between Hilton Head and Savannah. Many visitors do come just for the day, to have lunch or dinner at the Old Daufuskie Crab Company or to party at Freeport Marina, where the tiki bar whirrs out frozen concoctions as bands play blues and rock and roll. The island also has acres of unspoiled beauty. On a bike or in a golf cart, you can easily explore the island. You will find remnants of churches, homes, and schools—some reminders of antebellum times. Guided tours include such sights as an 18th-century cemetery, former slave quarters, a "praise house," an 1886 African Baptist church, the schoolhouse where Pat Conroy taught, and the Haig Point Lighthouse. There are a few small, artsy shops like the Iron Fish Gallery.

GETTING HERE AND AROUND

The only way to get to Daufuskie is by boat, as it is a bridgeless island. The public ferry departs from Broad Creek Marina on Hilton Head Island several times a day. On arrival to Daufuskie you can rent a golf cart (not a car) or bicycle or take a tour. Golf carts are the best way to get around the island. If you're coming to Daufuskie Island for a multiday stay with luggage and/or groceries, and perhaps a dog, be absolutely certain that you allow a full hour to park and check in for the ferry, particularly on a busy summer weekend. Whether you are staying on island or just day-tripping, the ferry costs $35 round-trip. Usually the first two pieces of luggage are free, and then it is $10 apiece.

TOURS

Freeport Marina, where the public ferry disembarks on Daufuskie Island, includes the Freeport General Store, a restaurant, overnight cabins, and more. A two-hour bus tour of the island by local historians will become a true travel memory. The ferry returns to Hilton Head Island on Tuesday night in time to watch the fireworks at Shelter Cove at sundown.

Tour Daufuskie is an owner-operated company that offers kayak tours, historical and cultural tours, and golf cart rentals.

Tour Contacts Tour Daufuskie. ☎ 843/842–9449 ⊕ tourdaufuskie. com.

WHERE TO EAT

$$ ✕ **Old Daufuskie Crab Company.** *Seafood*. This outpost, with
FAMILY   its rough-hewn tables facing the water, serves up surprisingly good fare. The specialties are deviled crab and chicken salad on buttery grilled rolls; many diners also enjoy the Lowcountry buffet with its pulled pork and sides like butter beans and potato salad. Dinner entrées include shrimp, rib eyes, and the catch of the day. **Known for:** incredible sunsets; colorful bar; reggae and rock music. ⑤ *Average main: $17* ✉ *Freeport Marina, 1 Cooper River Landing Rd.* ☎ *843/785–6652* ⊕ *daufuskiedifference.com/menu.*

8

WHERE TO STAY

$$$$ ⌂ **Sandy Lane Villas.** *Rental.* A luxurious, oceanfront low-rise
FAMILY condominium complex, the twin Sandy Lane Villas buildings look out to the simple boardwalk that leads directly
to a nearly deserted beach. **Pros:** spacious and private;
unobstructed ocean views; complimentary golf cart. **Cons:**
not a homey beach cottage; it's a 20-minute golf cart ride
from Freeport Marina; very few restaurant options for a
week-long vacation. $ *Rooms from: $475* ✉ *Sandy Lane
Villas, 2302 Sandy La.* ☎ *843/341–3030* ⊕ *www.bloody-
pointresort.com/sandy-lane-villas/* ↝ *32 villas* ⧦ *No meals.*

TRAVEL SMART
SAVANNAH

GETTING HERE AND AROUND

▮ AIR TRAVEL

Savannah/Hilton Head International Airport caters to both destinations, though it is an almost half-hour drive from either. For transportation into the cities, taxis circle outside the baggage claim area and rideshare apps like Uber and Lyft pick up at the north entrance of baggage claim. Some of the larger hotels offer shuttles.

▮TIP➔ If the flights into Savannah/Hilton Head International Airport aren't convenient, consider the international airports in Jacksonville and Charlotte. The drive time to Savannah is just shy of two hours. Low cost carriers like JetBlue and Frontier now offer flights to and from Savannah—but if you have to drive from Jacksonville, approaching Savannah from the south gives you an opportunity to stop at Jekyll Island and other treasures of southeastern Georgia. From the north, visit scenic Beaufort or Bluffton.

AIRPORTS

Savannah/Hilton Head International Airport (SAV) is 11 miles west of downtown. The airport is only 20 minutes by car from the Historic District and around 40 minutes from Hilton Head Island. Another option is the tiny Hilton Head Island Airport.

Airport Information Hilton Head Island Airport.⊠ *120 Beach City Rd., North End* ☎ *843/255–2950* ⊕ *www.hiltonheadairport.com.* **Savannah/Hilton Head Interna-**

tional Airport.⊠ *400 Airways Ave., Northwest* ☎ *912/964–0514* ⊕ *www.savannahairport.com.*

GROUND TRANSPORTATION

There are no airport shuttles other than those operated by hotels, so visitors not renting a car must taxi to their lodging accommodations. The going rate for the approximately 11-mile trip to the Historic District is about $30. Several limousine and sedan services allow you to choose your vehicle with rates starting at less than $100 an hour. Another option for transporting groups into Savannah, Old Savannah Tours has larger vehicles that can be chartered.

Airport Transfers Old Savannah Tours.☎ *912/234–8128* ⊕ *www.oldsavannahtours.com.*

FLIGHTS

Savannah is serviced by American, Delta, JetBlue, United, Allegiant, Frontier, and Sun Country.

▮ BOAT AND FERRY TRAVEL

Located on the Savannah River, the Port of Savannah is the busiest port between New Orleans and New York. Savannah Belles Ferry is part of the citywide transit system and provides regular service from the City Hall dock in the Historic District to the Westin Savannah Harbor Golf Resort & Spa at the International Convention Center, on Hutchinson Island.

Contacts **Savannah Belles Ferry.**
✉ *City Hall Dock, River St., Historic District* ☎ *912/447–4029* ⊕ *www.catchacat.org.*

▮ BUS TRAVEL

Savannah is a coastal stop for Greyhound. The newly renovated station is conveniently located on the western edge of the Historic District.

Contacts **Greyhound.**✉ *610 W. Oglethorpe Ave., Historic District* ☎ *912/232–2135* ⊕ *www.greyhound.com.*

▮ CAR TRAVEL

Interstate 95 slices north–south along the Eastern Seaboard, intersecting 10 miles west of town with east–west Interstate 16, which dead-ends in downtown Savannah. U.S. 17, the Coastal Highway, also runs north–south through town. U.S. 80 is another east–west route through Savannah.

Unless you have plans to explore beyond the Historic District, Savannah is one destination where smart city planning and abundant public transportation render a rental car unnecessary. If you'll be centrally located during your visit, choose from the plentiful buses, taxis, pedicabs (up to two persons can be pedaled in a cart attached to a bicyclist), horse carriages, trolley tours (some of which allow on-and-off privileges), free ferries, and rental bikes, scooters, and Segway rentals. This is a walking city, so bring a pair of comfortable shoes.

GASOLINE

In general, gas prices in Savannah hover around the national average. Gas stations are not difficult to find; there are several on Martin Luther King Jr. Boulevard and 37th Street, the thoroughfares that access Interstate 16 to route back to Interstate 95 and the airport.

PARKING

Downtown parking can be a challenge; there are often more options in nearby residential neighborhoods. Tourists may purchase a Visitor DAYPASS at Savannah Parking & Mobility for $24 for two days and $15 for a single day. Rates vary at local parking garages, but in a City of Savannah–owned lot you should expect to pay at least $1 to $2 per hour during business hours on weekdays, a $2 flat rate in the evenings, and a flat rate of $3 on weekends. Special events parking can double the rates. Metered parking from Oglethorpe Avenue to River Street is a maximum of $2 an hour, while metered spots from Oglethorpe Avenue to Liberty Street are a maximum of $1 an hour. Meters do not have time limits and are enforced from 8 am to 8 pm Monday through Saturday north of Liberty Street. On weekdays, south of Liberty Street, meters are enforced 8 am to 5 pm. Download the City's Park Savannah app and feed the meter online. Most downtown hotels have paid parking, and some B&Bs and inns have their own parking lots or advise guests on how to park on the street. Few restaurants have parking.

Contacts Savannah Parking Mobility. ✉ *100 E. Bryan St.* ☎ *912/651–6470* ⊕ *www.savannahga.gov/2519/Mobility-Parking-Services.*

RENTAL CARS

Major rental agencies can be found in town and at the airport, and many provide pickup and delivery service. Almost all car-rental offices are closed on Sunday.

RENTAL CAR INSURANCE

When renting a car, is the added insurance a necessary expense? No one—including us—has a simple answer. If you own a car, your personal auto insurance may cover a rental to some degree; always read your policy's fine print. If you don't have auto insurance, then seriously consider buying the collision- or loss-damage waiver (CDW or LDW) from the car-rental company, which eliminates your liability for damage to the car. Some credit cards offer CDW coverage, but it's usually supplemental to your own insurance and rarely covers SUVs, minivans, luxury models, and the like.

If your coverage is secondary, you may still be liable for loss-of-use costs from the car-rental company. But no credit-card insurance is valid unless you use that card for *all* transactions, from making a reservation to paying the final bill. It's sometimes cheaper to buy insurance as part of your general travel insurance policy.

ROADSIDE EMERGENCIES

Discuss with the car-rental agency what to do in the case of an emergency, as this sometimes differs from company to company. Make sure you understand what your insurance covers and what it doesn't, and it's a good rule of thumb to let someone at your hotel know where you are heading and when you plan to return. Keep emergency numbers (car-rental agency and your accommodation) with you, just in case.

ROAD CONDITIONS

Roads in Savannah are a mixed bag. Certain streets in the Historic District are brick or cobblestone, which makes for a bumpy ride. In other areas—particularly in the Midtown and Southside neighborhoods—roads are paved and in good condition. Traffic can be tricky in the Historic District, with one-way streets and large numbers of pedestrians, cyclists, and other vehicles; you may encounter slow-moving trolleys and horse-drawn carriages, but please don't honk at the horses. There's heavy truck traffic on Interstate 95, where the speed limit is 70 mph. Interstate 16 gets backed up for about an hour around rush hour.

▮ PUBLIC TRANSPORTATION

Chatham Area Transit (CAT) operates buses in Savannah and Chatham County Monday through Saturday from just before 6 am to just shy of midnight, Sunday from 7 am to 9 pm; download the app to see the full schedule. Visitors can also take advantage of Dot, Savannah's fare-free downtown transportation system. The express shuttle serves 24 stops through the Historic District and runs from 7 am to midnight weekdays, 10 am to midnight on Saturday, and 10 am to 9 pm on Sunday; it does not run on most holidays.

Contacts Chatham Area Transit(CAT) ☎ 912/233–5767 ⊕ www. catchacat.org. **dot.**✉ 1 International Dr. ☎ 912/233–5767 ⊕ www.connectonthedot.com.

▮ TAXI TRAVEL

You can hail cabs on the street if they don't have riders or assignments. Most cab services offer flat rates to and from the airport, usually in the range of $30, plus $5 for each additional person. Yellow Cab Company charges $1.92 per mile.

Savannah Pedicab, Savannah's first pedicab company, is a people-pedaled vehicle that costs $45 per hour; if your ride is less than an hour, Savannah Pedicab abides by a "trips for tips" policy in which the passenger pays whatever they see fit for rides (most riders pay somewhere between the value of a sandwich and a pizza). Savannah Pedicab operates from 11 am to midnight (2 am on weekends). A second pedicab company, Royal Bike Taxi, charges a dollar per block per passenger for trips less than a half-hour, $25 for half-hour trips, and $45 for hour-long trips.

Contacts Savannah Pedicab. ☎ 912/232–7900 ⊕ www.savannahpedicab.com. **Yellow Cab.** ☎ 912/236–1133, 912/236–1133 ⊕ www.yellowcabofsavannah.com.

▮ TRAIN TRAVEL

Amtrak runs its Silver Service/Palmetto route down the East Coast from New York to Miami, stopping in Savannah. The station is about 6 miles from downtown.

Contacts Savannah Amtrak Station.✉ 2611 Seaboard Coastline Dr. ☎ 800/872–7245 ⊕ www.amtrak. com.

ESSENTIALS

▮ COMMUNICATIONS

INTERNET

Many hotels and inns offer complimentary Internet access. The City of Savannah offers free Wi-Fi via "surfsavannah"; it can be picked up on River Street, Bay Street, Reynolds Square, Ellis Square, Franklin Square, and the south end of Forsyth Park. It can also be accessed along Martin Luther King Jr. Boulevard from Victory Drive to River Street. Users must register. Usage is limited to two hours a day, though, if you're planning an extended stay, purchase a 30-day Wi-Fi pass via Seimitsu by calling ☎912/525–0345. Live Oak Public Libraries also offer free Internet access at all of its branches.

PHONES

The area code in Savannah is 912.

▮ EMERGENCIES

St. Joseph's/Candler Hospital and Memorial Health University Medical Center are the area hospitals with 24-hour emergency rooms.

Hospitals Memorial Health University Medical Center.✉ *4700 Waters Ave., Midtown* ☎ *912/350–8000* ⊕ *www.memorialhealth.com.* **St. Joseph's/Candler Hospital.**✉ *11705 Mercy Blvd., Southside* ☎ *912/819–6000* ⊕ *www.sjchs.org.*

▮ HOURS OF OPERATION

Most businesses operate on a 9-to-5 basis, although some offices open at 8:30. Boutiques and shops that are geared to tourists usually open daily at 10 and close around 6, including Sunday.

▮ MAIL

There is a post office in the Historic District on the corner of Barnard and State streets, as well as Federal Express and UPS outlets within a couple of blocks.

▮ MONEY

Bank of America, Wells Fargo, Suntrust, and other major financial outlets have branches in Savannah; most operate normal office hours weekdays, with half days on Saturday.

ATMs are numerous, especially on River Street, around Johnson Square, and in City Market.

▮ SAFETY

Savannah officials are serious about your safety, and you'll notice both police cars and security patrol cars throughout the downtown area. The streets are safe for pedestrians during the day, but at night you should exercise reasonable caution, especially in poorly lit areas along the perimeter of the Historic District. Always lock your car and remove valuables that are visible through the windows. Utilize your hotel's safe for your cash and valuables. Keep handy phone numbers for taxi companies.

▮ TAXES

The sales tax is 7%; hotel room tax is 13%.

▮ TIPPING

Tip as you would in any other U.S. city; waiters in restaurants expect to receive 15% to 20% (the larger amount in more upscale establishments); 15% is still the norm here. Tip hotel maids about $1 or $2 per day.

▮ TOURS

Savannah boasts tours aplenty and offers comfortable prospects of the city's history, landmarks, and landscapes.

BOAT TOURS

Savannah Riverboat Cruises has daily departures from docks on River Street. The causeway is mainly commercial, with many deserted warehouses, so it's not a terribly scenic ride, but it is narrated, has a bar, plays Jimmy Buffet, and is a relaxing trip on the river. The 1½-hour ride costs $24.95 per person, and departure times change seasonally. The Monday Gospel Dinner Cruise has a Southern buffet and a choir to entertain and goes for $53.95.

Contacts Savannah Riverboat Cruises. ⊠ 9 E. River St. ☎ 912/232–6404 ⊕ www.savannahriverboat.com.

BUS AND TROLLEY TOURS

Operating out of City Market, Carriage Tours of Savannah travels the Historic District at a 19th-century clip clop pace, with coachmen spinning tales and telling ghost stories along the way. A romantic evening tour in a private carriage costs $160 per couple. Regular tours start at $25 per person.

Savannah's rich African American history can be experienced via the daily departing Freedom Trail Tour. This comprehensive black-history tour visits significant landmarks like the First African Baptist Church, the Ralph Mark Gilbert Civil Rights Museum, and the slave burial grounds at Laurel Grove Cemetery.

Historic Savannah Carriage Tours specializes in private tours aboard a picturesque European carriage. The romantic Moonlight and Roses Tour includes a dozen roses and a stop at a beloved local bar. Private tours cost $170 for two people. Tours open to the public are a little easier on the wallet: $25 per person. Either tour includes a horse-drawn amble through Savannah's historic streets.

Old Savannah Tours is the city's award-winning company with years of experience and the widest variety of tours. Popular options include the historic hop-on, hop-off trolley tour, the 90-minute Historic Overview, and the ghost tour that includes dinner at Pirates' House. Prices start at $28 per person.

Old Town Trolley Tours has narrated 90-minute tours traversing the Historic District. Trolleys stop at 15 designated stops every 30 minutes daily from 9 to 5 (August to March) or 9 to 6 (April to July). You can hop on and off as you please. The cost is $33, with discounts for purchasing ahead online.

Mix it up by exploring downtown with a Segway tour via Segway of Savannah. With two-way radios, it's easy to hear the guide and ask questions. A one-hour tour is $40 from December through March and $49 from April through November.

Hearse Ghost Tours may be like nothing you've ever experienced before. For 15 years these hearses did the job they were intended for; when they were retired, their roofs were removed to make space for eight live bodies cruising around the haunted sites in the Historic District. Count on macabre guides for irreverently funny narration throughout the tour.

Contacts Carriage Tours of Savannah. ☎ *912/236–6756* ⊕ *www. carriagetoursofsavannah.com.* **The Freedom Trail Tour.** ☎ *912/398– 2785.* **Hearse Ghost Tours.** ✉ *412 E. Duffy St., Historic District* ☎ *912/695–1578* ⊕ *www.hearseghosttours.com.* **Historic Savannah Carriage Tours.** ☎ *912/443–9333* ⊕ *www.savannahcarriage.com.* **Old Savannah Tours.** ☎ *800/517–9007* ⊕ *www.oldsavannahtours.com.* **Old Town Trolley Tours.** ☎ *855/245– 8992 toll-free* ⊕ *www.trolleytours. com/savannah.* **Segway of Savannah.** ✉ *234 Martin Luther King Jr. Blvd.* ☎ *912/233–3554* ⊕ *segwayofsavannah.com.*

SPECIAL-INTEREST TOURS

Personalized Tours of Savannah is a small company offering upscale and intimate tours of the city, with customized themes covering movies filmed in Savannah, the city's amazing architecture, and a highly recommended Jewish-heritage tour. The friendly owner is a longtime Savannah resident, and tours are peppered with plenty of insider knowledge.

Contacts Personalized Tours of Savannah. ✉ *425 E. President St., Downtown* ☎ *912/234–0014* ⊕ *www. savannahsites.com.*

WALKING TOURS

A Ghost Talk Ghost Walk tour should send chills down your spine during an easygoing 1-mile jaunt through the old colonial city. Tours, lasting 1½ hours, leave from the middle of Reynolds Square, at the John Wesley Memorial at 7:30 pm and 9:30 pm, weather permitting. The cost is $10 per person.

Savannah Tours by Foot's Creepy Crawl Haunted Pub Tour is a great option for anyone who loves a good ghost story and a visit to local watering holes. Believers say there are so many ghosts in Savannah they're actually divided into subcategories. These charismatic guides specialize in tavern ghosts, and they'll regale you with tales of secret sub-basements, possessed gum-ball machines, and animated water faucets. Tours traditionally depart from the Six Pence Pub at 8 pm. Because this is a cocktail tour, children are not permitted. Routes can vary, so call for departure times and locations; the tour costs $20 and lasts for 2½ hours.

Cobblestone Tours provides a deep historical context for Savannah's spooky occurrences. Audiences of all ages can take the Savannah Ghosts & Folklore tour by candlelight, or grown-ups can get scared with a drink in their hand on Cobblestone's Haunted Pub Crawl. Tours start at $20 and last 1½ hours. Another spooky option is Sixth Sense Savannah, which gives an insider's perspective of Savannah's poltergeists.

Historic Bonaventure Cemetery is the final resting place for notable Savannah greats like songwriter Johnny Mercer and author Conrad Aiken. Fifth-generation Savannahian Bonaventure Don is the perfect guide to share the history of the marshside cemetery, its monuments, and the tales of its final residents; guests name their own price for a 2½ hour tour.

On the First Squares Food Tour, lead by Savannah Taste Experience, visitors try classic dishes from several of Savannah's favorite locales, all while learning about the city's history and culinary scene; tours start at $54.

For a comprehensive history of slavery in Savannah and the role African Americans have played in shaping the Hostess City's story, schedule a walk with Footprints of Savannah. Tours, lasting 1½ hours, depart from Wright Square and are $20 per adult.

For an upscale take on the walking tour experience, stroll Savannah with Genteel & Bard, a luxury storytelling company that lets guests wander thanks to a miked tour guide and complimentary earbuds. The tours—Historic Savannah Daytime Walking Tour or Savannah Ghost Encounter Tour—are $25 per adult.

Contacts Bonaventure Don.
☎ 912/658–1748 ⊕ bonaventuredon.com. **Cobblestone Tours.** ☎ 912/604–3007 ⊕ www.ghostsavannah.com. **Creepy Crawl Haunted Pub Tour.** ☎ 912/238–3843 ⊕ www.savannahtours.com. **Footprints of Savannah Tours.** ✉ Historic District ☎ 912/695–3872 ⊕ www.footprintsofsavannah.com. **Genteel & Bard.** ☎ 912/373–6651 ⊕ genteelandbard.com. **Ghost Talk Ghost Walk Tour.** ☎ 912/233–3896 ⊕ www.ghosttalkghostwalk.com. **Savannah Taste Experience.** ✉ 426 Barnard St., Downtown ☎ 912/221–4439 ⊕ savannahtasteexperience.com. **Sixth Sense Savannah.** ☎ 912/292–0960 ⊕ www.sixthsense-world.com.

▮ VISITOR INFORMATION

The MLK Visitor Information Center is easily accessed from all major thoroughfares and is open daily 9 to 5:30. The center has a useful audiovisual overview of the city and a staff of knowledgeable trip counselors. Other downtown information centers include the River Street Information Center, open from 9 to 8 from February to November and 9 to 6 in December and January. The glass-enclosed Visitor Center at Ellis Square offers a convenient, centrally located information station.

For detailed information about Tybee Island, drop by the island's visitor center, just off Highway 80. It's open daily 9 to 5:30.

Contacts **The River Street Visitor Information Center.** ✉ *1 West River St., Historic District* ☎ *912/651–6662* ⊕ *www.visitsavannah.com.* **Savannah/Hilton Head International Airport Visitors Center.** ✉ *400 Airways Ave.* ☎ *912/966–3743* ⊕ *visitsavannah.com.* **Savannah Visitor Information Center.** ✉ *301 Martin Luther King Jr. Blvd., Historic District* ☎ *912/944–0455* ⊕ *www.visitsavannah.com.* **Tybee Island Visitor Information Center.** ✉ *802 1st St., Tybee Island* ☎ *877/344–3361* ⊕ *www.visittybee.com.* **Visitor Center at Ellis Square.** ✉ *26 Barnard St., Historic District* ☎ *912/525–3100* ⊕ *visitsavannah.com.*

INDEX

PHOTO CREDITS

Front Cover: Tetra/Getty Images [Description: Houses in residential district, Savannah, Georgia.] Spine: PhilAugustavo/iStockphoto. Insert: Dndavis/Dreamstime.com (1). Jeff Greenberg/age fotostock (2). David Davis / age fotostock (3). Ferne Arfin/Alamy (3). Savannah Music Festival (4). ZUMA Wire Service/Alamy (5). Danita Delimon/Alamy (5). Richard Cummins/age fotostock (6). Andy Palmer/Alamy (6). Katherinedavisgothel/Dreamstime.com (7). Scott Anderson/Alamy (8). Cindy Roberts (8). RiverNorthPhotography/iStockphoto (8). **Chapter 1:** Experience Savannah: Jesse Kunerth/Shutterstock (11). **Chapter 2:** Exploring Savannah: Lane V. Erickson/Shutterstock (21). **Chapter 3:** Where to Eat: dbimages/Alamy (45). Chapter 4: Where to Stay: Courtesy of The Kessler Collection (71). **Chapter 5:** Nightlife and Performing Arts: Courtesy of Savannah Music Festival/Ayano Hisa (87). **Chapter 6:** Sports and the Outdoors: Steve Nudson/Alamy (101). **Chapter 7:** Shopping: ralph daniel photography, inc (113). **Chapter 8:** Hilton Head and the Lowcountry: LeeAnn White/Shutterstock (127). **About Our Writers:** All photos are courtesy of the writers.

*Every effort has been made to trace the copyright holders, and we apologize in advance for any accidental errors. We would be happy to apply the corrections in the following edition of this publication.

Fodor's InFocus SAVANNAH

Publisher: Stephen Horowitz, *General Manager*

Editorial: Douglas Stallings, *Editorial Director*; Margaret Kelly, Jacinta O'Halloran, Amanda Sadlowski, *Senior Editors*; Kayla Becker, Alexis Kelly, Teddy Minford, Rachael Roth, *Editors*

Design: Tina Malaney, *Design and Production Director*; Jessica Gonzalez, *Graphic Designer*; Mariana Tabares, *Design & Production Intern*

Production: Jennifer DePrima, *Editorial Production Manager*; Carrie Parker, *Senior Production Editor*; Elyse Rozelle, *Production Editor*; Jackson Pranica, *Editorial Production Assistant*

Maps: Rebecca Baer, *Senior Map Editor*; Mark Stroud (Moon Street Cartography), *Cartographer*

Photography: Jill Krueger, *Director of Photo*; Namrata Aggarwal, Ashok Kumar, Carl Yu, *Photo Editors*; Rebecca Rimmer, *Photo Intern*

Business & Operations: Chuck Hoover, *Chief Marketing Officer*; Robert Ames, *Group General Manager*; Tara McCrillis, *Director of Publishing Operations*; Victor Bernal, *Business Analyst*

Public Relations and Marketing: Joe Ewaskiw, *Senior Director Communications & Public Relations*; Esther Su, Senior *Marketing Manager*; Ryan Garcia, Thomas Talarico, Miranda Villalobos, *Marketing Specialists*

Fodors.com: Jeremy Tarr, *Editorial Director*; Rachael Levitt, *Managing Editor*

Technology: Jon Atkinson, *Director of Technology*; Rudresh Teotia, *Lead Developer*; Jacob Ashpis, *Content Operations Manager*

Writers: Anna Chandler, Stratton Lawrence

Editor: Alexis Kelly

Production Editor: Jennifer DePrima

5th Edition

ISBN 978-1-64097-214-8

ISSN 1943–0116

Library of Congress Control Number 2019938165

All details in this book are based on information supplied to us at press time. Always confirm information when it matters, especially if you're making a detour to visit a specific place. Fodor's expressly disclaims any liability, loss, or risk, personal or otherwise, that is incurred as a consequence of the use of any of the contents of this book.

SPECIAL SALES

This book is available at special discounts for bulk purchases for sales promotions or premiums. For more information, e-mail SpecialMarkets@fodors.com.

PRINTED IN CANADA

10 9 8 7 6 5 4 3 2 1

21982319426742

ABOUT OUR WRITERS

A native Southerner, **Anna Chandler** was born in Tennessee, raised in South Carolina, and has made Savannah, Georgia home for more than a decade. She is a writer, editor, musician, and visual artist who loves kayaking, going to concerts, day-tripping through the Southeast, and studying Southern folk art. The former Arts and Entertainment editor of *Connect Savannah*, her writing has also appeared in *BUST, Savannah* magazine, *South, Savannah Morning News,* and more. She updated the Savannah content for this edition

Stratton Lawrence lives by the sea with his wife and two children on Folly Beach, just up the coast from Hilton Head. When he's not in the waves or the sand, he's navigating Icelandic backroads or hiking the Pyrenees with a toddler on his back. Stratton is a frequent contributor to *Fodor's, AFAR,* and *Charleston Magazine*. He updated the Hilton Head chapter for this edition.